YOUR CHILDREN ARE UNDER ATTACK

How Popular Culture Is Destroying Your Kids' Values, and How You Can Protect Them

a new book by

Jim Taylor, PhD

SOURCEBOOKS, INC.®
NAPERVILLE, ILLINOIS

Published by Sourcebooks, Inc.
P.O. Box 4410, Naperville, Illinois 60567-4410
(630) 961-3900
FAX: (630) 961-2168
www.sourcebooks.com

Taylor, Jim
 Your children are under attack : how popular culture is destroying your
kids' values and how you can protect them / Jim Taylor.
     p. cm.
 Includes bibliographical references and index.
 1. Mass media and children--United States. 2. Popular culture--Moral and
ethical aspects--United States. 3. Social values--United States. 4.
Parenting--United States. 5. Child rearing--United States. I. Title.

HQ784.M3T39 2005
306.874'0973--dc22

2004029937

Printed and bound in the United States of America
QW 10 9 8 7 6 5 4 3 2 1

Also by Jim Taylor, PhD

Positive Pushing: How to Raise a Successful and Happy Child

Table of Contents

Acknowledgments

I would like to express my greatest thanks and a debt of gratitude to Scott Shea, whose tireless—and unpaid—research efforts and keen insights were invaluable to what you see here.

Special Thanks To...

Mentors that I have been fortunate to have throughout my life and career—Marty Heib, Dr. Marc Reiss, Dr. David Chiszar, Larry Abrams, Dr. Ted Millon, and Dr. Frank De Piano—for your faith, support, and feedback that shaped me as a person, a professional, and an author.

Gerry Sindell of Thought Leaders International—my friend, manager, and, most recently, officiant at my wedding—what more can be said that hasn't been said before? My esteem for you is immeasurable.

Jim Levine, my agent. Your guidance has made my journey into the world of publishing meaningful, fulfilling, and successful.

Peter Lynch, my editor at Sourcebooks, whose knowledge of and insights into popular culture helped take my book to the next level.

Everyone at Sourcebooks, including Jill Amack and Vicky Brown, for their commitment and efforts in making this book possible.

The young people, parents, and educators who have taught me so much and whose lessons I share in this book.

My father, Shel Taylor, my late mother, Ceci Taylor, and my sister, Heidi, because you've always been there for me.

Finally, Sarah, my wife and the love of my life, because you complete me.

A CALL TO ACTION!

Your children are under attack. This assault is not coming from terrorists within or outside our borders. It is not coming from disturbed people in our communities. This onslaught is coming from our own American popular culture. It is ever present, intense, and unrelenting. There is rarely a moment in your children's daily lives in which they are not being bombarded with messages from popular culture. This siege is also in disguise; most parents cannot sense the harm inflicted on their children any more than fish can sense that their ocean is becoming more polluted. And children find these messages so fun and entertaining that they couldn't imagine that they are bad for them. Many of parents seem to have been fooled into believing that popular culture cares about their children. It doesn't! American popular culture cares about only one thing—money—and it will say anything and do anything to make more money. It can no longer be trusted to communicate healthy, life-affirming values to your children. This ever-growing juggernaut of money, materialism, and conspicuous consumption is now left ungoverned, unchecked, and dangerously out of control. This beast has an unquenchable appetite that will consume anyone in its path. The Golden Rule has been distorted into: Whoever has the gold, rules!

As a parent, you might say, "Our generation had popular culture when we were growing up and we turned out okay." Yes, the current generation of parents had popular culture, but it wasn't the same as today. Popular culture was once overseen by numerous public and private agencies, and guided by an agreed-upon value of "in the public interest." You had a handful of regulated television and radio stations that offered a variety of mostly positive programming. But those forces have all but disappeared.

In previous generations, parents and children lived lives that were busy and full of activities. Back then, though, popular culture was not the detrimental force that it is today. At most an irritant, popular culture at that time didn't make life for families more difficult because its messages were generally consistent with those that parents wanted their children to hear.

Today, children have access to hundreds of TV and radio stations, movies, DVDs, video games, the Internet, cellular phones, saturation advertising, and consumption-driven magazines that celebrate avarice, blatant sexuality, and violence. Children are inundated with popular culture everywhere they go. "The digital media are likely to have a more profound impact on how children grow and learn, what they value, and ultimately what they become than any medium that has come before," asserts Kathryn Montgomery, president of the Center for Media Education.

The messages that American popular culture communicates to children today are in direct conflict with what is best for them. Popular culture is now a truly counterproductive force in families' lives and, without societal support, parents have a harder time knowing what is in their children's best interests and an even more difficult time acting on that knowledge. Children, in turn, are being led farther down a road that makes them less receptive to their parents' positive efforts and more vulnerable to messages that prevent them from developing into healthy, happy, and contributing people.

The messages from American popular culture can be found in every part of children's lives; the clothes they wear, the friends they socialize with, in the food they eat, and the way they spend their free time. For example, the website of the fast-food restaurant chain, Burger King, exhorts children to "Fuel up like a superhero with fun stars and lightning-bolt-shaped Chicken Tenders…Just look in your Big Kid's or regular Kid's meal, because now and for a limited time you can find two great toys and two exciting new shapes. Now go and save the world! What are you waiting for?" Advertisements like this encourage unhealthy eating habits and foster obesity. And I doubt that Superman or Wonder Woman got their powers from fast-food. Another example is the BratzPack dolls—the "Girls with a Passion for Fashion"—who have bare midriffs, hip-hugging jeans, pouty lips, and absurdly skinny figures. They tell their fans, "Until next time, take care, be good, and above all else *be beautiful.*" These messages brainwash young girls into believing that physical attractiveness is all-important and may contribute to body-image distortions and eating disorders in adolescence.

At a deeper level, these messages influence children's views about the world at large, their life goals and dreams, and most fundamentally, the values that they hold dear. *Your Children Are Under Attack* explores how the messages from American popular culture directly influence and distort the values that your children adopt.

Protection, Past and Present

In the past, the protectors of children could be found in our government, businesses, schools, and at home. But the U.S. government can no longer be expected to safeguard our children—the Office of Homeland Security can't protect your children against this threat. Our government long ago gave in to big business, special interests, and "the bottom line." In doing so, it rejected the very values on which our country was founded and has shown only politically expedient concern for our children.

Big business will not show restraint either. Its very existence is predicated on placing profit above all else. Even so, in generations past, civic-minded business leaders did their best to contribute to the public good by, for example, establishing foundations to support worthy causes (e.g., Ford, Carnegie, Rockefeller). But in recent years, with an uncertain economy, little governmental oversight, and pressure from stockholders, many members of big business have jettisoned whatever humanitarian values or ethics it once held in a desperate and greedy grab for greater profits.

Even schools have become corrupted. With budget shortfalls, deteriorating facilities, and teacher shortages, schools have turned to popular

culture—in the form of fast-food, soft drink, and candy companies—
to help subsidize the costs of educating children. In doing so, schools
have sacrificed their values to remain viable. Once a safe haven from
popular culture, schools are now complicit, exposing children to
destructive and inescapable messages that support the unrelenting pressure to adopt the values forced on them by American popular culture.
The result is a decline among children in moral behavior, scholarship,
and social awareness, and an increase in materialism, violence, obesity,
eating disorders, substance abuse, criminal behavior, and suicide. Unless
you're homeschooling your children with no communication with the
outside world, there may be nowhere for your children to hide from this
mind-boggling assault.

The only hope of protection your children have left comes from inside
your home—from you. *Your Children Are Under Attack* is a "call to action"
for you to wrest power from American popular culture, put a stop to its
destructive Pied-Piper allure, and regain influence over your children's
lives. If you want your children to have a reasonable chance at developing
into healthy and happy adults, you need to understand that your position
as the most powerful force in their lives is in jeopardy. It is being replaced
by a voracious machine that cares nothing for your children and genuine-
ly has the capacity to destroy their chances to mature and thrive. Only by
maintaining your stature in their lives can you forcefully, yet lovingly,
guide your children toward a life that is not dominated by valueless
dreams of wealth, celebrity, power, and physical attractiveness, but rather
is grounded in life-affirming values that can contribute to your children's
possibility of leading lives of meaning and fulfillment.

Times Have Changed

Has there ever been a more difficult time to raise children? Have you
ever been faced with more choices, conflicting influences, and less ability to affect your children's growth than today? Have children ever had
more information and resources available to them, yet had a less clear
compass to guide them in using this knowledge? In today's society, people have unprecedented time, opportunities, and freedom with which
to shape their lives. Yet the same aspects of American society that give
us such a wonderful quality of life also present new demands, obstacles,
and risks in raising our children.

Ironically, all of the modern tools that you have available to make your family's lives easier and more efficient seem to work against your child-rearing efforts. Technology should enable you to make better use of your time and to have more free time to spend with your children. Yet the single greatest complaint that I hear from parents is that they are always rushing around trying—often unsuccessfully, they say—to meet their children's most basic needs, much less focusing on instilling values in their children. Despite technology that allows parents to keep in better contact with their children, many parents seem to be losing touch with their children rather than becoming closer to them. This disconnection makes children even more vulnerable to the influence of popular culture.

Cars, cellular phones, microwaves, and other modern conveniences are also supposed to save you energy that you can then devote to the joys of parenting—teaching, encouraging, and sharing with your children. This wonderful form of "multitasking"—another dreaded term foisted on us by American popular culture—has been replaced by scheduling, organizing, feeding, and driving. Parents now complain that they have a hard enough time just getting their kids through the day, much less have the time and energy to be concerned about values.

These technological advancements should encourage greater access to what Thomas Jefferson believed were our inalienable rights: life, liberty, and the pursuit of happiness. Yet these rights seem more distant and difficult to achieve today than ever before. These rights seem to have been co-opted and distorted by the very culture that was meant to help us realize them.

A New Parenting Culture

The culture of parenting has changed. An unfortunate phenomenon that I have observed increasingly over the last two decades can only be described as "lazy parenting." More and more, many parents are choosing the path of least resistance in raising their children. They are making decisions about their children that are in their own best interests rather than those of their children. Instead of taking full responsibility for raising their children, many parents today cede responsibility to others—organized sports, tutors, babysitters, TV, DVDs, video games. I call it *child rearing by committee*. In doing so, many parents have become enablers of American popular culture, giving in to these unhealthy forces rather than resisting them, simply because it's easier, less time-consuming, and less tiring. Unfortunately, in doing so, parents abdicate their ability to influence their children positively and open them up to ready conquest by American popular culture.

Some parents might get a bit defensive when accused of lazy parenting and cite all the things they do for their children (for example, paying for piano lessons, buying them expensive sports equipment, driving their children to soccer practice, etc.). But these efforts, though certainly time-consuming, actually absolve parents of many of their responsibilities. Parents who have succumbed to the over-scheduled life that American popular culture imposes on them have less quality time to spend with their children. They are required to set fewer boundaries, impose less discipline and consequences, and share fewer meaningful experiences. In general, parents don't have to assume their traditional—and essential—responsibilities in raising their children.

Lazy parenting has led to the two greatest obstacles I have seen to raising successful, happy, and contributing children: fatigue and expediency. In their hectic lives, many parents are simply too exhausted to do what's best for their children, and often make decisions—consciously or by default—that simply reduce their fatigue. Also, much of raising children involves a battle over who will tire out and give in first. Because your children always have more energy than you do, they can nag, cajole, whine, and complain until you throw up your hands in frustration and give your children what they want, even when it is not what is best for them. In a battle of attrition, only the strongest and most resolute parents will win. For those other parents, not only do they lose, but their children lose as well.

Expediency may be the most powerful manifestation of lazy parenting. Lazy parents raise their children in the most convenient way. The choices they make are aimed at making child rearing as easy and stress-free as possible. Television has always been the most universal tool used by parents in the name of expediency. The image of young children sitting entranced in front of television sets while their mother is on the phone or cooking in the kitchen, or their father is working in the dining room, was as common in the 1950s as it is in the

2000s. Says the mother of a fourteen-month-old, "Sometimes it's a necessary evil. We all know what it feels like to come home and flip on our favorite TV show and just veg for an hour. It feels really good, and so it's really easy to do that for children. Unfortunately, easy isn't always the best way to go."

Recent advances in media technology show how parents have been able to expand the scope of expediency in twenty-first-century America. For example, long family drives have always been a difficult part of parenting. Keeping children from being bored and whiny during long road trips—"Are we there yet?"—have always tested the patience of parents. In the late 1990s, carmakers began installing video systems into automobiles that allowed children to watch DVDs and play video games during trips. As one parent, unwittingly illustrating the power of expediency, said, "Now we always use it on long trips. It turns the drive into a dream date for my husband and me. We actually get to talk up front while the kids are busy watching in back." I wonder if these parents thought about card games, audio books, or road bingo, or how about plain old conversation? So these parents' lives are a little easier, but at what cost to their children?

A recent personal experience further highlights the influence of expediency today. I was eating at a restaurant recently and saw a couple with boys who were about four and two years old. During the entire dinner, the boys had headphones on and were watching a movie on a portable DVD player. What a truly painful illustration of lazy and self-ish parenting! These two parents didn't have to engage their children, put any effort into their family dinner, and could take care of their own needs. If this dinnertime practice is a common occurrence, they are unwittingly harming their sons. At a very basic level, the boys are learn-ing that they don't need to participate in family dinners or be engaged with others during dinner. They're not allowed to be bored or required to overcome their boredom with their own initiative. The boys don't have to assume their share of responsibility as part of the family dinner. Imagine what would happen at future dinners if their parents forgot the DVD player or the battery died?

Why there has been this epidemic of lazy parenting is unclear. Most likely, parents' lives are so busy that they don't believe that they have the time or the energy to devote to their children. Two-income households, divorce, loss of extended-family support, and disconnected communities contribute to the lack of available time and the stress parents experience. Being a parent may have become so complicated and unclear that parents may simply feel overwhelmed by the unceasing demands and helpless to overcome the obstacles. There may also be so many mixed messages from all aspects of our society—popular culture, parenting experts, family, friends—that parents just throw up their hands in confusion and exasperation. Or maybe many parents have bought into the messages of American popular culture telling them that they shouldn't have to be so selfless, that they shouldn't have to sacrifice their own lives, that having a family shouldn't have to mean that their children become their life's priority—basically, that raising children shouldn't have to be that hard. Regardless of the reasons, lazy parents become unwitting accomplices to American popular culture and their children become its unfortunate victims.

A Distorted American Dream

The American Dream is what has made America special since its inception. Every immigrant who sailed by the Statue of Liberty saw hope and possibility for a new and fulfilling life. The American Dream inspired millions of parents to work hard in often difficult and unrewarding jobs to give their children the opportunities that they never had. And so many Americans realized their American Dream of affluence and material comfort. In generations past, parents were happy when their children got good grades, played sports for fun, and learned a musical instrument. But somehow, that isn't enough for this generation of children. We now live in a culture in which good is no longer good enough. The standard of what had once been considered average, the 50th percentile, has been mysteriously raised to the 80th percentile, and this new "average" is still not adequate for children. It's as if parents who achieved the American Dream decided that being above average wasn't sufficient, so they raised the bar impossibly high. Today's parents place expectations on their children that are considerably more demanding. Children are expected to achieve straight A's and get accepted to the best schools, be star athletes with professional and Olympic aspirations, excel in music or dance, and, in their spare time, save the world.

This new culture has contributed to the emergence of American popular culture, the corruption of American values, and the decline in the American family. Parents are stressed out trying to provide their children with every opportunity, yet have lost sight of why they are giving their children these opportunities. Children are blinded by destructive messages from popular culture and their parents, and burdened with having to achieve unattainable standards that are not of their own choosing. Families are so busy chasing this distorted American Dream that they don't stop to see the damage it is causing to them. What began as the American Dream is slowly but surely becoming an American Nightmare from which it seems that families will never awake.

The Stakes Are High

What is at stake in raising your children in the early part of the twenty-first century? Nothing less than the future of your children and American society itself. This generation may very well determine the direction that our society takes in the next millennium. As a 2002 *San Francisco Chronicle* editorial asserted so passionately, "Parents must take the lead in reclaiming childhood...protected from a value system that emphasizes material wealth, products, looks, and sex above all else...Anyone who cares about the future of our society, and the values it stands for, must fight back...The challenge is not only to reclaim childhood. It is also to reclaim our nation's more enduring—and child-nurturing—values."

We are currently on the cusp of the old world and a new cultural frontier. The present generation of parents was raised with the old values that lead America to the forefront of modern civilization. You haven't been thoroughly corrupted by our profit-driven popular culture because of the values you learned when popular culture wasn't so ubiquitous or powerful. But what of the next generation? What will happen to your children's children where culture that is not driven by greed and other unhealthy values is just a distant memory, and your children and grandchildren only know American popular culture as we know it now—or worse? Can our grandchildren learn healthy values when their parents grew up immersed in negative value messages? Can they instill positive values in their children while living in a culture where the value messages are predominantly destructive? Future generations of children have only one hope—that you take a stand, say no to American popular culture, teach your children healthy values, and start a counter-cultural—a counter-American-popular-cultural—revolution that will halt the vicious cycle in which we currently find ourselves caught. This revolution can turn the tide of your children's futures against the destructive force of American popular culture.

The Pulse of American Families

Since the release of my last book, *Positive Pushing: How to Raise a Successful and Happy Child*, in April 2002, I have been traveling around the country speaking to thousands of parents at public and private schools in big cities and small towns. I have listened to the concerns they've expressed about raising their children in a mass culture whose values conflict with their own. What has become clear is that many parents have lost their bearings, and are overwhelmed in managing their family's overscheduled and stressful lives. I have spoken to educators who, by the very lives they have chosen, are powerful allies for children in the war against American popular culture. They describe the frustration and feelings of futility they experience daily as they try to teach children and ignite interest and caring against a tidal wave of messages from American popular culture that works to extinguish the flames of passion and compassion.

I have also spoken to the kids themselves who, surprisingly, recognize how destructive American popular culture is, but lack the experience and tools to resist its messages on their own. I have sought to understand how and why American families seem to have gotten so lost in a world that offers so many opportunities. I believe that I have found the answer. Just as in politics, where the guiding principle is, "It's the economy, stupid," in our society, our communities, and our families, the guiding principle must be "It's the values, stupid!"

So What Do We Do?

Raising children today is not unlike driving somewhere without a map, or even a destination. You know you want to go somewhere, but you're not quite sure where or how to get there. Even more challenging, it's as if all of the road signs are wrong and people you stop to ask for directions keep telling you to go every which way but the right one. *Your Children Are Under Attack* offers you a destination of where you want to go and a road map to get you there. Having this road map will save you both time and energy that you can devote to enjoying your children and seeing them grow into mature and value-driven adults.

This book will help you to regain your moral compass, identify and reconnect with your values, and make those values the guiding principles in your children's lives. In doing so, you will have the ammunition to join forces with your children, reestablish a line of resistance, and together defend against the massive, seemingly inexorable, and soulless force of American popular culture.

Your Children Are Under Attack will show you how to identify the dangerous messages that American popular culture imposes on your children. You will learn the media through which these messages are communicated. And, importantly, you will come to recognize the unhealthy messages that are embedded in the otherwise entertaining and seemingly innocuous television shows, movies, DVDs, video games, and music that are a regular part of your children's daily lives.

Your Children Are Under Attack will also explore the battlefield where this war is being fought. You will learn about the primary areas in which American popular culture insinuates itself into your children's lives. You will also learn the insidious ways in which popular culture seduces your children. We will look at the specific values that are under attack and what values your children are learning from American popular culture, while describing the values that are essential for your children to become successful, happy, and principled people. Finally, I will show you how can you can take sides with your children to instill healthy values and help them to repel the destructive values that are impressed on them by popular culture.

The values I write about focus on areas of your children's lives that are most threatened by American popular culture. These areas also emphasize essential values you must help your children develop to resist the pull of American popular culture. Identifying these crucial values evolved out of my twenty years of working with young people and their parents, and seeing the increasingly invasive and toxic effect our popular culture has had on children.

The first thing I had to do was identify which values are most important to children's development. To do so, I asked two questions:

1. What would happen to children if they didn't have this value?
2. Is the value necessary for families, communities, societies, and civilizations to function and thrive?

If a value passed this test, it was added to the list.

Through these years of talking with and listening to parents and children, I added and removed values, and honed the list until I arrived at the six values that provide the framework for *Your Children Are Under Attack*: respect, responsibility, success, happiness, family, and compassion. You might not agree with some of the values. You might have other values that you think are more important than those I describe in this book. If so, ask yourself the same questions that I did in testing your values and see if you can get closer to your own values in raising your children.

Your Children Are Under Attack will give you clear information and practical solutions to the unique challenges you face in instilling essential values in your children. You'll gain insights into the values your children need, presented in a focused and "to the point" format that bypasses the minutiae and skips the rhetoric found in many parenting books. *Your Children Are Under Attack* will enable you to do more than just try to fit effective child rearing in your family's busy lives. Rather, this book will show how you can be the kind of parent you really want to be every day without running yourself into exhaustion.

The ideas I discuss in *Your Children Are Under Attack* come from real parents faced with serious challenges in raising their children in today's complex world. *Your Children Are Under Attack* offers you solutions that are clear, practical, and grounded in the real world of parenting in twenty-first-century America. With the information and tools you learn from *Your Children Are Under Attack*, you will again have the power and the means to ensure that your children grow up with the values, attitudes, and skills to become positive, strong, and caring people.

The goal of *Your Children Are Under Attack* is to help you provide your children with special gifts that only you can give them. These gifts will allow your children to not just survive, but to thrive in these challenging times. Your children can be professionally successful, have healthy relationships with family and friends, be happy and contented in their lives, and, ultimately, be valuable contributors to the community in which they live and society as a whole. You can give your children the values and perspectives that will enable them to resist the destructive force of American popular culture. You can instill in them a value system that they can share with their children, extended families, and communities. These gifts not only strengthen your children's resolve against the power of American popular culture, but it also extends the size and capabilities of the resistance against it. Every child that is saved from popular culture is another recruit into a growing opposition in our society that is healthy and life-affirming and, with time and determination, can triumph over the destructive forces of American popular culture.

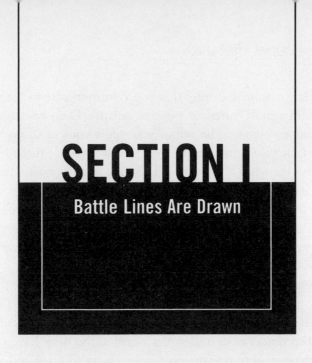

SECTION I

Battle Lines Are Drawn

The only chance your children have in winning the war against American popular culture is if you take sides with them. Use your power to protect them from the hypnotic allure of popular culture's damaging values, beliefs, and attitudes. An essential part of being their ally is to know your children's enemy. American popular culture is a master of disguise that can slip through your defenses and attack your children without you or them realizing it. Popular culture is also a massive and unrelenting force that can overwhelm your defenses and reach your children before you can regroup. Understanding American popular culture—its soldiers, tactics, strengths, and weaknesses—will help you prepare a strong and resolute defense against its assault.

Understanding your own capabilities to protect your children is also essential. You may not know it, but you have a powerful arsenal that you can use against American popular culture: your values. They are the most necessary and potent weapons at your disposal. Your values are powerful because they provide you with the clarity of mission and the resolve to be ever vigilant. Your values also act as the armor that can shield your children against popular culture's insurgencies and as weapons that you and your children can use to fend off the assaults.

The healthy value messages that you communicate to your children protect them against American popular culture. Every message that you convey that emphasizes the values you want your children to live by gives them the values and perspectives that will enable them to see popular culture for what it is, what it believes, what it wants from them, and how it can harm them. This awareness and understanding is your children's best defense because they will see popular culture's messages for what they are: manipulative, deceitful, and unhealthy communications aimed at meeting the needs of its voracious appetite without regard for the cost to children.

But good values and healthy messages aren't enough in the face of American popular culture's constant and concentrated assault on your children. It's easy to get worn down by American popular culture, lose hope, and surrender to its unflagging assaults. You must have a deep and resilient conviction to do whatever is necessary to safeguard your children. This resolve is necessary because popular culture never rests—and neither can you. You must become your children's allies, who stand by them in the siege. Your home must become a refuge for your children from the incessant and seemingly inescapable strikes from popular culture. This safe haven will allow your children to rest and marshal their resources so they don't lose their resolve. Your home will also become a supply depot where they can take on healthy values and perspectives that act as armor to deflect assaults when they reenter enemy territory.

CHAPTER 1

Know Thy Children's Enemy
(Beware of the Dark Side)

American Popular Culture on the Offensive

From the 1994 movie, *True Lies*, starring Arnold Schwarzenegger, Jamie Lee Curtis, and Tom Arnold.

They are driving through Washington, D.C. Harry (Arnold Schwarzenegger) is still shocked by his daughter's behavior. [In the previous scene Harry watched his daughter steal money from Gib's (Tom Arnold) wallet]

Gib: Kids. Ten seconds of joy. Thirty years of misery.
Harry: She knows not to steal. I've taught her better than that.
Gib: Yeah, but you're not her parents anymore, you and Helen [Jamie Lee Curtis]. Her parents are Axl Rose [Lead singer of Guns 'N' Roses] and Madonna. The five minutes you spend a day with her can't compete with that kind of constant bombardment. You're outgunned, amigo.

And you are outmanned as well. There is no more destructive force in your children's lives than American popular culture. It promotes the worst values in people, and disguises them all as entertainment. Reality TV, for example, has made the "seven deadly sins"—pride, avarice, envy, wrath, lust, gluttony, and sloth—attributes to be admired. Throw in selfishness, deceit, spite, and vengeance—all qualities seen and revered in popular culture—and you have the personification of the worst kind of person. American popular culture makes heroic decidedly unheroic values, characters, and behavior.

Most parents realize that popular culture conveys unhealthy messages to their children. In a recent survey conducted by Common Sense Media, three-fourths of parents believed that materialism and the negative influences from television, movies, and music were a "serious problem" in raising children. It further reported that 64 percent of parents believe media content today is inappropriate for children. Over 85 percent of parents believe that marketing contributes to children being too materialistic, sexual content leads children to become sexually active at a younger age, and violent content increases aggressive behavior in children. And 66 percent of parents think they could do a better job of supervising their children's media exposure.

Your challenge is to *know thy children's enemy.* In order to fight back against popular culture, you need to understand what it is, the many forms it takes, how it seduces children, and the messages it sends.

What Is American Popular Culture?

What is American popular culture, you ask? We all know it when we see it, you say. It's Shaquille O'Neal, J-Lo, Ludacris, McDonald's, Toys 'R' Us, Instant Messaging, Coca-Cola, and on and on. But this list only gives examples of popular culture. They are, if you will, some of the weapons that popular culture uses against your children. But they don't really tell us what popular culture is.

Ray B. Browne, a professor at Bowling Green State University in Kentucky, defines popular culture as "the way of life in which and by which most people in any society live. In a democracy like the United States, it is the voice of the people…that forms the lifeblood of daily existence, of a way of life. Popular culture is...the seedbed in which democracy grows. It is our heroes, icons, rituals, everyday actions, psychology, and religion—our total life picture." This definition sounds like it might have characterized popular culture fifty years ago, but it seems far too idealistic given how most of us see popular culture today. The voice of popular culture is no longer that of the people, but rather of the companies imposing its values on the people. It has co-opted rather than infused the lifeblood of daily existence. Popular culture hurts democracy by fostering conformity of thought and action and by controlling our choices. Many heroes offered by popular culture are not heroic, many of its icons represent unhealthy values, and many of its rituals, everyday actions, psychology, and religion are in its best interests, not those of the people.

Angela M. S. Nelson, a professor at Angelo State University in Texas, says that "Values are at the core of popular culture. It embodies popular objects or icons, heroes and heroines, and the rituals, myths, and beliefs surrounding these." She adds that popular culture both reflects *and* manipulates values and beliefs. Other experts assert that "popular culture is undeniably associated with commercial culture and all its trappings: movies, television, radio, cyberspace, advertising, toys—nearly any commodity available for purchase." Popular culture once mirrored our society's values, but now the reverse is true; popular culture determines society's values to a large extent.

Additionally, popular culture is pervasive, dominating virtually every part of our lives. Interestingly, Dr. Nelson says that popular culture relies on formula and repetition to influence people, repeating consistent themes to instill in people the values and beliefs that are endorsed and permitted in the culture. This notion is clearly evident in formulaic television shows (e.g., situation comedies, game shows, soap operas), common genres of movies (e.g., action, romantic comedies, animation) and music (e.g., hip-hop, country), cross-pollination of media (e.g., product placement in movies, films based on video games and theme-park rides), and represented by the profound redundancy of much of the media expressions of popular culture (e.g., repeated advertisements, replaying of music on radio). This unavoidable inundation of unhealthy messages makes it difficult for children to get away from its messages or to resist its influence.

The Profit Motive

Popular culture now exists for a singular purpose: to increase the profits for the companies that now control it: fast-food, soft drinks, candy, fashion, electronics, and so on. They accomplish their goal by brainwashing your children in two ways. Popular culture is like a network of saboteurs that infiltrate your family's lives with stealth and deception. You don't even notice its influence on your children—until it's too late. It is also an invading army that overwhelms your children. It attempts to control every aspect of your children's lives: their values, attitudes, and beliefs about themselves, their communities, the society of which they are a member, and the world that they inhabit; their thoughts, emotions, and behavior; their needs, wants, goals, hopes, and dreams; their interests and avocations; their choices and their decisions. With this control, popular culture can tell children what to eat and drink, what to wear, what to listen to and watch, and children have little ability to resist.

Not All Popular Culture Is Necessarily Bad

Though I will probably come across as militantly against any and all forms of American popular culture, I actually believe that there can be a place for some of it in our society. I confess that I like my share of "trash" movies, including star-driven romantic comedies, action adventures, and sci-fi. Whether popular culture is dangerous or benign depends on its true intention and how it's received by people. Popular culture that is simply aimed at entertaining people has its place in our society. Whether film, music, theater, books, or sports, activities that transport us from our daily lives into temporary alternative realities can play healthy and essential roles in our lives. These diversions act as brief respites from our otherwise busy lives. They give us a "time-out" that relieves stress, provides a small amount of escapism, creates pleasant vicarious emotions, and just plain entertains us. As long as the messages communicated in the media aren't implicitly bad for children, far be it from me to judge whether Spielberg is worse than Fellini or Aerosmith is worse than Beethoven.

However, popular culture that is intended to or inadvertently results in children learning bad values, attitudes, or beliefs, manipulating needs and wants, creating markets, selling goods and services that have no redeeming value, or impressing upon children anything that is unhealthy psychologically, emotionally, socially, or spiritually, physically is by its very nature, destructive. Examples include advertising that connects certain toys, clothes, food, or drinks with being popular or cool, or music that encourages racism, sexism, drug use, or violence.

The way in which children perceive popular culture also determines whether it is harmful. If children see popular culture as simple entertainment, as I mentioned above, and don't use, for example, unhealthy characters, lyrics, images, or words, as sources of their values, attitudes, and beliefs, then this kind of popular culture is mostly harmless. But, if children, as naïve observers, draw their values and their basic beliefs about the world from popular culture, then, regardless of its intention, it will hurt your children.

But let's be clear here. Even "good" popular culture isn't that good for children. Though there is certainly educational television, video games that encourage creativity, problem solving, and decision making, movies with positive messages and role models, these media, however good their messages are, teach children bad habits. Most of these forms of American popular culture foster passivity, limit meaningful social interaction, discourage physical activity, and take time away from engaging in value-driven pursuits. They waste your children's time— time that could be better spent participating in activities that teach healthy values and habits, and that support their intellectual, emotional, cultural, spiritual, and physical development (for example, reading, sports, arts, unstructured play, and talking with others).

In Your Children's Face

The presence of American popular culture in children's lives is constant, intense, and omnipresent. Your children are exposed to hundreds of television channels. They have free and immediate access to an almost unlimited array of information through the Internet, some of it quite harmful. They have free and immediate access to other people near and far through email and Instant Messaging. And when they're not on the computer, DVDs, video games, magazines, advertising, vending machines at school, and shopping malls fill your children's lives.

Research has shown that typical American children between the ages of two and eighteen spend well over five hours each day consuming popular culture, such as television, music, movies and videos, magazines, video games, and the Internet. It is likely that there is little time during your children's waking hours that they are not being influenced by popular culture.

But the presence of American popular culture shouldn't be your greatest worry. Rather, your greatest concern should be the influence that this presence has on your children. Few people really understand how popular culture affects children's lives. Even fewer people realize how truly harmful it is to children, families, communities, and to our society as a whole. For example, popular culture encourages your children to:

- be observers rather than participants;
- experience life vicariously instead of directly;
- engage in virtual reality rather than reality itself;
- be sedentary instead of physically active;
- have indirect social contact with others rather than real contact; and
- play it safe instead of take risks.

Is American popular culture beneficial to your children and your family? You decide. How pervasive is American popular culture's presence in children's lives? Let's take a look.

Television

A recent Kaiser Foundation study reported that children under the age of six spend about two hours a day in front of a screen (e.g., television, video games, DVD, computer), as much time as they do playing outside and three times as much time as they spend reading. Two-thirds of children are in homes where the television is on at least half the time and one-third where the television is on almost always, even when no one is watching. Even more disturbing, despite the recommendations from the American Academy of Pediatrics that children under two years old should not watch any television, two-thirds of toddlers spend over two hours a day in front of some form of screen media.

The Kaiser Foundation study offers some compelling findings on the effects of various forms of screen media on children. For example, reading is fundamental to a child's development, ability to learn, and success in school. Yet children in "heavy TV households" are less likely to read on any given day compared to children who watch less television. When they do read or are read to, less time is devoted to reading. Even more significant, children who are heavily exposed to television are less likely to be able to read at ages two and six than children who watch less television. And it's not just reading that's affected. Heavy television watchers spend, on average, thirty minutes less per day playing outside than do other children. Not only does this hurt their social development, but it also contributes to the epidemic of obesity among children. Yet despite all this evidence, over 40 percent of parents still believe that television helps their children to learn, while only about a quarter believe that it hurts their learning. Perhaps this mistaken belief is based on the educational television programs parents grew up with, for example, *Sesame Street* and *Mr. Rogers' Neighborhood,* but it is no longer the case. If you think children are watching such kid-friendly shows today, think again. You might be surprised to learn that *Desperate Housewives,* the 2004 ABC hit series about unhappy housewives in upscale suburbia, is the number-five-rated prime-time show among 12- to 17-year-olds. Notes David E. Kelly, the critically acclaimed television writer and producer, "There has been erosion in respect for the media by its guardians…While in years past network executives championed quality scripted television, today they celebrate the junk. Once, they were ashamed of it; now they throw parades for themselves."

The impact of television on children, particularly in the relationship between violence and aggressive behavior, is well documented. Extensive research has demonstrated that violent images are related to increases in violent thoughts, emotions, and behavior in children. Despite this irrefutable evidence, surveys have shown that over 60 percent of television shows portray violence. Even more damaging, the violence is often associated with humor, the perpetrators are attractive, no immediate punishment is meted out, and few negative consequences for the perpetrators are evident. The messages that children receive from violent television tend to glamorize the violence, minimize its harm, and suggest that they won't be held accountable for their aggressive actions. The findings of a review of over one thousand studies concluded that children who watch a substantial amount of violence on television are more likely to demonstrate aggressive values, attitudes, and behavior. A congressional summit involving children's health groups held in 2000 concluded that media violence will:

- increase aggressive behavior;
- desensitize children to violence and to its victims;
- cause children to view the world as violent and threatening; and
- encourage children to see violence as an acceptable means of resolving conflict.

Yet parents are clearly not getting the message.

Video Games

Video games have quite simply become the latest and most potent force for American popular culture, as evidenced by the *New York Times Magazine* cover story, "Joy Stick Nation!: How and why video games conquered music, TV, and the movies to become America's *popular* pop culture." The explosive growth of video games has been nothing less than staggering. For example, sales of video games have topped 220 million at $20 billion annually. Despite the strong evidence of the unhealthy effects of video games on children, 67 percent of households with children own a video-game system. Though there certainly are educational video games that can foster critical thinking, creativity, and learning, most children are not playing those games. Surveys estimate that 80 percent of the most popular video games have violent themes, and 50 percent of video games that were chosen as favorites by fourth- through eighth-grade children had violent content. A survey of video-game use found that, of 118 M-rated games (for mature audiences, over 17 years old), 70 percent were targeted to children under 17 years of age. Even more disturbing, younger children had ready access to these supposedly restricted video games. Unaccompanied children between 13 and 16 years old were able to buy M-rated video games 85 percent of the time. The video-game industry that produces and markets these games, the retailers who sell them, and the parents who allow their children to buy and play these games obviously do not have children's best interests at heart.

And it's not just that children are playing unhealthy video games, but that they are devoting incredible amounts of time to them. A recent survey indicated that about 70 percent of children play video games one to four hours a day with 12 percent playing a whopping five to nine hours a day. Moreover, just under 60 percent of parents don't set limits on their children's video-game playing. Says a college freshman who plays video games every day because it gives him something to do, "It's an activity that wastes a lot of time. When you're playing a video game, you really get into it and you lose track of time. Before you know it, an hour or so has passed you by." Not only is this student sacrificing study time, but he is also missing out on the valuable social experiences of college and wasting his parents' money.

The video-game industry vigorously defends itself by saying that they are just giving children what they want and that kids know that video games aren't real. They say that parents should be the ones governing what video games their children play. The video-game industry also denies that violent video games increase violence in children, despite the growing body of research that is finding that video games negatively affect children, particularly those games with violent themes. Studies have shown that children who play violent video games, particularly boys, are more likely to exhibit increased aggressive thinking, emotions, and behavior, and delinquency. They also found that video games can foster social isolation, as many video games are played alone. Gender stereotypes of women as helpless and sexually provocative are commonly portrayed. Some research has reported that academic achievement is negatively related to the amount of time spent playing video games. Not only is it harmful to children in many ways, but it keeps them from engaging in activities and having experiences that would encourage their health and development.

Music

Over the past decade, there has been a public outcry about music lyrics, particularly in hip-hop and hard rock songs. The concern has been that violent and sexually explicit lyrics could lead children to develop aggressive attitudes and violent behavior. This uproar led to Congressional hearings that pressured the recording industry to adopt a voluntary rating system for all popular music similar to that devised by the film industry. Anecdotally, the young perpetrators of the

Columbine school massacre were said to listen to heavy metal music with violent lyrics. Additionally, considerable hip-hop music is sexually exploitive and demeaning of women.

Though less often studied, music may affect children negatively. For example, correlational research has found that listeners of rap and heavy metal music had more hostile attitudes and more negative attitudes toward women, below-average school performance, behavioral or drug problems, increased sexual activity, and more arrests, though a cause-effect relationship can't be determined from this type of research (i.e., does the music cause these problems or are children prone to this kind of behavior drawn to violent music?). One study did report that listening to violent lyrics increased aggressive thoughts and feelings of hostility.

Magazines

The power of magazines to influence young lives has never been greater, particularly among girls, who comprise one of the largest segments of purchasers of magazines (along with adult females). Magazines such as *Cosmopolitan*, *Glamour*, *Seventeen*, *YM*, and *Teen People*, shape the way many girls think, look, dress, and feel about themselves. In recent years, there has been a shift in these magazines toward addressing issues of real concern for young women, for example, health, diet, and stress. But the overriding messages, particularly visual messages, in these magazines' content and advertising focus on beauty and thinness. The images and words that are the focus of these magazines have a powerful impact on girls' perceptions of their body weight and shape. For example, in one study, 69 percent of girls surveyed said that magazine content influenced their view of an ideal body type and 47 percent said the content caused them to want to go on a diet to lose weight. The study found that there was also a significant relationship between the frequency with which girls read women's magazines and girls' desire to lose weight, and the rate at which they dieted and exercised. Also, the more girls read these magazines, the more likely they were to be unhappy with their bodies.

Advertising

The presence and influence of advertising on children has been growing exponentially in recent years. According to a survey conducted by the Center for a New American Dream, children view an average of fifty television ads each weekday. If you include the ads children hear on the radio, read in magazines, and see on billboards and in storefronts, the number easily climbs into the hundreds and perhaps thousands. Asserts James U. McNeal, a professor of marketing at Texas A&M University, "Not long ago we considered children vulnerable beings to be nurtured. However, today we increasingly see kids through an economic lens. In our business culture, children are viewed as an economic resource to be exploited, just like bauxite or timber." Adds Wayne Chilicki, a General Mills executive, "When it comes to targeting kid consumers, we at General Mills follow the Procter & Gamble model of 'cradle to grave.' We believe in getting them early and having them for life." Now, these companies have your children's best interests at heart (note the strong tone of sarcasm, in case you missed it)!

Advertising taps into and manipulates children where they are most vulnerable, in their needs for self-esteem and peer acceptance. Over 50 percent of the children surveyed by the Center for a New American Dream said that buying certain products made them feel better about themselves. This number was even higher for 12- and 13-year-olds. A third of the children indicated that they felt pressure to buy the "right" products. Observes Betsy Taylor, the executive director of the center, "They are being made to feel that if they don't have the right low-cut designer jeans, the right video game, or the right designer watch—that they're going to be rejected by other kids."

Unfortunately, our government seems to have little concern for this manipulative and, some might say, abusive treatment of American children. Many European countries have regulations limiting advertising to children. But the U.S. government actually revoked the authority of the Federal Trade Commission to set such limits when the FTC threatened to do so to protect children. It should also come as no surprise to anyone that, as the *Mothering* magazine writer, Gary Ruskin, observes, "The rise in advertising to kids coincides with the rise in childhood problems of obesity, diabetes, gambling, and smoking. It also coincides with a rise in materialism and a decline in interest in political affairs." The uncontrolled exposure of children to advertising may be the greatest weapon that American popular culture uses against your children.

Given the significant evidence of the unhealthy effects of video games on children, you would expect that the video-game industry would act responsibly in their marketing to children. Yet video-game manufacturers are especially guilty of inappropriate and manipulative advertising. According to one report, video games designed and rated for mature audiences are being marketed to younger children. For example, an advertisement for Resident Evil 2 appeared in *Sports Illustrated for Kids* and the action figures based on the video game, Duke Nukem, are sold in toy stores. Even more egregious, the marketing messages for many video games encourage wanton violence and savagery, even for games that are rated E (Everyone—well suited for a general audience; these games have minimal violence but may contain some crude language), and T (Teens—for older kids, ages 13 and up; these games often have violent content and can contain strong language). For example, an ad for Dead in the Water (rated E) states, "I will kill you, maggot," an ad for Point Blank (rated T), says, "More fun than shooting your neighbor's cat." Even more extreme, an ad for Carmageddon, rated M (Mature—for people 17 and older; these games usually have very violent or gory content, strong language, and possible nudity): "As easy as killing babies with axes." Says George Broussard, cofounder of 3D Realms, who sells Duke Nukem, an extremely violent video game, "Duke is a mass-market character that can sell two million games. It'd be suicide to make the game unplayable by younger people." Does the video-game industry have no shame? Obviously not.

Internet

In this age of technology, one of the best measures of what values and messages are most present in your children's lives is the most searched topics on the Internet, particularly so because young people are its most frequent users. A perusal of the most commonly used search engines demonstrates how overwhelmingly powerful the presence of American popular culture is on children, and offers a rather sad commentary on what interests American children today. For example, Yahoo's most searched topics in 2003 were: Kazaa (the music file-sharing website), Harry Potter, American Idol, Britney Spears, 50 Cent (a hip-hop artist), Eminem (another hip-hop artist), WWE (the professional wrestling organization), Paris Hilton, NASCAR, and Christina Aguilera.

Conspicuously absent are *any* searches outside of popular culture.

Top-ten lists of the other leading search engines—Lycos, AOL, and Google—show a similar pattern. Two of the four search engines were comprised entirely of popular culture queries. The only significant topics that appeared on any of the search engines' top-ten lists were Iraq, affirmative action, the IRS, and Korea. Even Google's top-ten news stories of 2003 were dominated by popular culture (in order): the Iraq conflict, the Laci Peterson murder trial, the Kobe Bryant sexual assault trial, the Bertrand Cantat murder case (he is a French music star accused of killing his girlfriend, Marie Trintignant, a well-known French actress), the Recording Industries Association of America battle over music sharing, the Jessica Lynch capture and rescue, the Michael Jackson molestation case, the Elizabeth Smart kidnapping and escape, the Korean conflict, and the Dixie Chicks (who were excoriated for criticizing the Iraq invasion).

These search lists paint a richly textured—and painful—picture of what interests people, notably young people, and what they think about, care about, and focus on. The lists reveal the profound inanity of what occupies the time and energy of young people today and their thoughtless disregard for matters of substance and consequence. Predictably, they also reflect the priorities that lie at the forefront of American popular culture and the knowledge that it values. Even worse perhaps, Google's top-ten news stories demonstrate how America's news agencies, once bastions of integrity and depth, have become unwitting accomplices to popular culture; if the news industry didn't focus on the many meaningless stories, they would not likely lodge themselves so firmly in the psyches of young people.

In Harm's Way

Twenty-first-century America offers parents plenty of things to worry about regarding their children. But almost every parent in America is most noticeably concerned about three areas that threaten their children: alcohol, cigarettes, and sex. These three can do the most harm to your children's physical and mental health, and interfere with their development and futures. American popular culture has the most powerful influence on children in these areas and, unfortunately, that influence is pushing your children in the wrong direction. Popular culture has made drinking alcohol (and, by extension, taking drugs), smoking cigarettes, and having sex attractive and wanted by young people, despite their obvious dangers. In the case of the first two, those industries reap huge profits from getting children to drink and smoke at an early age. As for sex, it has quite simply become the most potent marketing tool in history. Products, from clothing and cars to food and beverages, are advertised ensuring that the buyer will be attractive and popular, and the products' use will result in increased sexual activity.

Alcohol

Alcohol use is one of the most significant areas in which American popular culture influences children because of its immediate and long-term health risks. Various forms of alcohol are the most frequently presented beverages on television. Research has found that alcohol is typically depicted in a positive or neutral light with little or no evidence of negative consequences. Television and radio advertising for alcohol rose over 1,000 percent between 1997 and 1999, after the alcoholic beverage industry lifted a voluntary ban against such advertising. During that same period, the number of websites devoted to the sale and consumption of alcohol rose by 80 percent. Alcohol appeared in over 65 percent of all television shows (an average of over eight times an hour) and in approximately 20 percent of music videos. Alcohol is also one of the most frequently advertised products on television, representing about 77 percent of all beverage commercials shown during sports events.

Not only is alcohol presented to children in incredible frequency, but also in a way that maximizes its allure to children. Drinking is commonly associated with attractive people, popularity, sexual behavior, sports, and fun. Sex is the primary vehicle for most alcohol advertising. For example, ads for beer are the most frequently broadcast and their messages are marketed predominantly to young males. Not surprisingly, these ads (and similar ones for hard alcohol) involve attractive male actors whose sexual attractiveness is enhanced by drinking the advertised beverage and by beautiful young women who are drawn to the actors because of what they are drinking. These ads are especially influential on adolescent males who are just starting to learn about their emerging sexuality and are vulnerable to simplistic and unrealistic messages about sexuality.

Young people learn more about alcohol use from advertising than from more responsible outlets, such as parents and educators. This imbalance of information causes children to be more aware of the images connected with alcohol and its purported social benefits than of the dangers related to drinking. Young people are particularly drawn to the images and lifestyle aspects of the ads, including humor, celebrities, animated characters, animals, and popular music. Research has shown that frequent contact with media depictions of alcohol and alcohol advertising creates positive perceptions about alcohol use and, in particular, viewing music videos was related to drinking at a younger age. Exposure to alcohol advertising also results in decreased concern for the dangers and greater interest in the social benefits of alcohol consumption, and higher expectations of drinking alcohol in the future. Other studies have shown that the liking of ads and the recall of brand names were related to recent and long-term consumption of alcohol.

Smoking

Smoking is another high-risk area in which American popular culture has a significant influence on children. Research shows that 90 percent of smokers begin before they reach legal age to purchase cigarettes and a third begin smoking by age 14. An astounding 10 percent of smokers begin as early as 10 years of age. Much like alcohol use, the research indicates clearly how popular culture, in the form of cigarette advertising and the presence of smoking on television and in film, encourages children to begin smoking. For example, children have been found to be three times more susceptible to cigarette advertising than adults, and such inducements are twice as powerful as peer pressure. Children who spend more time watching television (including movies and music videos) are more likely to engage in high-risk behavior, such as smoking and drinking alcohol.

Connecting interesting animated characters (e.g., Joe Camel) and fun images has enabled the tobacco industry to pique the interest of very young children and plant the seed for future cigarette use. As children get older, the focus of the influence shifts. For example, the onset of smoking in children was related to whether children's favorite film stars smoked. The ready adoration of celebrities by children and their desire to emulate them increases the risk that children will smoke just to be like them. The presence of smoking in movies was also found to be associated with a greater risk of smoking. The characters portrayed in film who smoke are often macho, feminine, sophisticated, sexy, popular, chic, mature, or mysterious, all qualities that are very attractive to children. With such powerful messages, popular culture lures children into a habit that has well-known health risks to children and significant costs to our society. As with alcohol, the depictions of smokers in film and other media predictably never illustrate the long-term health dangers associated with continued tobacco use.

What attitude does the tobacco industry have toward children? The following is excerpted from Congressional testimony by Dr. Jeffrey Wigand, the "whistle blower" who became the subject of the 1999 film, *The Insider,* starring Russell Crowe: "Children are the mainstays of the tobacco industry. Youth is the key to tobacco industry expansion. In order for tobacco industry profits to be sustained and to rise; in order for company stock to thrive, the tobacco companies must have replacement smokers, smokers who take the place of those who quit, but mostly those who die from a tobacco-related disease. In terms of maximizing profit, children are the most efficient replacement smokers. I heard firsthand from the highest officials at Brown & Williamson [one of the leading cigarette producers] that the company philosophy towards children is simply this: 'Hook 'em young, hook 'em for life.'"

Sex

The influence of American popular culture on children's beliefs, attitudes, and behavior toward sexuality has never been greater, particularly in light of the reluctance of many parents and schools to educate children about sexuality. The portrayals of sexuality on television, in music, movies, magazines, and advertising, and its ready access through the Internet offer children messages that are enticing, yet rarely accurate or responsible. For example, over two-thirds of television programming has sexual content, yet only 10 percent mention the potential consequences of sexual activity. Up to one-half of all music videos (depending on the genre) portray sexuality or eroticism.

Two-thirds of movies are R-rated, yet most children under 17 have no trouble getting into to see them. Over 20 percent of radio segments— both music and talk—have sexual content. Each of the top-ten CDs had at least one song with sexual content. Little of the music on CD or the radio communicated sexually responsibly content to listeners. The messages that children get from this inundation of sexual content is that sex is cool, fun, and risk-free. These messages are in sharp contrast to the reality of sexual activity that includes sexually transmitted diseases and pregnancy.

Magazines that target girls use sexual themes in much of their advertising and devote much of their content to how girls can get a guy. The Internet has become a significant source of exposure to sexual content. For example, 25 percent of children aged 10 to 17 encountered unintended sexual content while on the Web. With few controls built into Web browsers, children can access sexual material at will. "Sex" is the most searched word on the Internet. Research indicates that the sexual content and messages in American popular culture influence young people's beliefs, attitudes, and behavior about sex. For example, 75 percent of teenagers indicate that the fact that popular culture makes sex the normal thing to do encourages them to have sex, and its portrayals encourage irresponsible sex. Young teenagers rate popular culture as their top source of information about sex. This finding is a sad commentary on parents and schools, who should be the primary sources of accurate information about sex. Experts on youth sexual behavior suggest that popular culture affects children's attitudes and behavior toward sex in several ways. The ongoing presence of sexual content in popular culture keeps sexuality in the front of children's minds. It reinforces a generally accepted set of norms about sex. And popular culture offers little sexually responsible information or models from which children can learn.

The ideas and research I have just discussed and the plethora of other findings that are too numerous to describe here illustrate the overwhelming presence that American popular culture has in your children's lives and the destructive influence it has in so many areas of their lives. But there is not, to date, any data about the impact that American popular culture has on the values that children adopt. For now, we can only extrapolate the meaning of the available research and intuit what values are reflected in the children's behavior that the research has observed. Without too much of a stretch, we can assume the values that your children are adopting from popular culture are not healthy or life-affirming for them, your family, the community in which you live, and our country as a whole.

Popular Culture's Two Lines of Attack

American popular culture conveys its values through its many media. Though diverse in its tools of persuasion, popular culture relies on two primary avenues for communicating their messages and influencing your children. The first type of message that popular culture uses is what I call "loudspeaker" messages, in which the messages are deafening, constant, and ever-present. The shrillness of these messages is heard, seen, tasted, or felt, and cannot be readily avoided. Examples of these loudspeaker messages are most kinds of popular culture, including movies, video games, television, and music, in addition to less obvious loudspeaker messages from roadside billboards and magazine ads. Many aspects of children's daily lives have become loudspeaker messages from American popular culture. Many of children's peers and those they admire act as accomplices to popular culture sending clear and unavoidable messages: what they wear, what they eat and drink, what they talk about, how they behave. Just driving down the street in most cities, towns, and suburbs exposes children to bright and flashing lights aimed at luring them into stores (where they can buy products they don't need) and restaurants (where they can eat food that is unhealthy). Because of the invasiveness of these messages, children can't help but notice them and, for most children, can't avoid their influence.

Most parents are aware of these "loudspeaker" messages—they're hard to miss—and many try to avoid or resist them as much as possible. For example, many parents limit TV time, video-game use, and what movies their children see. At the same time, this constant barrage may simply inure parents to the point where they don't even notice them any longer. But don't be fooled into thinking that just because they don't affect you they won't influence your children. Vigilance to all forms of popular culture is essential to protect your children from its harmful effects.

The second type of message that American popular culture uses to seduce children are what I call "stealth" messages. These messages are usually hidden behind characters, images, words, and sounds that are fun and engaging, but are designed to subtly tap into children's unconscious needs and wishes. Messages that create positive emotional reactions, for example, dancing while drinking Pepsi, or winning a basketball game wearing a pair of Nikes, resonate at a deep and unconscious level with children, causing them to want to feel that way too. Other subtle messages, that tap into children's fears and insecurities related to self-esteem, social acceptance, and physical attractiveness, are particularly effective in manipulating children.

Using these messages, American popular culture deceives you and your children. What looks like fun and games is actually polluting your children's minds and spirits. It's corrupting their morals, taking away their initiative and creativity, and destroying their humanity. But you might miss this unhealthy influence seeing your kids having such a good time. And popular culture feels no sense of responsibility—or decency—toward your children. If you asked popular culture about its influence on your children, it would probably say something like, "I don't want to harm children. There is no research to support the claims of parents and educators. I'm just giving children what they want. TV shows, video games, music, and magazines that your children watch, play, listen to, and read are just harmless entertainment. I don't influence children, I only reflect our society." Or "It's not fair to blame me. What about parents taking responsibility for their own children? It's not my job to raise them. They should be the ones who decide what TV shows their children watch, what music they listen to, and what video games they play."

Examples of the unhealthy value messages that American popular culture conveys to your children are ubiquitous. According to the bestselling author, Larry Woiwode, "Television, in fact, has greater power over the lives of most Americans than any educational system or government or church…The growing influence of television has changed people's habits and values and affected their assumptions about the world." Reality TV, a recent spawn of American popular culture, is currently the hottest property on television. Most people assume that it arose out of popular interest, but in actuality reality TV was developed by networks as a means of curbing the costs of television production and enhancing profit margins. There was no clamoring by the American public for this genre of entertainment.

The values communicated on reality TV are truly destructive. Shows such as *Survivor* encourage deceit, manipulation, backstabbing, and "look out for #1" and "win at all costs" attitudes. Reality shows such as *American Idol* and *The Weakest Link,* though ostensibly about achieving the American Dream of wealth and fame (a false dream which few children will ever realize), places great emphasis on the rejection and humiliation of its losing contestants.

Advertising's clear purpose is to convince your children to buy products—or nag you into buying them for your children—that the ads are selling. Can you blame advertising for this? I would say not, as it is only doing what it was created to do. Yet the deceit and manipulation is powerful and without conscience. For example, a few years ago an ad for Lays potato chips encouraged viewers to "Get your own bag!" A commercial for Butterfingers candy bar featuring *The Simpsons* has Bart admonishing Homer to "Get your fingers off of my Butterfinger!" Though certainly entertaining, the values that these ads, and many like them, convey to kids is selfishness, hoarding, and lack of generosity, all in the name of greater profits for the companies who manufacture and sell these products. Value messages embedded in ads that are, on the surface, fun and often filled with celebrities, cute animated characters, or amusing people, communicate truly awful values. Advertisers clearly have no shame, even using meaningful values, such as patriotism, for its own greedy ends. For example, they have used the September 11, 2001, tragedy to sell products. Automobile companies draped themselves in patriotism and American flags to sell cars for "no money down and 0 percent interest." Hummer, the huge, gas-guzzling SUV, intimated that buying their vehicles would be a show of support for U.S. troops in Iraq.

Video games, such as the Grand Theft Auto series and Halo 2, aggrandize criminal behavior, stereotyping, violence, and murder without consequences. The Grand Theft Auto series exemplifies the kinds of lessons violent video games teach children. "This phenomenally popular video game allows you to hijack cars, shoot cops, kill women with baseball bats, have sex with prostitutes (and then kill them too)…In this game, you don't kill the bad guy, *you're* the bad guy," writes the *New York Times Magazine's* Jonathan Dee, "…it therefore seems undeniable that video games, compared to other forms of entertainment, are disproportionately concerned with violence. (Revenge is the back-story element in a great many games, if only to frame the violence in a justifiable context)…The gore and moral lassitude of games like Doom or Grand Theft Auto…have given rise to a parental panic…" Responds Bruno Bonnell, the CEO of Atari, a leading video-game producer, "I think the mass-market perception of video games…is 'Wow, those games are too violent…' But that represents only about 10 percent of the market." Well, as I mentioned earlier, about 220 million video games were sold in each of the last few years, meaning over 20 million of those games are violent. Assuming that most of these violent video games are played by children, that is an enormous number of children being exposed to unhealthy values.

I could write an entire book describing the truly appalling values that are expressed on television, video games, music, film, sports, magazines, the Internet, fashion, and toys. But the point of this book is not to catalog numerous and detailed examples of the pervasive and harmful effects of American popular culture on children—this topic has been studied and described extensively elsewhere. Rather, my goal is to provide a compelling overview that will convince you of the danger of popular culture and encourage you to explore how you can, for your children's sake, resist popular culture and teach them healthy, life-affirming values.

Your Children Know about the Danger

Over the years, having spoken to thousands of children, I have learned a surprising thing: most children aren't fooled by American popular culture. They know it's bad. They know that all American popular culture cares about is making money. They know that the messages it communicates are unhealthy. Most children also know what good and bad values are and what is right and wrong. But they lack the experience, perspective, and tools to withstand the attraction: its bells and whistles, its bright lights and loud music, its beautiful people, its short attention span. Children have good values deep down—they may even be born with that capacity—but they lose touch with them because the contradicting messages from American popular culture are so intense, invasive, and persistent. They are simply overwhelmed by the force of popular culture. If those same messages are also part of the messages communicated by you and are a part of your family, the valued goodness that your children have could be so suppressed as to be irrecoverable.

CHAPTER 2

Know Your Values (Armor Up)

American Popular Culture on the Offensive

Paris Hilton is 23 years old, an heiress to the Hilton hotel empire, and has a trust fund estimated at $30 million. According to media reports, Ms. Hilton barely graduated from high school and spends her time as a pampered, partying socialite, intent on flaunting her wealth and notoriety. Ms. Hilton got her first credit card at 9 years old, dressed in haute couture at age 13, started going to dance clubs at 16, and was seen in a sex video at 19. Reports have described her as self-centered, spoiled, obnoxious, and desperate for respect. Ms. Hilton receives over-the-top attention from the popular media despite the fact that she has accomplished little in her life. As many observers note, she is famous for being famous.

What values do you think Paris Hilton grew up with? What role did her parents, Rick and Kathy Hilton, the grandson of the founder of Hilton Hotels and a child actress, respectively, play in her development? How could a young woman who was given every opportunity become what appears to be an immature, vacuous, and unkind person? I pose these questions because I can't provide you with any clear answers. What I will say is that she seems to have learned no boundaries and few values of redeeming quality (e.g., humility, compassion), and has become a human sacrifice to the forces of American popular culture. Though few people would feel sympathy for Paris Hilton, she is a true casualty in the war with popular culture. At the same time, Ms. Hilton has become a ally and highly attractive symbol of popular culture to many young people. As with many examples of American popular culture, children, particularly girls, see Paris Hilton and want to look and dress like her, be treated the way she is, and be given what she has received. Children who admire her must learn, however, that without money, Ms. Hilton would be just another beautiful, promiscuous, vapid, and anonymous young woman looking for attention.

One of the most frequent comments I get from parents is, "We've never sat down and actually talked about what we value." Well, how can you teach values to your children if you don't even know what yours are? At best, you might communicate some positive values to your children in a trial-and-error way and they might pick up some of those desired values. At worst, your children will not receive your value messages at all and will look elsewhere—such as to American popular culture!—to decide what should be important to them. In either case, your children will not receive clear, direct, and positive messages about the values that you believe they should have.

Growing Concern about Values

In recent years, there has been a growing concern about whether America's children are learning good values. For example, a recent survey conducted by Public Agenda, a nonprofit research organization, found that many parents don't believe that they're doing a good job providing their children with essential values and skills. As the decline in values among our youth has become more evident, increased attention has been devoted to reversing this trend. For example, most states offer "character education" programs to schools to help teach children about values in the hope that it will reduce cheating, bullying, stealing, and the use of alcohol and drugs.

Given the significant concerns, it is paramount to understand what values are, what values you live by, the role that you play in teaching

your children values, and how you can encourage healthy values in
your children.

What Are Values?

Values have been the topic of extensive discussion and debate in America
during the past twenty years. Many have observed and commented on
the deterioration in adherence to positive values in our culture. This
moral decay has been blamed for everything from the rise in divorce rates
to crime to bad behavior among children. Yet there doesn't seem to be
great consensus on why the observance of values are in decline or how
they can be reasserted. Much of this confusion stems from a lack of real
understanding of what values are, their influence on people, and their
place in our everyday lives.

Webster's New Universal Unabridged Dictionary defines values as "the
ideals, customs, and institutions, etc., of a society toward which the
people of the group have an affective regard." Put simply, values are
guides that shape the members of a society in appropriate and acceptable ways for them to think, feel, and behave. Values are the foundation upon which civilizations, societies, communities, families, and
individuals are built. They are essential for maintaining the integrity of
every person and every group as a whole. As the dictionary definition
suggests, people develop intense emotional connections to their values;
values such as honor, integrity, and dignity evoke strong feelings in
many people. Values give clarity to moral and ethical choices that people face in their lives, preparing them to confront these choices when
they arise. For example, if someone values friendship, it means that
when they are faced with a choice between friendship and personal
gain, they would choose to protect their friendship and forego personal gain. Values give us standards of behavior toward which we can
strive. They shape who we are as people and as a culture, setting priorities, establishing norms, and creating expectations.

How Values Were Lost

If values are so important to individuals and societies, why have values
lost their luster and power in recent years? Unfortunately, values have
gotten a bad rap. Political, social, and religious groups have attempt-
ed to commandeer values to satisfy their own agendas. This hijacking

has turned values into exclusive "holier than thou" domains over which various groups claim control. This co-opting may have clouded the meaning of value to people and turned them off to their importance. We seem to have lost sight of what values really are, and lost consensus about what are considered healthy values, and how values benefit everyone.

Values are also hurt by the fact that they are so revered. Because of their lofty status in our society, many people think that values are ethereal entities, floating somewhere outside of the "real world." This perceived distance from everyday life is one cause of values losing their influence over people. People have become disconnected from the values on which our society was built. They no longer think about, see, feel, or experience them in their daily lives. But values—such as honesty, caring, and hard work—are very real and should express themselves throughout every day of our lives. When you tell your children to do their homework, bring their dishes to the table, or be nice to their sibling, you're not just enforcing family rules and regulations. More important, you're communicating essential values that your children must learn: discipline, responsibility, and consideration.

We have gotten lazy with our values. We've assumed that good values would continue to assert themselves simply because they always have. We have given little thought to or had meaningful dialogue about the role of values in our lives and, to a degree, have forgotten what they mean to us. We have taken for granted the values on which our country was founded, and this neglect has resulted in us veering off a value-driven course.

Our culture has also changed dramatically in the last thirty years. There is no longer consensus on what we should value as a society, due in large part to the influence of American popular culture. There is also greater fragmentation of families, separation of people, and disconnection between communities. This loss of social ties has made agreement on values more difficult and has made it harder for values to be kept at the forefront of people's lives, shared among people, and taught to subsequent generations.

Economic uncertainty may also be contributing to the decay of values in America. As the psychologist, Abraham Maslow, suggests in his "Hierarchy of Needs," people must satisfy more basic needs—food, water, shelter—before they can focus on other, higher-order needs, such as values. As concerns about the economy, jobs, and putting a roof over their heads and food on their tables grows, parents' attention to teaching values to their children may have diminished.

The frenetic pace of twenty-first-century life has also interfered with parents teaching values to their children. Overworked, overscheduled, stressed out, and exhausted parents no longer have the time or the energy to make values a priority in their families. Parents are just happy to get their children through another day. The rigors of daily life have taken precedence over the values on which daily life should be based.

These issues all inhibit the teaching of values to children, but none of them actually cause children to internalize an entirely different set of values. Unfortunately, other forces, namely American popular culture, have arisen and gained power in the last few decades, communicating values that are in direct conflict with our time-honored values. These forces (that are driven by profit at any cost and have little concern for the public good) have either seduced people into believing that unhealthy values, such as immediate gratification, greed, and hedonism, should be adopted and pursued, or caused them to feel helpless to resist them.

Teaching Values

Values are like plants that must receive regular attention for them to grow and flourish. Values must be nourished and tended to regularly. A watchful eye must be kept for any disease or parasite that might harm them. Values must be brought into the light daily so they can grow stronger and be appreciated by parents and children alike for their beauty, meaning, and importance in their lives. Values are "watered and fed" when they are brought down from that top shelf that is hard to get to and placed within easy reach in your daily life and your children. Values should be woven into the very fabric of your family's everyday life and should be connected to every thought you and your children have, every emotion you feel, and every action you take.

Types of Values

Values have a broad range of influence in your lives. To help you gain clarity of the values you hold and want to communicate to your children, I have placed this spectrum into categories of values that apply to every part of your life:

Personal values are those values that guide the kind of life you create for yourself. These values emphasize how you wish to live your life (e.g., honesty, integrity, independence, health, education, quality of life, intellectual, athletic, and creative avocations).

Social values determine what is important to you in your relationships with others (e.g., family, friendship, compassion, charity, communication, intimacy). These values are expressed in the connections you have with family, friends, community, society, and the world as a whole.

Spiritual values focus on the role that faith plays in your life (e.g., belief in a higher power). They can be related to a formal religious system or may simply be a personal set of beliefs about spirituality. Spiritual values can also encompass personal and social values (e.g., "love thy neighbor").

Achievement values relate to the importance you place on striving for and attaining goals in your life. These goals are found in your educational, career, athletic, artistic, and other endeavors. As you explore your values, these categories can help you to organize them and get a better understanding of how they fit together.

How Children Learn Values

Though there is evidence that children are born with the ability to be moral, children learn specific values from the forces in their lives to which they have the most exposure and that they perceive as the most influential. The most common sources of values in children are parents, educators, American popular culture, and peers.

Unfortunately, many people have an oversimplified view of instilling values in children, believing that children will naturally embrace values because they are simply the right way to live. In reality, though, teaching children healthy values must begin at an early age and be nurtured throughout childhood.

Children are easily influenced when they're young. They will absorb the values that they view as most beneficial to them. Early in your children's lives, you have the most frequent and powerful impact on their lives. Less healthy forces, such as American popular culture and peer pressure, do not yet exert a strong influence on them. If you can instill healthy values in your children when they're very young, you inoculate them against the destructive forces of popular culture before they enter later childhood and adolescence. If your children don't have well-developed value systems before they are fully immersed in popular culture, much like a weakened immune system, they are more vulnerable to being infected with the unhealthy—and highly contagious—values from popular culture and its many carriers, such as the media and peer pressure.

The process of helping your children instill healthy values begins with your understanding of what your values are. With that clarity, you can then take a variety of deliberate and active steps that will encourage your children to think about, feel, act on, experience, and choose values that you deem important.

What Do You Value?

The first step in teaching your children healthy values is simple: "Know your values!" You need to take a long, hard look at your life. Identify what you value. Look in the mirror and ask yourself whether these values are positive and the kinds of values that you want your children to adopt. Will your values help your children to become successful, happy, and contributing adults? See what values you are communicating to your children. Are you sending the right value messages and are your children getting them? See what other forces are imposing their values on your children. What is American popular culture communicating to your children and how vulnerable are they to its messages? Make sure that the values your children are getting are the values you *want* them to get.

We rarely choose our values. Most of the time we simply adopt the values of our parents and the dominant values of our community and society. Perhaps later in life some of us examine our values and reevaluate our lives, but, in general, the values that we internalize as children remain with us through adulthood and are the basis for the direction our lives take. Given how values develop and their influence on your children's future, you must ensure that the values you expose your children to will be in their best interests for their futures.

What were the values you were raised with? What do you value now? Are they the same or different? Which values are you now living in accordance with? Do your values bring you meaning, satisfaction, and happiness? These are essential questions that you must ask yourself if you want to instill healthy values in your children. Yet finding the answers to these questions is a challenge. Ensuring that what you value will help your children is a bigger challenge, and the greatest challenge is instilling those healthy values in your children.

The most difficult aspect of answering the question "What do you value?" involves avoiding clichés and not describing values that have high social desirability, but may not actually reflect what you value. For example, hard work, generosity, consideration, discipline, responsibility, commitment, faith, and health are values most everyone would say that they believe in. Yet if most of the people looked carefully at their lives, another very different set of values might present themselves.

To truly understand what values you possess and live by, you must deconstruct your life until it is reduced to its most basic values.

Your Childhood

Looking at the way you were raised is the first step in identifying the values that you adopted. What values did your parents impress upon you—achievement, generosity, wealth, education, kindness, status, civic duty, appearance? Do you still have those values? Or did you choose other values to guide your life?

Your Career

What do you do for a living—are you a corporate employee, a small-business owner, a teacher, salesperson, caterer, or social worker? This is a common question that people ask in social gatherings. Periodically, I have seen people get rather defensive in response to this question. They say, "Who cares what I do for a living? What I do is not who I am." I would suggest otherwise. Assuming people have choices in the career paths they take, which path you choose is a reflection of what you value. Though a bit of a generalization, it is probably safe to say that someone who becomes an investment banker has different values than someone who becomes an elementary school teacher. What those underlying values may be might vary, but one could assume that the investment banker values money, while the teacher values helping children.

Your Social Life

You can also look at with whom you socialize. The people you choose to interact with are a reflection of what you value. We generally spend time with people with similar values, so you can use your friends and acquaintances as a mirror to see what you value.

Where You Live

Where do you live—in a high-rise apartment in a city, in the suburbs, or on a farm—and what caused you to choose that location? Did you move to the city for the social life? Did you move to the suburbs because it is safe? Did you move to the country because you wanted quiet and to be closer to nature? In answering these questions, you learn what values are reflected in where you live.

What You Talk About

What you talk about is another indication of what you value. You talk about topics that interest you and what you find interesting is based on what is important to you. What do you talk to others about mostly— politics, gossip, religion, sports, the economy—and what does that tell you about your values?

How You Spend Your Time

Time is perhaps our most precious commodity because it is nonrenewable. Because of this, we value our time above most everything else and we are careful how we spend it. As a result, how you spend your time is another useful measure of what you value. Invariably, you will spend time doing things that are most important to you. Your choice of avocations can tell you a lot about what you value. What activities do you engage in most frequently—cultural, physical, religious, political, social—and what values are reflected in those choices?

How You Spend Your Money

Money is another resource that we hold dear. Although, unlike time, it is renewable, money, for most people, is not easily obtained. Because of the difficulty of earning money, how you spend it is another powerful indicator of what you value. What do you spend your money on— a home, cars, travel, clothing, education, art, charity, entertainment?

You use your money in ways that you value most. Over and above what you say and other indicators in your life, where you spend your hard-earned money says the most about what your values are.

You can then ask yourself whether your current values are the same as those you grew up with. Have you gone through a period of examination and reconsideration? Have you consciously chosen to discard some values from your upbringing and adopt new ones? Are the values you identified when you deconstructed your life consistent with what you thought they were? Are they the values you are communicating to your children? Are your values, now that you have a more complete understanding of them, ones that you would like your children to adopt and live their lives by?

I have found that parents who never questioned their values, bought into them early in their lives, and built their lives around those values, often had values that were less healthy and were not always conveying healthy values to their children. In contrast, parents who consciously examined their values early in life and made deliberate choices about what they valued tended to have more life-affirming values and passed those values on more clearly to their children.

A difficult aspect of exploring your values is having to admit that you have values that may not be healthy or life-affirming for your children. Perhaps you find that your interest in making money exceeds your concern for those less fortunate. Maybe you believe that health and fitness are not that important to you. Or you may believe that achievement is all about winning or that appearance and status influence how you live your life. If you come to this realization, I implore you to make the necessary changes in your values. Raising your children with positive values is the most important gift you can give them.

I urge you to seriously consider the values that I discuss in this book. While I'm not saying that everyone should have the same set of values, I do believe that there are some values that are universal and can be shared regardless of your race, ethnicity, religious faith, or political persuasion. Additionally, my judgments are grounded in over twenty years of work with young people and their parents and seeing which values lead to the development of happy, successful, and mature people and which result in people who are selfish, immature, and unfulfilled. Having to admit that you have values that may not be healthy for your children is the second most difficult part of exploring your values. The hardest part is deciding to change your values because it is in the best interests of your children. I believe there is nothing more courageous than parents who are willing to look in the mirror, see something they don't like, and commit themselves to change because they know it is best for their children (and, by the way, these changes usually make parents happier, more fulfilled people too). So I challenge you to look openly at your values and, if necessary, make changes to them and to your life so your children have the best chance to live lives of meaning, satisfaction, and joy.

Emerging Values

The most important emerging value that can come out of this discussion is for you to *value values*. I know that sounds redundant, but for you to instill healthy values in your children, you must see values as essential to your children's healthy development and a priority in their lives. When you value values, you will make them the guiding force in your child rearing. Values will be the foundation on which everything you do with your children is based. All of the ways that I showed you how to determine your values (i.e., your career, your friends, where you live, how you spend your time and money) should now be the basis for how you shape your children's values. All of these areas not only tell you what you value, but, more important, they will tell your children what you value and what they should value. You want to ask yourself, are these the values I want my children to have?

CHAPTER 3

Create a Family-Value Culture (Construct a Defense System)

American Popular Culture on the Offensive

The Osbournes, an MTV reality TV show, chronicles the lives of Ozzy Osbourne, considered the father of heavy-metal music, his wife and manager, Sharon, and their two children, Kelly and Jack (a third daughter, Aimee, chose not to participate in the show). Ozzy, who has a long history of drug and alcohol abuse, is famous for his shocking on-stage behavior and outrageous lifestyle. Sharon, the rock of the family, appears to spend much of her time holding her family together and recently was diagnosed and treated for cancer. Nineteen-year-old Kelly dropped out of high school in tenth grade and is pursuing a singing career. Jack, 17 years old, was admitted to a drug rehabilitation clinic in 2003 and acknowledged attempting suicide. As described in the July 6, 2000, issue of *Rolling Stone*, Ozzy has a difficult time asserting himself as his children's father, "'Now listen to me, children,' he says. And then they start snickering and giggling. For, indeed, what dadlike words can he say to them? What is he, Ozzy Osbourne, legendary drug-addled Prince of Darkness, the very founder of parent-freaking-out heavy-metal music, going to do to them if they don't settle down? 'How can I give out the rules when I'm worse than them most of the time? When they've seen me coming home in police cars, in f——ing ambulances, in strait-jackets and chains?... I try to be a figure of authority, but do they listen to me? F——, no!'"

The Osbournes has been a huge success and the family is adored for its quirkiness and honesty. The Osbournes are portrayed by the media as being a loving and supportive family with positive values. At the same time, it seems clear that the Osbourne parents expressed values that have hurt the children. Though an extreme example of family dysfunction to be sure, most parents that are influenced by American popular culture will create some form of dysfunction that hurts their children. The degree of that dysfunction and the harm it does to children will depend on how immersed parents are in popular culture and how much they ally themselves with its values.

Pick a Side

Now that you've explored and identified your values, you can see whose side you are on. Have you bought into American popular culture and are you passing its values on to your children? Or are your values in clear contrast to popular culture and are you helping your children to resist its messages? Picking sides is no small task because the same messages that your children are drawn to can be equally attractive to adults. Images of success, happiness, fame, popularity, power, and physical attractiveness that American popular culture exposes you to can be an irresistible intoxicant for parents. Who do you think buys those magazines in the supermarket checkout line? Hopefully, what enables you—or will enable you—to take the side of your children is that, as a mature adult, you have the capacity to think critically, look beneath the surface of messages from American popular culture, judge the true meaning of those messages, and consciously decide what you value and what is in your children's best interests.

You Have the Power

Many parents I speak to have almost lost hope in their ability to influence their children. They feel that their children have gotten away from them and that American popular culture now controls them. These parents seriously doubt that they can affect the values that their children adopt. Given the presence and influence of popular culture in your children's lives, you too may wonder whether you have the power to influence your children positively.

Fortunately, there is considerable evidence that you can have real impact on the values that your children embrace. For example, three factors have been shown to have a direct effect on parents' ability to instill healthy values in their children:

- *Family cohesion*, which involves the emotional bonds, boundaries, time spent together, inclusive decision making, and shared activities that families have, results in greater influence by parents over the values their children internalize.
- *Family adaptability*, the capacity of family members to change their roles (e.g., relationships, rules, control), assert control, and negotiate in response to varying situations and that allows children to participate in value-related interactions, discussions, and decision making, enables parents to influence the values that their children adopt.
- *Family communications*, comprised of positive conversations, empathy, and support, encourage parental influence over their children's values.

Because of the importance of values and the demonstrable influence you can have over your children's values, you can't leave their "value education" to chance. You can't assume that your children are just naturally going to adopt healthy values. And you can't expect that they will internalize your values just because you're around them. Your children will adopt the values that are most visible and influential in their lives. Though you may think you have the greatest impact on your children, your ability to affect them may be less than you expect and your influence diminishes with every year. Unless you take steps to the contrary, American popular culture will become the most dominant force in your children's lives by the time they reach 10 years of age (if not sooner). Children are being overwhelmed by the value messages from American popular culture, and it affects what they think, feel, and do, what they want, and, yes, what they value. Do you know where your children are getting their values?

What Is a Family-Value Culture?

Everyone needs and wants to be part of a culture. Belonging to a culture offers people a sense of identity, feelings of connectedness, shared values, beliefs, and attitudes about the world, and support when faced with the challenges of life. Children will seek out a culture that is most present in their lives and that provides the most rewards. How can you ally yourself with your children and protect them from a culture that will do them harm? It begins with creating a culture in your family that reflects the values you hold most dear. Much as American popular culture causes children to adopt unhealthy values from the sheer force of its presence, you can establish a "family-value culture" that has an equally powerful—but positive—influence on your children. The benefit of having a family-value culture that your children are raised in is that it precedes the presence of American popular culture and can fill the need for a culture in your children's lives so they don't feel the need to adopt American popular culture.

For a family-value culture to protect your children, it must be evident from the beginning of their lives. If you can "indoctrinate" your children into your family-value culture early in their lives, the values espoused by your family's culture will become more deeply ingrained in their psyches (i.e., how they think, feel, and behave). These well-rooted values will be more resistant to the pull of American popular culture when they are exposed to it in full force. This early immersion will ensure that your family-value culture is the first culture your children experience and envelop themselves in.

At the same time, it is never too late to change the culture of your family. Children are never at a point of no return where they become inescapable converts to popular culture. As I mentioned before, most children know that popular culture is bad for them, but aren't capable of escaping its clutches on their own. They are often just waiting for someone with the capability to oppose popular culture with whom to ally themselves. A shift in your family-value culture as late as your children's teenage years can still free them from the grip of American popular culture and help them regain perspective, alter their values, and put them on a healthier road.

A key aspect of your family-value culture is that it should be woven into every area of your children's lives. It should communicate clear value messages to your children. Children should have regular opportunities to talk about, live by, and express the values underlying the family-value culture. A family-value culture should reward your children for acceptance of and engagement with the culture with love, respect, validation, self-expression, and autonomy. An effective family-value culture is self-reinforcing because it provides children with feelings of accomplishment, meaning, satisfaction, and just a general sense of doing the right thing.

Developing a family culture is also an essential part of the grassroots effort to fight American popular culture. Every family that rejects the values of American popular culture and raises their children with a family-value culture is one more recruit in the war against popular culture. Every family who commits to a family-value culture also influences society at large exponentially because these families exert a value-driven influence on their relatives and friends, the schools that their children attend, their places of worship, and the communities in which they live.

Your Role

Creating a family-value culture is a deliberate process. You start with understanding what you value, judging whether the values you possess are healthy and in the best interests of your children, and making conscious decisions about what values you wish your family culture to be founded on. Then, as your children grow, you can educate them about what a family-value culture is, what the values that underlie the culture are, and why the values are so important to them, your family, and the world in which they live.

The first step in this process is to understand your involvement in creating a family-value culture. Your role in building a family-value culture is comprehensive and sometimes complex. Your primary responsibility is to teach your children about the value culture to which your family adheres and create an environment that will encourage your children to adopt the family-value culture (that's what this chapter is about). At the same time, you have several other roles that will help your children buy into the value culture and give them the means to resist American popular culture.

Be the Adult

Your first role as a value-driven parent is to be the adult. Being an adult is not something that automatically comes with age, experience, or having a family. Being an adult means responding to your children, your family, and the world in which you live in a way that is in their best interests. It also means expressing and teaching not only healthy values, but, just as importantly, offering a healthy family process that will support and encourage the values. These processes include viewing the culture in which your family lives in a conscious and deliberate way. It involves thinking through the choices that your family has to make rather than responding with a knee-jerk reaction or simply following the dictates of American popular culture. Acting as an adult means responding in ways that are emotionally beneficial to your family and, in fact, that emotional maturity—expressing emotions, both positive and negative, in a constructive way—is an essential part of your family-value culture. Being an adult involves having the capacity to delay gratification of your own needs and often putting the needs of your children ahead of your own. Adults are also capable of intellectual and emotional openness, and are able to engage in a dialogue with their children to address value dilemmas that arise.

For example, an 8-year-old boy, Eddie, comes home from soccer practice excitedly telling his parents that he's been invited to be a member of an elite traveling team. Participation in the team would require that Eddie attend practice four times a week and play in tournaments in other cities twice a month. American popular culture's notions of success, having what Eddie's coaches tell his parents is a "gifted" athlete with huge "potential," and pressure to "keep up with the Joneses" could cause his parents to give an automatic reaction of telling him that he can be a part of the team. But as adults who are concerned about their family-value culture and their son's best interests, Eddie's parents would step back from the situation and look at the ramifications of the decision. They would consider whether it was consistent with their family's values and what effect it would have on Eddie's overall life and that of their family's in terms of time, energy, stress, and finances. From these deliberations, his parents would judge what is best for their son and family, and make a decision that is in harmony with their family-value culture.

Teach Value Tools

As I mentioned earlier, children appear to be born with the capacity to act morally, and most children know right from wrong and want to do the right thing. But the pull of American popular culture often causes children to act in ways that they know are wrong. So instilling values in your children is not enough. You must also give them the tools to bolster their values in the face of attack from popular culture. For example, a 10-year-old girl, Kim, comes home after school and tells her parents that several of her friends were saying mean things about another girl she liked and teasing the girl about how she dressed. Kim felt bad about it, but wasn't sure if she should say anything. Her parents can help her decide what is best by guiding Kim through the use of the value tools.

One tool that your children need is *awareness* of when these assaults occur. At a young age, before your family-value culture has been fully ingrained, unless your children are consciously aware of American popular culture's influence, they will be vulnerable to its unhealthy messages. Continuing the previous example, Kim already demonstrates awareness by recognizing that her friends' treatment of the other girl is not nice. Kim's parents can expand her awareness by asking questions, such as whether this treatment has occurred more than once and whether the other girl has provoked it.

An awareness of popular culture enables your children to use another essential value tool, *critical thinking*, to judge what the message is and whether they should accept it. Without critical thinking, your children are at risk to accept popular culture's messages blindly, based on peer pressure or some other unhealthy need. With it, they can examine the message, see what values underlie the message, and decide whether it is a message they want to listen to. Kim's parents can continue their line of questioning by asking why her friends would be so mean, how she thinks the girl feels about being teased, and whether anything good can come from this type of treatment.

The tools of awareness and critical thinking enable your children to engage in good *decision making*. They learn to evaluate popular culture through the lens of your family-value culture and make deliberate decisions about what messages from American popular culture they choose to accept. Decision making based on your family-value culture can help your children look at their choices, weigh the costs and benefits to each option within the context of their values, and make a decision that is best for them. Kim decides that her friends' treatment of the other girl is wrong and chooses to tell them. Kim understands that she is risking her friendships, but she also realizes that she doesn't want to be friends with girls who are that mean.

Act as a Filter

When your children are old enough to be immersed in American popular culture, but are still too young to have fully embraced your family-value culture, they are at their most vulnerable to popular culture's unhealthy messages. At this point, an essential role you play for your children is as their filter for information from popular culture. You must act as the gatekeeper of information they are being exposed to. In this very active role, you must maintain conscious awareness and control over potentially harmful aspects of your children's lives and make thoughtful decisions about what aspects of popular culture your children are allowed to experience. For example, you should pay attention to what television shows your children are watching, what music they are listening to, what they eat away from home, what video games they are playing, what they are viewing on the Internet, and what they are doing at their friends' houses. If they are doing things that are inconsistent with your family-value culture, you need to set limits and, importantly, explain the decisions you are making.

This role also involves helping them understand the messages that will inevitably get through to them to ensure that, rather than being harmful, act as lessons about values and the kind of culture they wish to be a part of. By acting as filters early in your children's lives, you assume two important functions. You protect them from unhealthy messages from American popular culture *before* they have the values and tools to safeguard themselves. You also teach them, over time, to act as their own filters so that as they get older and have increasing exposure to popular culture they're able to separate the "wheat from the chaff." For instance, while watching television, you can help them to understand the purpose of advertising and show them how it is designed to manipulate viewers into wanting to buy the products.

Offer Another Perspective

Perhaps the most important role you can play with your children is to offer them different perspectives on their experiences with popular culture. Remember that your children have limited ability to consider different ways of looking at their world. Because of their lack of experience, lack of cognitive sophistication, and emotional vulnerability, they will accept the perspective that is most powerfully evident and immediately attractive to them. When they, for example, play a violent video game, they simply don't have the wherewithal to consider what value messages, above and beyond the entertainment, are being conveyed to them and whether the messages are unhealthy. As I have already discussed in chapter 1, the violent images and actions that are so common and brutal in many popular video games seep into your children's brains without them realizing it. If you allow your children to play these video games, you must offer them another perspective about the violence in these video games, show them that this violence is an unacceptable value, and that, however fun the video games may be, they offer little redeeming value in their use.

It is your responsibility to offer them another point of view that will keep them from buying into the harmful messages of American popular culture. This perspective begins with you being a "critical" parent. When I say critical, I don't mean critical of your children. Rather, I mean you need to look critically at the many forms of American popular culture that your children are interacting with, judge what messages your children might be getting from them, and then provide them with insights and perspectives that will mitigate the negative messages or discourage your children from wanting to expose themselves to that aspect of popular culture. In offering different perspectives to your children, they learn to view their experiences with American popular culture in a more sophisticated—and skeptical—way and, with time and more experience, to be able to gain a realistic perspective of American popular culture on their own.

Educate Your Children about Values

Educating your children about your family-value culture can begin as soon as they develop the ability to talk, listen, and to understand consequences. (Note: I don't like to offer suggestions on age appropriateness because children of the same age can vary greatly in their ability to understand and learn new ideas. You should judge when your children are ready for these discussions based on their maturity.) You want to introduce them to what values are, the role they play in their lives, and their importance to the family.

What Are Values?

Using my ideas about values from chapter 2 (and your own ideas as well), you should talk to your children about what values are. Give them a clear definition of values and discuss with them how values affect their lives and those of others. Key issues that you should emphasize are that values are principles that:

- establish priorities for what is important;
- guide the decisions they make; and
- act as a road map in determining the direction of their lives.

You should also highlight values that your children can understand and relate to. When your children act in ways that express a family value, you can point out what the value is and why what they are doing reflects the value. For example, when they bring their dishes to the sink after dinner, you can point out that they are being cooperative. When they devote considerable time to a project at school, you can show them how that demonstrates commitment and hard work. Asking your children to come up with practical examples of values in their own lives is another way to engage them and to make this process a dialogue rather than a lecture.

Why Are Values Important?

You should then talk to your children about why values are important and how values benefit them and others. What do values offer your children as individuals? How do they affect your family? And what role do values play in your community and society in general? The answers to these questions will help your children recognize the essential importance of values and why they should adopt healthy values. Again give examples, such as generosity, accountability, and honesty, and show how these specific values affect your children's lives. Recognize experiences that reflect values and connect them with your values for your children. For example, when your children are considerate of their siblings, show them how it benefits them (e.g., their siblings are nice to them) and the family as a whole (e.g., everyone gets along).

What Are Unhealthy Values?

A useful teaching tool that you can use in your discussions about values with your children is to identify unhealthy values and explain why they are destructive. This will help your children to see clearly the differences between positive and negative values. Using examples, such as greed, selfishness, and dishonesty, can help you illustrate how these values hurt your children, your family, your community and American society as a whole. When your children express unhealthy values, show them how the values hurt them and your family. You can also point out examples of bad values in other people and from the media and describe why the values are unhealthy.

Expressing Values

Many people think that values are lofty ideals that have little connection with their daily lives, but this is not true. You need to show your children that values are expressed constantly every day. Tell your children how values are seen in what they think, how they feel, and how they behave. Show them how values are reflected in the activities in which they participate, how they spend their time, and the choices they make. For example, finishing a school project on time, taking out the garbage, and reading with a younger sibling all express positive values of discipline, responsibility, and caring, respectively. When your children express positive values, you want to praise their value-driven actions (I will discuss praise/punishment in more detail in chapter 4). What is so important to creating a family-value culture is for your children to connect their values with all aspects of their lives.

Again using contrasts as a learning tool, show your children how negative values are expressed. Show them, for example, how laziness, condescension, and lying are conveyed. There is no better "classroom" for teaching about unhealthy values than in the popular media. Television, radio, video games, and magazines are all rife with destructive values from which your children can learn. If you allow your children frequent access to popular media, instead of letting your children experience the values of American popular culture alone, watch TV, listen to music, play video games, and read magazines with them.

Use these opportunities to highlight healthy and unhealthy values by talking to them about the media messages, what underlying values are being communicated, and why they are unhealthy.

One down-to-earth place where values are expressed is in the rules, boundaries, and expectations that you establish in your family-value culture. Each of these prescriptions is based on the values that you hold and the messages you want your children to get about your family-value culture. But your children don't necessarily make this connection. Many children simply see rules, boundaries, and expectations as limitations placed on their freedom without rationale or purpose. By explicitly linking your values with these directives, your children understand the reasoning behind your dictates, see their value, and directly connect their actions with your family-value culture. You can make these connections for your children by not simply "laying down the law," but rather by discussing how the limits you place on them are related to your family-value culture and how the boundaries benefit them and your family in the long run.

Consequences of Values

Perhaps the most powerful way to help children understand the importance of values is to discuss with them the consequences of healthy and unhealthy values. A valuable lesson for them is to learn that if they act in a valued way, good things will happen, and if they act according to bad values, bad things happen. Examples of this relationship can include good effort in school results in good grades and your approval, being compassionate to others causes others to respond in kind, selfishness causes children to lose their friends, and being caught stealing results in punishment and a loss of trust.

An unfortunate obstacle to teaching children about the consequences of living by one's values is that acting on good values are not always rewarded and bad values are not punished. To the contrary, American popular culture often glorifies and rewards bad values. For example, domestic violence, drug use, infidelity, and other criminal and immoral behaviors don't prevent professional sports teams from forgiving talented athletes for their behavior and paying them extravagant salaries. Remember that American popular culture doesn't have values. It is driven solely by the profit motive and will accept even the most egregious behavior if that serves its needs. Most painfully, the limits of what can be accepted by popular culture in the name of profit continue to be pushed, for example, the continuing career of the boxer, Mike Tyson, despite a conviction and jail sentence for sexual assault and other criminal behavior, and the frequent DWI and drug arrests of numerous NFL and NBA players. The recording industry persists in promoting hip-hop artists and rock stars despite rap sheets that continue to grow. Product sponsors continue to use troubled athletes, pop-music stars, and other celebrities in advertising campaigns. And, worst of all, young people continue to worship them. It is these conflicting messages that your children receive every day that confuse the teaching of healthy values.

Value Dilemmas

A powerful way to foster your children's understanding and appreciation of values is to talk to them about value dilemmas that they will face as they move through childhood and into young adulthood. For younger children, topics might include lying, stealing, and cheating. Issues for older children can include sexual behavior and alcohol and drug use. You can also identify value breakdowns from popular culture, for example, the poor behavior of actors, athletes, musicians, and politicians, to help them understand that being rewarded for bad values not only doesn't justify the values, it also has costs that may not be readily apparent to children, such as loss of self-respect and admiration from others, threats to health, and lost opportunities. Value dilemmas arise every day in your children's lives. Either they are faced with dilemmas themselves or there are examples of value dilemmas in popular media, such as newspapers, on TV, and in movies. You should have your "radar" attuned to these dilemmas and use them as opportunities to educate your children about these quandaries. With younger children, you will want to emphasize the tangible consequences of the choices presented in the dilemmas, for example, what trouble they would get in if they stole a piece of candy that they really wanted because they didn't have any money to pay for it. With older children, you can have more sophisticated discussions about self-respect, dangers to themselves and others, and implications for their future as well as the more concrete consequences of their actions (e.g., legal and health problems) in response to the value dilemma. For example, what are the personal, criminal, physical, and social ramifications of drinking and driving under pressure from friends?

In presenting these value violations, you can explore with them the benefits and costs of following and disregarding healthy values, the short- and long-term consequences of a breach of values, emotions associated with adhering to and violating values, and the choices that they will have to make about values. Children who have experience in facing value dilemmas—even if only through discussion and vicarious experience—and understand the reasons behind responding in a valued way are more likely to make value-driven decisions with such predicaments when they actually present themselves.

Family-Value Culture Is Your Family's Life

Because of the multifaceted influence of a family-value culture on your children and the strong pull that American popular culture exerts on them, simply talking about values is not enough. You must express your family-value culture in all of the ways that your children can learn healthy values. Most important, you must believe deeply in and be wholly committed to your family-value culture. Values can't just be what you say or do, but rather you must *be* your values. You must be a walking, talking, feeling, acting, living expression of your family-value culture.

Values Are You: Make Sure You Walk the Walk on Values

Knowing what you value is one thing, but communicating those values to your children is an entirely different challenge. Are the values that you believe in the values that your children are getting from you? You must ask yourself whether you are "walking the walk" on your values because, when your children are faced with conflicting messages in what you say and what you do, your actions will win hands-down every time. For example, if you say that hard work, not grades, is what is important in school, but you are constantly asking them about their grades, they will get the message that grades *do* matter.

For the duration of your children's early years, you are their most powerful influence and role model. With little question, they will look to you to decide what they should think, how they should feel, how they should behave, and, yes, what they should value. To see the significance of the effect you have on your children as role models, you need to look no further than how readily they adopt your vocabulary, voice intonations, facial expressions, and body language. You may not realize that just being who you are and behaving as you do powerfully influences the values your children learn from you. For example, the physical affection you show your spouse and children communicates to them that open expressions of love are valued in your family, or being involved in a charitable organization tells your children that compassion and giving are important family values. Anything you say, the emotions you express, how you interact with your spouse, family, and friends, and, more directly, how you relate to your children, are all expressions of the family-value culture that sends to your children subtle, yet influential, messages about your values. Being aware of your words, emotions, and actions around your children is essential to ensuring that your children buy into your family-value culture.

These messages are especially influential when you act in ways that place the needs of your children ahead of your own. For example, after a long and tiring day of work, do you choose to take your daughter to the park to kick the soccer ball around or help your son with his homework, even though you would rather sit on the sofa and read the newspaper? In doing so, you are communicating to your children that you value your family more than you value yourself and are willing to make them a priority even when it's not easy.

The question of conveying values to your children is further complicated by the fact that there is not always agreement between what values you intend to communicate to your children and the values they are perceiving from you. What you think you are teaching them is not always what they are learning from you. This disconnect can occur because your actions that are meant to reflect your values and are obvious in their intention to you, are not always clear to your children, particularly when they are young. For example, let's say you have a great passion for your work, you work very hard, and you're nicely rewarded for your efforts, enabling your family to live an affluent lifestyle. The values that underlie your efforts may be a love for your job, a work ethic, and a desire for quality in everything you do. Unfortunately, these values are not necessarily what your children see. Invariably, young children explain things in their lives in the simplest and most obvious way. In the case of your work, what your children may see is that Daddy or Mommy work really hard and make lots of money, so money must be really important to them. With this line of thinking, your children can thoroughly miss the actual values behind your work efforts and, instead, internalize something that is not part of your family-value culture, in this case, the value of money. This is why you should not only make sure you are living a life that expresses your values, but also combine it with discussions of your values. Periodically ask yourself whether your actions clearly express the values underlying your life or whether your children could misinterpret them. Also ask your children what value messages they are getting from you. For example, you can ask them, "Why do you think Daddy (Mommy) works so hard?" Their answers will tell you whether they are getting the right value messages.

Values are Thoughts: Talk to Your Children About Their Values

"Talk to your children" is perhaps the most commonly offered recommendation from parenting experts. Yet it may also be the least adopted, particularly when it comes to values. Whether because of lack for clarity of what their values are or simply the lack of time and energy to have these discussions, many parents don't sit down and talk to their children about the most important topic they should talk to their children about, namely, values.

Talking to your children about values can occur in a spontaneous or structured way. As I mentioned above, your family's daily life is filled with value lessons waiting to be taught. Having your antenna up for these opportunities allows you to spot them immediately and use them to teach your children about values. You can also make value discussions a part of your family-value culture. For example, you might designate one dinner per week to the discussion of a particular value. To get your children more involved, you can, when they are young, offer them the choice of several topics to talk about and, when they are older, ask them to bring a value topic from their lives to the dinner table for discussion. Asking your children for experiences they have had or seen in their daily lives that illustrate the value under discussion can really bring values to life.

Talking with your children about values and your family-value culture accomplishes several essential goals in helping your children adopt the family-value culture and learn healthy values. It communicates to them that values are important enough to spend time and energy talking to your children about them. Talking with your children gives them an opportunity to learn about what values are, what specific values are important to you, why they are important, and the role they play for your children as individuals, in your family, and in the community, country, and world in which you live. This value education, as I mentioned earlier, provides children with the foundation of knowledge from which they can further explore values. Perhaps most important, by talking with your children about your family-value culture, you create a dialogue in which they begin to talk about values too. By talking with your children about values, they can understand them, clarify confusion, question you about the "whys, hows, and whats" of values, and challenge you about your values. Finally, the ultimate aim of talking with children about values is for them to think about values. This ongoing thought process enables children to develop their own unique relationship with values, figure out what values mean to them, and decide how values fit into and influence their lives. Exploring all of these relationships helps reify values in children and prepares them to make moral and ethical decisions when faced with conflicting needs and goals.

Values Are Emotions: Let Your Children Feel Values

The lessons children learn from others and the thought processes that they go through help children adopt and adhere to certain values. Yet it appears that emotions have the most persuasive influence on whether children act in valued ways. Some experts believe that emotions, such as empathy and guilt, are inborn and serve an adaptive purpose by helping to ensure that people behave in ways that benefit themselves, their families, and the communities in which they live. Growing up in an environment in which values are thought about, talked about, and experienced, children learn to connect their emotions with the values that are expressed in their family-value culture.

Some emotions restrain children from acting badly. Fear, for example, is a visceral deterrent that makes children uncomfortable when contemplating immoral behavior. Guilt causes feelings of regret and shame after children have violated a value. Because children don't like to feel bad, they are less likely to act against their values again. Allowing children to experience "negative" emotions has become somewhat taboo in our society in the mistaken belief that these feelings will hurt children. But protecting your children from so-called bad emotions can keep them from making the connection between their feelings and their values, and hinder their ingraining healthy values. Empathy enables children to feel how others would feel if they treated someone in an unethical way. Empathized feelings of hurt and sadness in response to, for example, anger or cruelty, would inhibit unprincipled behavior because children wouldn't want to feel the way that others would feel if treated badly.

Other emotions encourage the expression of positive values. Emotions such as inspiration and pride motivate children to act in a moral way because they connect valued behavior with the good feelings associated with those emotions. Following ethical behavior, children experience other emotions, such as satisfaction, contentment, and joy, which reinforce their moral behavior by enabling them to associate those good feelings with their previous value-driven actions.

Values Are Action: Let Your Children Act on Values

Values are most important "where the rubber meets the road." Values are such an essential part of children's lives because they ultimately dictate how they behave. Children will engage in behavior based on what they think, how they feel, and the options they have before them. If the thoughts, emotions, and decisions are guided by values, children will most often act in accordance with those values.

The best defense against the values of American popular culture is to create a family-value culture that encourages your children to think, feel, choose, and act in accordance with their values early and often in their lives. The more they experience their values, the more ingrained they will become and the more resistant they will be to other, less healthy values. Much like a vaccination against an illness, these early experiences with positive values inoculate your children against an assault from destructive values.

An essential aspect of this inoculation process involves allowing your children to violate the values on which your family-value culture is based. Part of children learning about values is acting against them and seeing what happens. How do your children feel? What is your reaction? What are the consequences? How do others respond to the violation? The answers to these questions help children figure out why the value is important and should be followed in the future. These "failures of values" allow you to use these opportunities to talk to your children about values and explore with them what they were thinking, how they were feeling, what outside forces contributed to the value breach, and how they made their decision to act as they did.

Violating a value also enables children to gain ownership of their values. Early in children's lives, they adhere to values to earn your love and out of fear of consequences. As they mature, they learn that you will always love them and that the consequences are usually not so dire as to act as an effective deterrent. They must then decide for themselves whether the values are ones they want to adopt. This deliberate choice allows your children to take full ownership of their values, which means that they choose to follow them because they understand that these values are in their best interests.

Values Are Choices: Let Your Children Make Decisions about Values

Values provide the compass that children can follow in the choices they face and the decisions they make throughout their lives. When faced with competing options, for example, whether a child will lie or tell the truth to his parents after breaking a dish, the values they have internalized and the emotions they link to those values will dictate what value choice they make. Children who are given the opportunity to talk about and experience values, and connect positive emotions with those values have a much better chance of making value-driven decisions—consider their options, weigh the benefits and costs, and make a choice that is consistent with their family-value culture—rather than ones based on self-interest, immature needs and wants, or in response to the urgings from American popular culture.

Enabling children to make the choice of what they value is another essential part of creating a family-value culture. The notion that values are choices also means that children must, in the end, choose the values they want to live by. Early in life, they will probably adopt the values that you espouse because they want to please and emulate you. But an essential part of instilling values in children involves allowing them, as they move through adolescence, to look critically at your values and choose for themselves whether the values they have adopted from you are the values by which they want to live their lives. All of the ways to create a family-value culture I have discussed so far also encourage your children to think critically about their values and to make decisions about the values they choose to adopt. Ongoing discussions between you and your children should ultimately communicate that their values, as they approach adulthood, become entirely their decision. This choice gives them ownership of their values and will more likely guide them in their lives.

Recognize that your children will periodically make bad choices, act counter to your values, test the boundaries you set for them, and disobey the rules you establish. Rather than resisting these challenges, you should use these opportunities to help your children learn more about their values and to make better choices. For example, if you catch one of your children in a lie, you can ask several questions:

- •Why did you lie?
- • What were the benefits of lying?
- • What were the costs and consequences of lying?
- • What have you learned from being caught in a lie?

This discussion, accompanied by appropriate punishment, helps your children understand why they made a poor choice and see the consequences of the bad decision, and shows them why it is in their best interests in the future to tell the truth. In making their own choices—even bad ones—your children figure out what good choices are and take responsibility for what they come to value.

In accepting this reality, I encourage you to be open to adjusting the boundaries and rules that you establish for your children if they can convince you that the limits are unfair or they demonstrate that they can be trusted with more freedom. If your children feel overly constrained, they may feel the need to not only step over the boundaries you set, but blow the limits up completely by going well beyond them.

Giving your children small victories by loosening your reins when appropriate will prevent them from needing to look for big victories that grossly violate your family-value culture and which may be truly harmful. Allowing your children to have input into and influence over what they are allowed to do and what you expect of them can make them feel more like they are choosing, rather than being forced, to follow your dictates. With young children, you can give them a limited number of choices from which they can choose, for example, when they do their household chores each week. As your children approach adolescence and they have demonstrated their ability to make good choices, you can offer them more options from which to choose and, over time, give them open-ended control of their choices by asking them, for example, what time they believe they should be allowed to stay out until on weekends. This personal sense of commitment and ownership can encourage them to feel that the rules, boundaries, and expectations that arise from your family-value culture are their own.

I want to alert you that giving your children ownership and choices may cause conflict between you and your children. They may decide that they value something different than what you value and, even worse, something that is in direct opposition to what you value. For example, you might value a formal education and a traditional lifestyle. Yet one of your children may not want to go to college, but rather wants to travel the world and work for a nonprofit organization.

You have several options if this disagreement arises. Your first inclination might be to resist your children's wishes and try to force their values in line with yours, with threats of disownment or bribes of material inducements. I can assure you that not only will you fail in these coercive attempts, but you will drive your children away quickly and ruin your relationship with them.

Another option is to consider that the values that your children are expressing may not be permanent. Rather, they may be part of the natural experimentation that young people go through as they find their place in the world and settle on values that they are most comfortable with and connected to. With this openness, you can maintain a dialogue about their values and the choices they're making to better understand where these values came from and whether they are in your children's best interest. With an ongoing conversation, you can also provide input and perspective on the values they are exploring that might help them return to values that are in greater agreement with your own.

Finally, you can accept and respect their values and choices. Though you may not agree with them, as long as the values aren't destructive and they make your children happy, what more can you ask for? In the event that you don't think your children are making good choices or following good values, there is, once they grow up, little you can do about it, so taking steps to stay in their lives and maintain a good relationship with them is the best way to remain an influence on them.

Values Are Social: Let Your Children Interact with Values

Values are influenced by the reactions that children get from others in response to their behavior. Value-driven behavior that is rewarded with social praise and validation will be internalized. Actions that are in conflict with values which are punished socially will be discarded. A problem is that children are vulnerable to social influence from many sources, including those that are not driven by your values. Peer pressure often interferes with children adopting healthy values. Children can be praised by their peers for acting immorally and punished for behaving in a valued way. For example, in some schools in America, children who study hard and have educational goals are ostracized, and stealing, teasing, bullying, and being a "slacker" are behaviors that are admired. Common forms of popular culture exert a similar influence. Advertising, from fast-food and soft drinks to clothing and athletic shoes, convey the message that buying certain products will make children popular and winners, and if they don't buy them, they will be social outcasts and losers.

As your children get older, your influence over them will decrease and other social forces, such as their peers and American popular culture, will become greater. As they enter adolescence, the pressure to conform and be accepted will grow substantially and they may feel compelled to make choices based on their need for acceptance rather than on their values. This is one of the most common struggles you face, maintaining your influence in the face of increasing opposition from popular culture, and will be discussed at length later in the book.

In brief, your best defense against this social influence is instilling at an early age positive values, effective decision making, and self-respect through your family-value culture, so that your children will recognize bad influences and unhealthy values, and not feel the need to adopt values and act in certain ways just to be accepted. Rather they will seek acceptance from peers who share their values and who will encourage healthy values and good choices.

Given these significant challenges that children face if their values conflict with American popular culture, you may wonder if it is worth the fight. You may ask, Is there an upside to my children living by my family-value culture? The benefits, though less tangible as those offered by popular culture, are much more compelling. Most basically, children who live by healthy values will lead lives that are genuine and can be true sources of meaning, satisfaction, and joy. Children who are seduced by American popular culture are seeking the pot of gold at the end of a rainbow that is just an illusion. Value-driven children will find others like themselves with whom they can develop rich and lasting relationships. Children who go to the dark side are destined to have shallow and unfulfilling relationships. Children who are raised in a family-value culture will choose life paths—education, career, marriage, avocation—that will allow them to be vital, successful, and contributing members of society. Children who are not driven by healthy values will pursue life goals that will ultimately leave them bored, unsatisfied, and disconnected.

Fortunately, you aren't alone in your battle against harmful social influences. You're not the only positive role model in your children's lives. Siblings and extended family members, friends, teachers, coaches, and clergy can all have a significant influence over what your children come to value. To ensure that you maximize the influence of positive others on your children, create a valued social world that supports the value culture that you have created in your family.

Building a value-driven social world that envelops and protects your children requires that you take a conscious and active role in determining the people who influence your children. Deliberate choices about the communities you live in, the schools your children attend, the friendships they develop, and the houses of worship that your family visits provide you and your children with allies in your fight against American popular culture.

Values Are Experiences: Let Your Children Encounter Values

Many parents believe that children learn values best when the messages are loud and obvious. So parents talk to their children regularly about values, post lists of values on the refrigerator, children take values courses at school and in their houses of worship, and watch videos and television that's specifically aimed at teaching them values. Though this organized approach to teaching values is important, it may not be the most effective. In all of these cases, children know that they are being taught values and they may or may not find it interesting or care enough to pay attention. They may even decide to ignore or resist its messages because they feel like they're being force-fed their values. This "formal" value education can also be somewhat one-dimensional in which parents and others are doing the teaching and the children are mostly passive recipients.

As I have mentioned before, the most powerful and lasting lessons are often the most subtle. Children learn values most effectively and lastingly when they're highly engaged in an activity that they don't even realize is teaching them values. The best way to instill values in your children then is to immerse them in activities that reflect and express your family-value culture. For example, when your children participate in charitable work, the arts, athletics, family events, or political or environmental efforts, you aren't telling them that they will be learning about values that are important to your family-value culture. Instead, your children are living your family's values, interacting with others who share your values, accomplishing goals that are consistent with your values, and experiencing positive emotions connected to those values.

The value experiences they participate in implicitly communicate value messages. Children see a positive connection between the experience and the value, and they ingrain the value without full awareness. Children come to see that acting a certain way—a way that reflects the value—"is a good thing to do." For example, having your family help prepare a Thanksgiving dinner at a homeless shelter—without telling them its purpose—would be fun for your children because they would get to meet new people and help cook a big meal. They would also learn about people who are less fortunate than they are and appreciate the value of giving to others because seeing the completed meal and receiving thanks from the diners would naturally make them feel good. The value-driven event alone enables them to think about what they are doing, why they are doing it, and, importantly, connects positive emotions, such as pride and satisfaction, with their involvement. All of these experiences encourage the adoption of life-affirming values without your children even realizing it.

Value-driven experiences are most influential on children when they have to "get their hands dirty." For example, although donating money to a charity can certainly teach the value of caring and giving, children aren't really able to connect with the meaning of those values because they can't see the end result of their actions. In contrast, spending a day in a home for the elderly, for example, exposes children to what the true meaning of the values are, connects the actions of caring and giving with an immediate beneficial result, and causes children to feel deep emotions—empathy and kindness—which lie at the heart of children "buying into" the values.

Early in your children's lives, you should expose your children to a variety of value-driven activities to help them find those with which they resonate. You can expect that your children will respond to different experiences in different ways. For example, one of your children may get scared in a nursing home, but is excited to "buddy" with a disabled child. Forcing your children to participate in activities that make them uncomfortable may undermine the values you want them to experience. Additionally, exposing your children to many value-lesson experiences may cause them to truly connect with one activity, not only teaching the value, but fostering a deep and lasting connection with a cause that they can carry into adulthood.

Ideally, your children should experience these values at a young age, so by the time they reach adolescence, these experiences are a part of their lives that they appreciate and benefit from. However, it is never too late to expose your children to these life-altering activities. Resistance from teenagers who have never had these experiences can be expected because of its newness and unfamiliarity. At the same time, a thoughtful dialogue, your commitment, and positive experiences that show them the benefits of these activities can turn initial opposition into a growing interest. Of course, not every teenager is going to become enamored with a value-driven life, particularly those whose parents allowed them to become and stay immersed in the values of American popular culture. If the resistance becomes strong and counterproductive, children should not be forced to continue their participation. Such "indentured servitude" in the name of values will only cause them to resent the experiences and push away from the values they reflect. At that point, you must acknowledge that all you can do is expose your children to these experiences, encourage change, and then allow them to make their own decisions about their value. If new value experiences don't take root immediately, at least you have planted a seed that may grow as your children mature toward adulthood.

Values Are Life: Let Your Children Live Values

An important part of teaching your children about values is to bring values down to earth. Children can sometimes mistakenly see values as intellectual concepts or high-brow philosophies that have little connection with their lives. Make no mistake about it—values are heavy stuff. They provide the foundation for your children's lives. But just because values are serious doesn't mean that they should be out of touch with children's lives. Bringing values into your family's daily life grounds the philosophical notions of values in your children's day-to-day activities—school, family, play—and guides them without them realizing it.

Any discussion you have with your children about values should end by connecting a particular value with some action with which they are familiar, for example, practicing the piano (diligence), helping their father rake the leaves (cooperation), taking out the garbage (responsibility), or helping their little sister get dressed (kindness). But you shouldn't just talk about these seemingly insignificant, yet oh so important, actions. The real meaning and significance of values is how values are expressed in the minutiae of your family's daily lives; what you think and feel, how you behave, the choices you make, the interactions you have with others, and the efforts you put into your vocations and your avocations., The best way to teach your children value lessons is to disguise them as daily life. For example, giving your children household chores, limiting television viewing, and having dinners together are small but powerful messages that communicate your family-value culture to your children. You want to show them that these apparently small acts are actually significant deeds that reflect your family-value culture and are the stuff that their lives are made of.

Emerging Values

By creating a family-value culture, other essential values emerge that can further contribute to your children leading valued lives. The first emerging value that arises in children as they come to know their values is *self-awareness*. Children learn how and why they think, feel, and act. Self-awareness becomes the basis for personal growth, effective decision making, healthy relationships, quality work, and an appreciation of the world in which they live. Self-awareness enables children to understand their needs and motivations, consider short- and long-term consequences of their behavior, empathize with others, and learn from their experiences.

Growing up in a family-value culture also acts as an impetus for children to live lives of *principle*. Children who lead principled lives base the decisions they make on a set of values that they have considered and chosen deliberately. They are less likely to behave impulsively, be influenced excessively by others, make choices that are not in their best interests, put self-interest ahead of consideration of others, or, more generally, be tempted by American popular culture. Children who learn to lead principled lives also lead lives of meaning, fulfillment, and joy because they know what is important to them and they seek out relationships and activities that are of value to them.

Children who grow up in a family-value culture also lead lives of *purpose*. Their values provide them with a vision of the life they want to lead. This vision then offers them a destination and a road map that gives them a clear direction in the path that their lives will take. Children with a purpose are less likely to be lured from their chosen course by peer pressure and seductive messages from American popular culture. They will have a discerning eye for attempts by others to change their direction. The clarity of their values gives them the determination, patience, and resilience to stay the course in the face of obstacles with which they are presented. Finally, a life of purpose based on deeply felt values offers children meaning, satisfaction, and joy because they are on a road of their own choosing, engage in activities that they value greatly, and continually achieve goals that they have set for themselves and put effort into attaining.

Children who are raised in a family-value culture adhere to the value that everything they do should be in *their own best interests*. These children have a clear sense of what is good and bad for them and, when faced with choices that may be harmful, typically base their decisions on what they know will be best for them in the long run. This value-based sense of right and wrong allows them to resist external pressures—popular culture, peer pressure—and to act in ways that are consistent with their values.

CHAPTER 4

Stock Your Arsenal (Lock and Load Love)

American Popular Culture on the Offensive

A 2004 addition to the invasion of reality TV is *Nanny 911*, a show a *New York Times* review described as another "televised exercise in British-American sadism" in the same vein as *The Weakest Link* and *American Idol*, in which "infantile families are abused by prim, nasty nannies from Britain—and end up begging for more." The first episode introduces the Rock family: mother Karen, father Matt, 4-year-old Dylan, and 2-year-old Natalie. As the *Nanny 911* website describes, the Rocks "have a home where there are no limits or rules" and both children are completely out of control. "Dylan finds it amusing to...constantly talk back to people, screaming and cursing...by literally spitting in their [his parents'] faces. Karen's and Matt's response to this behavior is usually light punishment with no follow-through or no reaction at all. Two-year-old Natalie seems to be following very closely in her brother's footsteps..." Says Karen, "We don't know what we're doing, so we don't do anything." Karen is very supportive and loving with her children, but she sets no limitations and metes out no consequences. Matt offers Karen little support and provides no discipline to his children. Karen hasn't slept in the same room with her husband since Dylan was born and any attempt to extricate herself from her son's bed at night results in a temper tantrum. *Nanny 911* actually has some redeeming qualities as Nanny Deb coaches Karen and Matt on working together, setting appropriate boundaries, and giving their children firm and consistent punishment. Nanny Deb also establishes Rock family rules:

1. Respect each other.
2. Every action has a consequence.
3. "I want" does not get.
4. Hands are not for hitting.
5. Work together.
6. Be consistent.

Do Karen and Matt Rock love their children? Of course they do. Are they using that love to raise their children to be healthy and mature? Decidedly not. To the contrary, the Rocks' inappropriate use of love has turned their two young children into little monsters who are uncontrollable and heading down a bad road in their development. Only after a week-long intervention by Nanny Deb do the Rocks show signs of using love in a way that will benefit rather than hurt their parents.

The love you show your children is the foundation on which they develop their view of themselves, of others, and the world in which they live. Your love is the most powerful tool you have in helping your children resist American popular culture. Unfortunately, over the past thirty years, love has often become an unwitting weapon that parents use against their children in the service of American popular culture. Popular culture has communicated two conflicting messages to parents that has weakened their ability to influence their children and has made children more vulnerable to its assaults.

Unconditional Love

One message is that you should love your children "unconditionally." Unconditional love seems quite reasonable on the surface. You should love your children simply for who they are rather than for what they do. Unfortunately, many parents take this seemingly sensible goal and go too far, showing love to their children for everything that they are and do, and not holding them accountable for anything. Children are shown love even when they behave badly, do poorly in school, and treat others unkindly.

By showing love to your children unconditionally, your children experience the presence of your love without its power to affect them positively. This influence comes from the fact that, early in your children's lives, their greatest motivation is to gain your love. This desire for your love gives you the power to instill in your children healthy values, encourage them to adopt your family-value culture, and give them the tools to combat American popular culture.

Without the power of love, your ability to influence your children in any way is diminished. There are no limits, just total freedom to do what they want. Though this might sound desirable for children, the truth is that they want and need boundaries to safeguard and guide them. If you're unwilling to provide your children with clarity and direction, they will look elsewhere—like to American popular culture, which is only too happy assume power over your children. Popular culture is glad to guide them down a road that best serves its needs without regard for what is in your children's own best interests.

Whenever I tell parents that I don't believe in unconditional love, they cringe and get a bit defensive. "What do you mean I shouldn't love my children unconditionally?" they say. "No matter what they do, I will always love them!" Granted, you will always love your children in a very deep way no matter what they do. But I would guess that there are quite a few times when, though you may always love your children, you definitely don't express that love to them. You get frustrated when they don't try their best in school. You get angry when they're disrespectful. You're disappointed when they behave badly. Yes, you still love them, but that is not the message they get. Young children aren't sophisticated enough to tell the difference between disapproval at how they behave and withdrawal of love because of who they are. When you get angry with them and tell them, "What you did was very bad!" what they feel is, "Mommy doesn't love me anymore."

You probably communicate conditional love without even realizing it. When your children get bad report cards, you likely express disappointment or anger and you may threaten them with punishment, or even mete out some type of punishment, if they should continue to get poor grades. Do you still love them? Of course. Do they feel that unconditional love from you then? I don't think so.

Conditional Love

The other message from American popular culture is that parents should use "conditional love" to control their children. Because love and approval from their parents are like food to young children— essential to their existence and growth—they will do anything to gain that love. Parents who bought into this view used conditional love to force their children to live up to certain expectations. When children met their parents' expectations, they were rewarded with love, praise, and gifts. When they resisted their parents or failed to meet their expectations, love, rewards, and gifts were withdrawn. Where many parents get hung up on conditional love is that they define it in a way that is clearly unhealthy for children. This destructive conditional love—what I call "outcome love"—involves offering love or expressing approval to your children when they perform up to a particular expectation in school, sports, the arts, or some other achievement area. Classic examples of outcome love include the parent who berates his daughter for losing a tennis match or the parent who grounds her son for getting a B on his report card. This kind of conditional love is truly unhealthy, and I see it constantly with the young achievers I work with. So let me make it clear: outcome love is bad!

This traditional type of conditional love has been a strategy foisted on parents by American popular culture. Parents have been convinced that outcome love is best for their children because they are sure to get good grades, get into a good college, and find a well-paying job. What popular culture doesn't tell you is that it can also cause your children to become needy and dependent on receiving love and to seek out encouragement, approval, and reward from anyone willing to give it.

And you may not realize the messages of love, support, and acceptance that can be found in most media of popular culture. For example, if your children eat a particular kind of food, they'll feel good (Happy Meal!). Or if they drink a certain kind of beverage, they'll be popular. This outcome love is used as a weapon by parents against their children—however inadvertently—to mold them into the way they want. And, sadly, in doing so, parents become allies to American popular culture and against their own children.

Unfortunately, both approaches backfired. Unconditionally loved children remain children—immature, self-absorbed, spoiled, and unruly—ready victims of American popular culture. Because they are loved no matter what they do, they don't learn essential life lessons, such as consequences, responsibility, and patience, and never develop into mature adults.

Conditionally loved children respond in one of two ways. They are often initially acquiescent, but later become angry, resentful, and rebellious. As children get older, they learn to feed themselves—literally and figuratively—so they're no longer dependent on their parents for sustenance and are less willing to follow their parents' dictates. In reaction to this oppressive conditional love, they seek out "love" from other sources, for example, the open arms of American popular culture, which lavishes them with good feelings from fast-food, conspicuous consumption, and feelings of acceptance for being a part of its culture. These children's relationships with their parents are often ruined because of their reaction to being controlled and by listening to the "You don't need your parents, we'll take care of you" messages from American popular culture. Or, so starved for their parents' love, conditionally loved children become passive and compliant pleasers who will do anything for that love and who are so needy that they seek out approval from any place that is offering it, including a very approving popular culture.

The Right Way to Love Your Children

Your challenge is to provide a kind of love for your children that fosters positive values and maturity. This love is neither unconditional nor conditional in the way that you probably think of. This healthy kind of love is conditional, but based on criteria vastly different than the kind of conditional love defined by American popular culture. This different kind of love breeds positive values, confidence, responsibility, emotional mastery, and healthy relationships. Loving your children "the right way" involves striking a balance between showing too much love and not showing enough love.

Loving your children the right way involves knowing what is best for your children, showing them that everything you do with them is in their best interests—even if they're not thrilled about it—and that you'll do whatever you must to ensure that they become healthy and well-adjusted adults. Loving your children the right way means hugging, kissing, expressing your affection, rewarding, praising, reinforcing, supporting, and encouraging your children—but not constantly, indiscriminately, or when they don't deserve it. Just as importantly, loving your children the right way also means being tough. This doesn't mean being negative, angry, or controlling. It means sometimes forcing your children to do things they may not want to do, but you know what is best for them. Loving your children the right way also means establishing clear expectations connected with reasonable consequences, and administering those consequences firmly and consistently. And yes, it also means you can get angry with them and show your disappointment—but always expressed in a way that will help them learn and grow. This healthy love is about doing the right thing for your children—whether they like it or not. This can mean loving and praising them. It can also mean communicating to children what is acceptable and unacceptable behavior, what will and won't be tolerated, and holding them responsible for their actions. This tough love prepares your children for the battlefield of American popular culture by teaching them to be both loving and resilient, aware and open, and accepting and discerning.

Give Value Love
Not all conditional love is bad for children. If you use the right kind of conditional love, it can be a powerful tool to teach your children essential values and create healthy, happy, and mature adults. The type of conditional love that I advocate doesn't involve you giving or withdrawing love based on your children's accomplishments or their obedience. Rather, healthy conditional love—what I call value love—

involves you using love and approval to reward positive values, beliefs, attitudes, and skills in your children. Value love, rather than being a weapon against your children, is your most powerful defense against American popular culture. Value love is the best way to help your children learn good values, and positive values are your children's best protection against popular culture.

Value love communicates to your children what values are important to you. When you express love when they act in a valued way and you withdraw love when they violate your family's values, your children make the connection between your values and your love. Value love also provides children with an initial impetus to act in a valued way. Because they want your love when they're young, they're more likely to act in ways that enable them to receive your love. If your children view these first value lessons as positive, then they will in time internalize the values as their own. The difference between value love and outcome love is based on using love to instill healthy values compared to unhealthy values pushed on families by American popular culture. Perhaps most important, value love focuses on aspects of your children's lives over which they have control, in contrast to outcome love in which children often have little control (e.g., whether they win a chess tournament or are the class valedictorian). In other words, they have the power to either act in a valued way and receive your love or act badly and suffer your justified wrath. If your children choose to work hard, do their chores, are kind to people, and express other healthy values consistent with your family-value culture, they will be rewarded with your love. If they choose not to live up to your family's values, they will be punished with the withdrawal of your love. How your children choose to behave is up to them and they must decide what the benefits, costs, and consequences of their actions are (the specific techniques for using value love will be discussed shortly).

Offering your children value love begins with you knowing what you value (chapter 2 should have helped you here). You want to identify situations in your children's lives in which they may or may not behave in valued ways, for example, their efforts in school, their chores around the house, or how they play with their friends. You also want to recognize what specific behaviors might be valued or otherwise.

With this foundation for value love, you can now prepare your children by explaining the situations in which valued behavior is most evident in their lives and the valued behavior that you expect of them. Importantly, you must make clear to them the consequences—rewards or punishment—based on whether they act in accordance or against those value-based expectations.

You must then express value love clearly, firmly, and consistently. You need to be vigilant to your children's behavior, recognize when they are and are not acting in a valued way, and communicate your value love in a committed fashion. Only then will your children get the message loud and clear what you value and that they should value it too.

Praise Your Child...The Right Way

Praising your child the right way for the right things is a powerful way to instill positive values in your children. When you praise your children, they get the message that what they just did was a good thing. Praising your children the right way means you are praising them based on your values, not those impressed on you by American popular culture. It also means that they see the connection between what they did and what was good about what they did.

Praising your children is a much more complex process than it appears to be. The classic reward I hear from parents when their children do well at something is, "Nice job. Way to go." This is lazy praise. This is worthless praise! Why? Because it doesn't specify what you are praising them for. "Did my parents praise me because of what I did, who I beat, how hard I tried, or what?" The purpose of praise is to reinforce your children's behavior and the values that underlie them. Whatever you praise is what they will come to value. If they don't know what you're praising them for, they won't come to value anything. Or they may believe you're praising them for one thing (e.g., winning a sports competition) but you mean to praise them for something else (e.g., their commitment and persistence). Without this clarity of praise, they will probably assume that you are praising them for the most evident part of their behavior (for example, getting an A), which is exactly what American popular culture wants to happen, because it rewards the result.

Your praise should always specify that which you want to be rewarded. For example:

- "You really put in the time on that project." (hard work)
- "That was very considerate of you to help your sister." (kindness)
- "You could have played with your friends earlier in the week, but instead you chose to study for your test." (good decision making)

The tricky part of praising your children the right way is getting them to focus on the connection between their behavior and the praise rather than on the praise itself. Too much emphasis on the praise distracts your children from the value lesson you are trying to teach them. Praise that is out of proportion to the behavior ("You are the smartest boy in the world!") is wholly unrealistic, doesn't reward a value, and doesn't emphasize something that is within your children's control (they can't control how intelligent they are). Over-the-top praise causes your children to continue to behave in that way only as long as they know that they will continue to receive the praise. The emphasis of your praise should always be on the value that underlies your children's good behavior.

You also don't want the praise to be about you, such as "We are so proud of you" or "We think you did just great." When you praise your children in that way, you're communicating to them that their accomplishments are really about what they mean to you rather than to them. Your praise should always be about your children. "I'll bet you are proud of your effort today" or "That was a very nice thing you did for your friend."

This focus on your children enables them to more easily understand what they did to deserve the praise. Praising your children the right way emphasizes the intrinsic reward of behaving as they did. It creates positive emotions or produces a desired consequence. The best praise from you doesn't actually give your children anything, but rather simply points out the benefits they get from behaving as they did. For example, your daughter being nice to her younger sister can make her feel good.

Praising the right thing is also pretty tricky. Personal, social, and spiritual values are expressed in the act itself when values conflict.

These very acts express the values that underlie them and parents can praise the act alone to reinforce the value. For example, "It was so wonderful that you chose to donate some of your lawn-mowing earnings to your school's charity fund." They also create positive emotions, such as satisfaction, contentment, and gratitude, that make the act self-rewarding.

Achievement praise is traditionally based on the outcome of an effort rather than the effort itself. That is, achievement is about the destination, not the journey. This difference can make it difficult to teach your children about the true meaning of achievement, that the meaning, satisfaction, and joy are found in the experience of striving toward a goal rather than its attainment. Achievement values are further confused because American popular culture values the outcome—irrespective of how it is attained. For example, popular culture places such emphasis on winning at any cost that it implicitly endorses steroid use in the pursuit of athletic success, even though its use is illegal and unethical. Popular culture communicates to children that success is all that matters regardless of how it is achieved and that any and all attempts to achieve success are justified regardless of whether they violate all standards of decency or fair play. Is this a value that you want your children to adopt?

Praising the outcome of the achievement sends children the wrong message: that the result is what is important. For example, when your children come home with an A on a paper, you may praise them enthusiastically, "It is so great that you got an A on your paper." But what value does that praise communicate? "When I get A's, my parents praise me, so getting A's is really important to them." In making this link, they connect their test grade with the value—and importance—of getting straight A's.

The fact is you don't need to praise your children's outcomes. When your children do well in school, sports, the arts, or some other achievement area, they know it. Your saying so is not news to them. If it's not completely obvious to them, everyone else—teachers, coaches, friends—tells them. Your children don't need you to tell them that they "done good," so saying "Great win!" or "Nice performance!" has no value in teaching your children about positive achievement values. Rather, you need to ask yourself what value enabled them to achieve the desired outcome and what value do you want them to learn from the achievement experience—diligence, patience, perseverance?—and praise the expression of that value, for example, "You really stuck with it to do that well."

Whenever you praise an achievement value, be sure that the value is within your children's control. Though achieving a particular result (e.g., getting an A on a test) is a worthy goal, children don't often have control over it, for instance, a test may be very difficult, there are other students who do better, or they may simply not have the wherewithal to achieve a specific outcome. Without that control, they may not live up to that achievement value out of no fault of their own. They can't always control their outcomes, but they can control their effort, focus, and thoroughness, which are essential achievement values.

Finally, many parents believe that by placing the value of achievement on the outcome, their children are more likely to achieve the desired outcome. Not only does this emphasis teach the wrong values about achievement, but the irony is that stressing the outcome actually interferes with children attaining the outcome. Your children come to believe that results are what matters, yet they are less able to produce the results that you expect of them.

If your children are focused on the outcome, they're paying attention to something that occurs at the end of their efforts, which means they're not focusing on what they need to do to achieve the outcome they—and you—want. If they're not focusing on the process, they are less likely to perform their best. And if they don't perform their best, they aren't going to achieve the desired outcome. What many parents don't realize is that by praising healthy achievement values, such as diligence, patience, perseverance, and hard work, you actually increase the likelihood of your children achieving the desired outcome. So don't praise results—they're self-evident! Always praise behavior that is directly connected to the values you are trying to teach.

Reward Your Child...The Right Way

A common question I am asked is: "Can I reward my children after they have acted in a valued way?" The answer is "Yes, but..." I distinguish praise from rewards in that praise is verbal and rewards are material. Many parents think that rewarding children materially—with money or gifts—is a good way to influence and motivate them. But rewards are a slippery slope that once you get on you can often never get off.

The problem with material rewards is that children's behavior becomes about the rewards rather than the intrinsic value of their actions. This is particularly true for personal, social, and spiritual values. For example, if you pay your children for taking out the trash, they come to see this chore as a job that they should rewarded for instead of a responsibility they must fulfill as part of the family-value culture. "But I give my children an allowance for their weekly chores—is that bad?" you may ask. Not necessarily. In this case, you are rewarding them for fulfilling their family responsibilities, but it is not for a specific act. Rather, it is an appreciation of their commitment to your family-value culture. You are also teaching them another important value, that their actions have consequences: if they do good things, good things happen. They also learn a lesson about the market economy, namely that quality work is rewarded. Also, realistically, the allowance you pay your children is probably not great enough to fully justify their efforts (more on allowances in chapter 6).

Achievement values are a bit different. Providing a token reward for a job well done is a normal and not unhealthy thing for parents to do that shows appreciation for children's accomplishments. But you should never reward them for the result! Rather, you should reward them for what enabled them to achieve success.

A bad reward would be: "You can have your favorite dinner if you get straight A's on your report card this term." This reward is bad because it directly connects the reward to the outcome. The reward is also promised before the outcome occurs, thereby acting as the extrinsic incentive to produce the desired outcome ("If I get an A, I will get a reward"), which may undermine their intrinsic motivation to do well in school.

A good reward would be: "You can have your favorite dinner for having worked so hard and focused on your studies this semester." This reward is good because it encourages healthy achievement values (i.e., hard work, focus). The reward is also given after the effort, so it doesn't act as an incentive to work hard and focus in the first place. Rather, your children worked hard because they wanted to. And, realistically, the benefits of the reward are short-lived; the memory of the meal as a reward will fade long before the connection between the healthy values and doing good does. Whenever you offer material rewards to your children, be sure to explain exactly what you are rewarding them for so they clearly see what value you want them to learn.

Offering a reward can provide your children with an initial impetus to behave in a certain way. For example, a couple who are friends of mine has a simple arrangement with their children—something their children want for something they want. Their children can choose a camp to attend for part of their summer break in exchange for choosing a charitable activity they will participate in during another part of their vacation. With this agreement, there is an exchange (another good lesson for children to learn) and both the parents and the children gain from it. By providing some initial impetus, your children also see what you value enough to want to encourage them to internalize those values. These initial "bribes" should not continue however, because with ongoing external incentives your children will never learn the intrinsic value of behaving in a valued way. Hopefully, after engaging in the value-driven behavior, your children learn its intrinsic worth and you don't need to provide them with additional motivation.

Another mistake that parents make is to offer rewards that are not healthy or value-driven. These confusing messages encourage one value, but also teach them another value that is not life-affirming. Any material rewards you give your children should be positive and healthy, and should be consistent with other values of importance to you. For example, if you don't value junk food, a trip to McDonald's should not be a reward even for the most value-driven behavior. If you think video games are the bane of American youth, they should not be used as a reward no matter how much your children want them or how much you know you can use them to get your children to act in a valued way. Good rewards are those that encourage education, health, faith, and other fundamental values.

The reward should also be commensurate with your children's efforts in expressing a certain value. For example, you shouldn't buy your children an expensive toy for winning a basketball game or buy your children a gift for doing what is simply expected of them for being part of the family. Disproportionate rewards place the focus on the reward and distract them from the values you are trying to teach them, so the connection between the reward and the values is totally lost.

Winning the game and fulfilling their familial responsibilities should be reward enough. An appropriate reward for playing well in a basketball game might be their favorite dessert after dinner. Receiving their allowance is reasonable reward for completing their household chores.

Punish Your Child...The Right Way

Just as you want to praise and reward children for value-driven behavior, you also want to punish them for acting in ways that conflict with your family-value culture. Punishing your children for bad behavior communicates to them what is unacceptable behavior and what the consequences are of that behavior. With that knowledge, your children can then choose for themselves how they wish to act.

Punishment is always intended to teach lessons to children. Every time you punish your children it should be with their best interests in mind—though they may not necessarily think so at the time! The punishment should always communicate to them what they did wrong, why what they did was wrong, and what the correct behavior is. Your children must make these connections or the punishment will have no value and it will only engender anger and resentment toward you. If your children miss this link, not only will they not learn an important value lesson, but they will probably choose to do the exact opposite just to get back at you.

The $64,000 question that all parents ask is: "What is the best kind of punishment?" Unfortunately, there is no clear answer to this question. I can, however, offer some basic guidelines that you can apply to your children. The best place to start is to ask what the worst kind of punishment for your children is. Punishment shouldn't cause your children to feel frustration, anger, hatred, or sadness. Though your children will naturally not be very happy with you, the punishment shouldn't cause your children lasting negative emotions, nor should it cause them to feel badly about you or about themselves.

Punishment is *never* meant to satisfy your needs or assuage your emotions. You shouldn't punish your children because you are frustrated, angry, or disappointed. You will certainly feel that way—a lot!—throughout your child's early years, but your negative feelings should never be your impetus to punish. If you punish your children to make yourself feel better, they will get this message and come to the realization that you care more about yourself than about them. This "parent-centered" punishment can occur when you are tired and stressed, and lash out at your children's bad behavior. This punishment is neither thoughtful nor beneficial for your children. And their reaction to the punishment will never be good. They will feel demeaned and will respond with hurt, anger, resentment, and resistance. The punishment may make you feel better, but it offers nothing good to your children. When your children are focused on the punishment being in your best interests rather than theirs, they thoroughly lose sight of potential value lesson in the punishment. Your children may also learn a truly harmful lesson; that it is okay to hurt others when they're mad.

Bad punishment is also disproportionate to the severity of the "crime" they committed. Excessive punishment, such as grounding your son for a week because he was mean to his sister, can cause children to focus so much on the punishment instead of the lesson to be learned that they completely miss its point and, in fact, see the punishment as being about them rather than their behavior. Your children will feel that they are being punished far too much given what they did wrong. This perception of unfairness will make them angry and more prone to resist you in the future, thus the punishment has the opposite of the desired effect.

The best punishment has a clear goal of teaching your children a value lesson. It should make them feel bad, but the hurt should be about having acted badly, not about being a bad person or about directing it back on you for hurting them. Ideally, the punishment should cause them to feel disappointment (in themselves) or guilt at having acted against their family-value culture. The emotional pain they feel should not last long, nor should their ill feelings toward you. The punishment also shouldn't cause your children to feel demeaned or devalued. For example, if your children join a group of kids smashing pumpkins on Halloween, a reasonable punishment might be to have them apologize to the families whose pumpkins they destroyed, require them to pay the families out of their allowances to replace the pumpkins, and to clean up the messes they caused (this example comes from personal experience and I never smashed pumpkins again). In contrast, an inappropriate punishment might involve berating your children, grounding them for a month, and continually reminding them of how they humiliated you.

You need to apply the punishment in a firm, emotionally detached, and loving way. This approach will allow your children to focus on and get the value message you are communicating in the punishment. Your calm application of the punishment will also communicate that it gives you no pleasure and that it is about them, not you. They will also realize that, even though they may not like the punishment, at a deep level they will know that you are doing it for them. Your composed, reassuring demeanor will allow them to feel appropriate emotions after bad behavior, such as remorse, regret, and contrition. At the same time, your children will feel less intense negative emotions, such as anger, frustration, and resentment, that would keep them from learning the lessons underlying the punishment. The right type of punishment will ultimately foster positive emotions, such as empathy, inspiration, and pride, in recognizing their bad behavior as well as the desire to behave better in the future. For example, during a play date with several other families, you may be very angry when you see your daughter hitting a playmate and taking her toy. Your anger may come out of embarrassment from being judged by other parents. If you rush up to your daughter and banish her from playing with a harsh tone, she may become defensive and upset. However, if you remain calm, explain what she did wrong and why, and tell her that she has to take a time-out for five minutes, though she may still get upset, she will remain focused on what she did wrong rather than on how mad mommy or daddy is.

The best punishment is directly linked to the bad behavior. By relating the punishment to the misdeed, you ensure that your children see the connection and learn the value lesson. For example, if your son neglects to mow the lawn as he is supposed to, an appropriate punishment might be to withhold part of his allowance and require that he also rake the leaves.

The best punishment takes something of value away from children. This punishment removes the potential hurt of you "inflicting" punishment on your children and places the onus on them for losing something they value. This approach gets them to focus on how their actions caused them to lose something they care about and how they can keep from losing it in the future. For example, if your daughter did poorly on a school test because she was watching television when she should have been studying, you can take away her TV privileges for a week.

An essential part of effective punishment is that it gives children the power to show you that they have learned their lesson and to reduce or remove the punishment with valued behavior. Your punishment should include an "escape clause" that enables them to earn back with valued behavior the something that they lost. Returning to the previous example, if your daughter demonstrates sufficient effort and dedication to her studies for another upcoming test, you may shorten her punishment and allow her to watch TV after only four days.

You should also explain the punishment to your children. Don't assume your children get the message. Tell them why you are punishing them—what they did wrong—and outline the parameters of the punishment. Importantly, initiate a dialogue so you can help them—and you—understand why they acted badly. This conversation enables them to better understand their motivation for their bad behavior, pressures they may have felt from external forces, such as peers and popular culture, and what decision-making process they may have gone through. You can also talk to them about other options they had and how they might make a different choice in the future. Your children can express their views and feelings about their behavior and the punishment, allowing them to feel that they have some input into the process. By combining the punishment with a dialogue, you enable your children to experience the punishment at all levels of the behavior. They are held accountable for their misbehavior. They are able to think about what thoughts and decisions led to the bad behavior. Your children can re-experience the emotions they felt before, during, and after the bad behavior. They can clearly understand the values that were violated by their bad actions. And they can step back from the bad behavior and use the wisdom of hindsight to figure out whether they want to act badly again in the future.

Emerging Values

By using love as a weapon against American popular culture, you also use it as a tool to help your children develop healthy love and self-worth for themselves. Children learn about the emerging value of *loving and valuing themselves* from how their parents love and value them. Parents who express value love to their children teach them to love and value themselves based on who they are, what they value, and how they behave in accordance with those values. Because value love is always within their control, these children have the capacity to act in ways that allow them to give self-love when they behave in a way that is consistent with their values. Children who express value self-love have realistic expectations, are confident, patient, relaxed, and happy.

This healthy self-love provides children with the sense of security and comfort that enables them to be open with others and to express themselves in emotionally vulnerable ways. Their self-love fosters the emerging value of *quality relationships* because these children allow themselves to feel deeply and this emotional openness encourages others to act in kind, thus enabling these children to develop deep and enriching relationships in all parts of their lives.

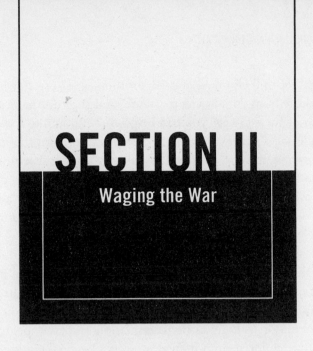

SECTION II

Waging the War

To help your children resist the onslaught of American popular culture, you must know and study the battlefield on which your children's futures will be fought. Early in your children's lives, they have little ability to defend themselves. Therefore, the two primary participants in this battle are you and popular culture itself (though you want to enlist allies, such as schools and places of worship). Who emerges victorious will depend on your commitment and resolve in protecting your children, your willingness to do whatever it takes to ward off the unhealthy influences of American popular culture, and your stamina in defending your children on a daily basis.

This war for your children's futures will be waged on battlefields in all areas of their lives. Section II is devoted to exploring where those battlefields are and how you can help your children successfully wage war against American popular culture in these different arenas. Each of the six chapters—fields of battle—is represented by a fundamental value that your children must learn to become principled, capable, and caring people: respect, responsibility, success, happiness, family, and compassion. If you can instill these values in your children, you can be confident that you will have given them the strength, resolve, armor, and weaponry to withstand American popular culture's continuing onslaught as they evolve into adulthood. You will also have created another capable recruit in the war to stop culture from dominating the value landscape of America.

In each of these arenas, you can help your children to look critically at the messages American popular culture imposes on them. You can teach them how to ward off these assaults by staying true to their values and making conscious decisions about whether they choose to accept those messages. This shield may be just enough to allow your children to come off these fields of battle bowed, but not broken, and with their values and integrity still intact.

American popular culture never rests. It relentlessly sends new and seductive messages to your children. Popular culture is in an unceasing process of mutation, constantly changing its form to trick you and your children into thinking it cares about your children and knows what is best for them. Or it disguises its true mission and attempts to distract you and your children from its real messages by cloaking itself in fun, excitement, and entertainment.

One of the most common themes in science fiction and fantasy movies and video games is that of a monumental threat to the future of humankind from alien or inhuman armies. The goal of these dark forces is to enslave or destroy the human race. This genre of entertainment is also a metaphor for what American popular culture is trying to do to your children. Like the Terminator, popular culture is programmed to do one thing—destroy human life as we know it (okay, perhaps that is a bit melodramatic, but you get the idea) and, every time it gets knocked down, the Terminator—and popular culture—gathers itself and keeps right on coming. Popular culture is also like the Orcs of *The Lord of the Rings* trilogy. There seems to be an unending supply of popular culture's foot soldiers—television, movies, music, magazines, ads—with which to attack your children. For every one that is destroyed, ten more seem to rise out of the earth and join the battle against your children.

Yet an important lesson can be learned using these two popular-culture staples: that ordinary beings have the power to turn back overwhelming threats to our way of life and emerge victorious. What enabled the humans and hobbits to triumph over the threats to humankind, and what will allow you to protect your children and overcome American popular culture, is a deep conviction in what is right, an unerring commitment to their values, perseverance in the face of unimaginable odds, and a dogged determination to defeat their enemy.

CHAPTER 5

Respect (R-E-S-P-E-C-T)

American Popular Culture on the Offensive

Headline: "Professional Athletes 'Dis' Opposition!" After scoring a touchdown, Terrell Owens, an All-Pro wide receiver formerly with the NFL's San Francisco 49ers, pulled out a Sharpie marking pen, signed the football, and gave it to a fan in the stands. Joe Horn, a wide receiver for the New Orleans Saints, after scoring a touchdown, pulled out a cellular phone hidden in the goal post padding and called his mother about his score. Chris Webber, an all-star forward for the NBA's Sacramento Kings, ran his hand across his throat in a slashing motion to celebrate a basket and taunt his opponents. Bill Romanowski, a linebacker for the Oakland Raiders, spat on San Francisco 49er wide receiver, J. J. Stokes, after a tackle. Each player, who earns millions of dollars a year, incurred five-figure fines, which most observers characterized to be a slap on the wrist.

Professional athletes are revered in American popular culture. Children want to be like their sports heroes. They put their heroes' posters on their bedroom walls, wear their jerseys, and try to copy their athletic moves. Because of this influence on children, they are highly vulnerable to what athletes say and how they behave. What messages do these acts of "celebration" convey to your children? One message is that they should celebrate for simply doing their job. Can you imagine a college professor doing a "touchdown dance" after giving a particularly good lecture? Or can you envision an auto mechanic taunting fellow mechanics after diagnosing and repairing a car problem? How about a ten-year-old doing the "Ickey Shuffle" (a celebratory dance by former NFL running back, Ickey Woods) if he won a spelling bee? It sounds ridiculous and such behavior would never be tolerated in the "real" world. Yet this behavior is not only accepted, but admired, in the world of sports.

Another message is that it is all about putting the spotlight on themselves and that simply scoring a touchdown (or being successful in some other activity) isn't attention enough. These celebrations are most evident in the traditional team sports of baseball, basketball, and football. Not coincidentally, ESPN and other television sports shows highlight these antics among professional athletes and present them as cool, fun, and entertaining. The ESPN anchor, Stuart Scott, paid homage to Terrell Owens after one of his touchdown celebrations in which he danced with a cheerleader, "Yeah, what's up, girl. What your name is? How you doin'? Good, good, good. I love you, boo." In justifying Owens's behavior, Scott added, "All that is just T.O. being T.O." These antics have become such a venerated part of popular culture that they are included in sports video games, such as Madden NFL 2005. It is no surprise that young athletes see their sports heroes acting this way and want to emulate them.

I've seen gratuitous celebration at numerous youth sports competitions. For example, such behavior, including home run celebrations, taunting opponents, and mugging for the cameras, was commonplace at the 2002 Little League World Series (though only from American players). By the next year's event, players from Latin America and the Far East were also acting like bad sports (How is that for exporting American values?). If you stop by to watch almost any youth sports competition, whether on an urban basketball court, a suburban baseball field, or a rural football field, you will see many young athletes trying to shoot, hit, run, and behave badly like their professional-sports heroes.

What lies at the heart at these messages is a profound lack of respect. These celebrations have the more powerful effect of demeaning the opposition. Beyond the diminution of their opponents, this behavior is disrespectful to the celebrating athletes themselves (though they obviously don't see it that way), to the fans who come to see quality athletic performances (though admittedly many enjoy the antics as well) and to the sport itself (though league officials take only token steps to stop such behavior). And this disrespect isn't limited to sports. It can be found, in some form, in popular music (e.g., hard rock and hip-hop), on television and radio talk shows (e.g., Jerry Springer and Don Imus), and in politics (e.g., negative campaign ads).

American popular culture doesn't want your children to respect you, themselves, or others. If they don't respect you or themselves, they're more likely to resist you by doing the opposite of what you think is best for them. This reaction feeds right into popular culture because most of what it tells children to believe, want, and do goes against what you know is right. Your children are drawn to popular culture because it is telling your children that it will respect them, even though it actually shows zero respect for your children by manipulating them for its own profit-driven ends.

Popular culture tells your children that respect comes from wealth, fame, status, power, popularity, and physical attractiveness. Real respect comes from people living value-driven lives, based on integrity, hard work, and compassion. Popular culture tells children that respect is a right that they deserve. Real respect is a privilege that is earned through good behavior and good works. Popular culture tells your children that respect is shown when they are given whatever they want when they want it. Real respect is gained by showing respect for oneself and others.

Nowhere is this culture of disrespect more evident than in the recent popularity of reality TV. These shows not only allow disrespect, but glorify it and make it a new art form. Failure alone is not punishment enough for the "losers" in reality TV. They must also be demeaned, dehumanized, and publicly humiliated. These losers must suffer the indignity of banishment from reality TV shows by hosts, such as the abusive, yet venerated, Ann Robinson—"You are the weakest link!"—and judges, such as American Idol's Simon Cowell—"You have zero talent!" Despite this despicable behavior, viewers are encouraged to feel excitement and glee in seeing others suffer. As viewers cringe outwardly at the barbs that are thrown at the well-meaning contestants, they inwardly giggle in guilty pleasure at seeing them in pain. Most of the joy of watching reality TV is not in seeing contestants succeed, but rather in seeing them not only fail, but fail in the most humiliating ways. Children who watch reality TV, among other forms of popular culture, are taught to celebrate every luscious moment and, in doing so, are unwittingly indoctrinated into the culture of disrespect that is growing with our society.

Children who buy into this unhealthy view of respect eat unhealthy food, waste money on clothing and shoes that they're told will get them respect, and drink alcohol and take drugs because then they'll be respected by the "popular" crowd. Children learn to trash-talk fellow sports competitors, bully vulnerable students, and "dis" their parents and teachers, all in the name of being respected. In falling for these lies about respect from American popular culture, children are not only disrespectful of others, they are unwittingly disrespectful of themselves.

Respect Starts at Home

There are so many forces in American popular culture that resist your efforts to teach your children respect as a value. It can sometimes seem futile. Yet you are not alone in your efforts. Schools, houses of worship, and sports and artistic organizations, among others, also aim to instill respect in your children. But, like most of child rearing, respect starts at home. If you can teach your children to respect you, themselves, and others when they are young, they are likely to carry that value with them as they enter the real world and use it to withstand American popular culture.

Be the Parent

One way that American popular culture insinuates its view of respect into families is by sending messages to parents about what they need to do to be good parents. The most recent message is that you should be friends with your children. You should be their chums, hang out with them, get them to want to be with you rather than with peers. You should be able to do anything with your children, tell them anything, and be able to treat them as equals. But when you're friends with your children, you actually detract from the strength of your relationship with them and surrender your moral authority over them. When you're friends with your children, you are ceding the respect that they should have for you as their parents. You give up your unique and special relationship with your children because they have many friends, but they have only two (hopefully) parents. Why would you want to be one of many when you could be the one (or two) and only and garner the respect that unique relationship allows?

Let me make this very clear: being you child's friend is *NOT YOUR JOB!* You cannot and should not be friends with your children. If you are friends with your children, you are hurting your children.

Why, you ask, is it such a bad thing to be friends with your children? It's simple. Friends have equal power with their peers, yet parents and children should not have power equality with each other. Parents have to do things that friends wouldn't do. Friends don't tell friends to do their homework and friends don't tell friends when it's time to go to bed. When you're friends with your children, they won't respect your power to say "No!" and mean it.

How many times have you said, "Which part of 'no' didn't you understand?" A recent survey by the Center for a New American Dream reports that when parents say no to a request, 60 percent of children keep nagging, on average, nine times after being told no. Ten percent of 12- and 13-year-olds even said that they nag their parents over fifty times. Even more troubling, 55 percent of the children surveyed said that their parents usually gave in. As their parent, you need to maintain that power and communicate to your children that you are in charge. If you don't show them who's boss, they will lose respect for you, take advantage of you, and you will lose your ability to influence them positively.

Your children don't *want* to be friends with you. When I ask children how they feel about being friends with their parents, they look at me as if I'm from another planet. It's just not in their mindset to be friends with their parents. You're their parents! Parents aren't supposed to be cool, phat, or down with it (using past popular-culture lingo). When parents try to act like their children's friends, they come across, as one girl once told me, "Oh so twentieth century. Acting cool makes them look so dorky and desperate." Despite their frequent protestations, your children want you to be their parents. Being friends with you was definitely not your children's idea.

Your children also *need* you to be their parents. Though children in the twenty-first century often look, dress, act, and talk like adults long before they actually are, the reality is that until they're 17, or 18, or even 21, they are still children in many ways—inexperienced, unskilled, emotionally immature—and living in a world that has never been more threatening. Your children need someone in their lives—*you*—who is more powerful than they are and who can protect them from the big, scary world (of course, they would never admit that to you). When children are the most powerful people in their families, they live in a constant state of fear because they're not ready to take on the world alone. When you're the parent, you can provide them with a safe haven—with direction, support, and boundaries—from which to explore the world. You show your children that you're there to protect them when needed.

When parents want to be friends with their children, they are doing it to meet their own needs. These parents are often unfulfilled in their own lives, lonely, and without adult friends. They share inappropriate information with their children (for example, about their relationship with their spouse or their unhappiness) and place the onus of their happiness on their children's shoulders. In placing the role of friend on their children's shoulders, parents place a burden on them that they're ill-equipped to carry. Because of their love for their parents, most children will accept this role of friend and confidante because they would feel guilty and ashamed if they didn't give their parents that support. Lacking the experience and emotional maturity to handle this responsibility, children slowly crumble under its weight. In time, their love, empathy, and compassion for their parents can turn to anger and resentment at having to assume a role that they neither asked for nor are capable of managing.

Here's a simple rule: parents should have adult friendships and children should have peer friendships. Make sure that you have adult family and friends with whom you have healthy, mature, and sharing relationships. If your needs for intimacy and support are appropriately satisfied by other adults, you won't need to turn to your children to have those needs met. Similarly, your children should have age-appropriate relationships with peers, with whom they can share and gain support from. Freedom from the responsibility of being friends enables you to fulfill your real parental responsibilities and allows your children to be your children.

In maintaining a healthy boundary for your children, be aware of what your needs are and by whom they are being met. Though a part of being a family involves spending time together, be careful that your children aren't being forced to unreasonably sacrifice time with peers to be with you. And never use guilt to force them to choose you over their friends. Also, monitor what you talk to them about, particularly concerns you have in your own life. Be sure the content of your conversations is appropriate for an adult speaking to a child. Ultimately, how much time you spend with your children and the types of conversations you have with them should be dictated by what is in their best interests in their development.

Being their parent instead of their friend doesn't mean that you have to be a harsh, restrictive ogre. You can be loving, fun, and supportive. But it also means earning your children's respect and being tough, though being tough doesn't mean being mean, angry, or controlling. You must know what is best for your children and do whatever is necessary—whether they like it or not—to ensure that everything you do is in their best interests. Being their parent also doesn't mean that they won't care for you any less. In fact, they will probably love and respect you more because you are doing what is best for them. Though they may not always show it, your children will respect and appreciate you being their parent much more than they would your being their friend.

Not being your children's friend when they are young doesn't preclude you from ever being their friend. Once your children become adults—no longer needing you to be such a powerful force in their lives and possessing the tools necessary to navigate their lives without your help—then you can be friends with them. This evolution from parent to more of a friend (though you will always be their parent and hopefully continue to receive love and respect from them) is a natural part of the parent-child relationship and one you can look forward to as your children enter adulthood. At that point, you will want to be friends with your children because you'll want them to allow you to live with them when you get old!

The feedback I get from many parents is that they feel that they have lost the respect from their children and feel hopelessly ineffectual about influencing their children positively. In a way, many parents have surrendered to what they believe is the inevitability of losing the war against American popular culture. When they do give up, popular culture wins by default and your children suffer for it. The reality is that you have a much greater impact on your children than you think. For example, a recent study reported that teenagers are less likely to begin smoking if their parents express disapproval. Surprisingly, the disapproval diminished the effect that peer pressure had on whether they took up smoking. This finding affirms similar research on the influence of parents in teenagers' use of alcohol and drugs.

When you assume the role of parent and earn the respect of your children, they learn the value of respect for themselves. When most of us think about respect, words such as esteem, worth, acknowledgment, acceptance, courtesy, consideration, deference, reverence, and honor come to mind. All of these words capture what we want children to feel about themselves and toward others who earn their respect. Yet a recent survey by the nonprofit group, Public Agenda, found that only 13 percent of respondents felt that respectful, friendly, and helpful children and teenagers were common. Respect is so important because, without it, children can't value themselves or others. Children who don't respect themselves are heading down a road that can lead to self-destruction. They are likely to act impulsively, take unnecessary risks, be more easily swayed by peer pressure and needs for acceptance, and be less concerned with the consequences of their actions. Children who lack self-respect simply don't care about themselves and don't see themselves as being worthy of the descriptors I just listed above. Children who don't respect others are selfish, uncaring, rebellious, and hurtful to others.

Children who have self-respect treat themselves well. They're less likely to do harmful things, they make mostly good choices, and they tend to act in ways that are in their own best interests. Children who respect themselves are more likely to be happy, successful, and have healthy relationships with their parents, siblings, and others in their lives. Children who respect others are generally unselfish, considerate, caring, and generous. They also better understand authority, defer to you and other influential adults, and will respect reasonable boundaries placed on them. These children also are more likely to trust you and abide by your directives.

Contrary to the assertions of American popular culture, when you act like parents—not friends—you engender healthy respect, encourage loving relationships with your children, and foster their development. Your job is to maintain healthy control over your children to provide them with a safe environment in which they can explore and grow.

Maintain Power

The depiction of parent-child relationships in American popular culture aim to undermine respect and authority. Think about how Bart Simpson treated his father, Homer, on *The Simpsons*. Or how Ed Bundy was treated by his children on *Married with Children*. Many of the situation comedies on network television portray fathers, in particular, as buffoons who are unworthy of respect and easily manipulated by their children.

Being the parent is about maintaining power. It means being tough, although tough doesn't mean being harsh and unfair. Being the parent means being firm and adhering to your family-value culture in the face of persistent and persuasive attempts to sway you. It also means being consistent. You must send clear messages about your family's values, your expectations, and the limits you set for your children. If you give in, adjust your message when it is convenient, or change your approach without reason, you're sending mixed messages that will only confuse your children and interfere with their getting the messages that you want them to receive.

Maintaining power communicates to your children that you're in charge, that you expect them to live by the family-value culture, and that you are ready to enforce the expectations and limits you set for them. Maintaining power doesn't mean being utterly dictatorial, particularly as your children move into adolescence. It means striking a balance between being completely permissive and overly strict. Parents who strike this balance allow their children to contribute to family decisions about limits, but ultimately decide for themselves what are reasonable limits for their children. They establish unambiguous expectations and make clear to their children the consequences of transgressions. Finally, these parents follow through firmly and consistently when their children violate the limits. Interestingly, in some important ways, children of permissive and overly controlling parents come out the same; they lack self-control, are self-centered, and have little social awareness. Maintaining power involves being firm, but flexible. You can foster this flexibility by talking to your children about your expectations and the limits you set for them, why they are important to you, why they should be important to your children, and encourage them to talk to you about them. Engaging them in a discussion of your steadfastness gives them the opportunity to convince you to be more flexible. Flexibility doesn't mean giving in to your children. It means being open to changing the expectations and limits you have placed on them. If your children can persuade you through their words or actions that they deserve more latitude, you should show flexibility and give them more rein. Of course, you have to make sure that they act responsibly with their new-found freedom. If they do, you may consider giving them more independence as a reward for your earned faith in them. If they abuse the privilege you've given them, you must take it away from them immediately. For example, if your 14-year-old son stayed out past his agreed-upon curfew, you should set his curfew earlier, have a discussion about why he broke curfew, and provide another consequence, such as cleaning out the basement, to show him that his actions affect all parts of his life. If you allow your children to keep their independence after violating curfew, they will not understand the special opportunity that they are given or that it is truly a privilege that must be earned. You must also hold them responsible for their transgressions. If they violate your trust, they must pay for it in a way that will help them clearly see the connection between what was expected of them and how they broke your trust. Your children need to understand that with freedom comes responsibility and that without being responsible, the privileges will be lost. Invariably, your children will break your trust periodically.

That's just part of being young. What's important is that they learn from these experiences so they don't continue to abuse the privileges you give them and misuse the freedom they will slowly gain.

Maturity

Maturity is essential for your children to learn respect. The perspective that comes with maturity allows your children to respect your efforts in raising them, as well as those of their teachers, coaches, and others who influence them positively. They respect others who act in ways that reflect your family-value culture and can look critically at those who don't, even if they are wealthy, powerful, or famous. Mature children respect their parents and recognize that (to paraphrase the Rolling Stones song) you won't always give them what they want, but you will always give them what they need (hey, popular culture isn't all bad).

Parents can be fooled into thinking that their children are mature enough to respect the freedom and responsibility that they are given. These days, girls are reaching puberty much earlier than in the past. Girls as young as 11 or 12 years old can be mistaken for young women. They are also dressing in more mature—and sometimes provocative— ways at increasingly younger ages. Because of weight-lifting programs and nutritional supplements, teenage boys seem bigger and more mature than ever. Young people are dressing, acting, and talking like adults.

Yet these physical and superficial changes belie the fact that immaturity among children in twenty-first-century America is an epidemic. Many parents, teachers, and coaches tell me that so many children they know are self-absorbed, spoiled, irresponsible, disrespectful, and lazy. Their sense of entitlement is profound and misguided, yet they learned it somewhere, most likely from American popular culture. They want what they want, when they want it, how they want it, and they want it given to them on a silver platter. That's the way it is for movie stars, pop music artists, and professional athletes. Many children these days don't want to do anything that they don't feel like doing. Hard work, discipline, and patience are just not cool these days! "Why should I have to earn it, when I can get rich and famous just by being on *Fear Factor* or *American Idol*?" If parents force them to do something, children give half an effort begrudgingly. And many parents let them get away with it!

American popular culture doesn't want your children to grow up. Why, you ask? Popular culture does everything it can to condition your children to become good little consumers, and keeping them immature fosters that receptivity to its influence. Children are more easily seduced, swayed, and tricked. They are more likely to bend to peer pressure and follow the crowd. Children are more naively open to messages with strong emotional content, for example, associating a certain kind of candy with having fun or a pair of shoes with being cool and popular. They are more susceptible to having their emotions manipulated, for example, an ad that triggers their fear of rejection for not wearing the right type of clothing. They're more impressionable to words and images that touch "hot buttons," such as social acceptance, physical attractiveness, immediate gratification, and envy. Children are more easily bored, have shorter attention spans, and are readily distracted, so they will look to the brightest lights and loudest sounds to stimulate and entertain them. Products connected with popular music, attractive people, and excitement draw children like moths to a flame. They are less likely to think critically, question the messages they see and hear, or make well-thought-out decisions; children are some of the biggest impulse buyers out there. Children are drawn to what is hip, groovy, cool, rad, phat, the bomb, or def (depending on your generation). Children aren't good at weighing options, considering long-term ramifications, or recognizing consequences. They're not driven by values or conscious decisions about what is in their best interests. Children are highly vulnerable to the simplistic, seductive, incessant, and overpowering messages from American popular culture. In other words, children are the ideal target for the messages offered so forcefully by popular culture, and keeping children *children* helps it maintain its bottom line.

American popular culture makes it harder to raise mature children. Many celebrities, such as professional athletes, musicians, and actors, are often no more than spoiled, entitled children who are given—and forgiven—everything. They receive special treatment and demonstrate no respect or appreciation for what they've been given. The media, including television, newspapers, magazines, and the Internet, focus their coverage of these celebrities on their bad behavior, for example, O. J. Simpson, Rush Limbaugh, Michael Jackson, and Ben Affleck, because it sells. Children see their idols acting this way and assume that it's not only okay, but absolutely appropriate—how could it not be, it's on TV! In the meantime, you're the one who has to try to show your children that the people they look up to are not good role models.

Your challenge is showing your children that the world just doesn't work that way. If you don't teach them this lesson when they're young, when they grow up and move out of the house, they'll be in for a rude awakening because entitlement rarely exists in the real world. Teaching your children this lesson means making sure they don't always get what they want, forcing them to do things they don't want to do, and requiring them to face the consequences of their actions.

Maturity comes from your children learning how the adult world really works and developing the values, perspectives, and skills that will enable them to thrive as adults. These insights about the world in which they live teach children to respect you, themselves, and others. Mature children learn that they can't always get what they want, when and how they want it. They learn that they might not get it at all. When they can get what they want, they usually have to work hard to get it—few things of worth in life come free or easily—and it might take a while. When they do get something they want, mature children appreciate it and are thankful to those who helped them. Mature children also realize that life is full of frustration and disappointment, and if they ever want to be successful and happy, they'll have to figure out how to deal with it—and running to their parents or quitting is not dealing with it!

Battles of Will

Whether your children learn the value of respect also depends on how you handle the inevitable conflicts that you and your children will have as they move toward adulthood. Though conflict is a natural part of childhood and an essential aspect of their separation from you into independent beings, it is also a battlefield on which you fight for your children against American popular culture—often concurrently with fighting with your children.

American popular culture wants to start a war between you and your children. By encouraging conflict, popular culture destroys the bridges that you have with your children and creates a rift that reduces your influence over them. If you're busy fighting your children, you will have little time to battle popular culture. If your children are fighting you, they will look for love, respect, and acceptance in other places—such as popular culture.

And American popular culture is only too ready and willing to take your children in and make them feel respected and accepted—"Drink Dr. Pepper and you'll get the girl [or the guy]" or "Wear Nike athletic shoes and you'll 'be like Mike.'" With you out of the way, popular culture can more easily seduce your children with messages that convey, "Your parents don't understand you, but I do. Listen to me and I'll take care of you." The combination of the messages from popular culture being attractive to your children and counter to your own messages makes them fodder for popular culture. When your children are mad at you, what better way to get back at you than to accept and act on the messages from American popular culture that they know you will hate. For example, why do you think children wear the low-hanging, baggy pants that are so much in fashion these days? Because they are good-looking or comfortable? Nope. Children wear them because popular culture has convinced them that the pants—how *do* they stay up?—will give them identity and acceptance, and they know their most parents will cringe when they see their children in them.

The challenge is not that you are going to have conflicts with your children from time to time—that's just part of the parent-child relationship—but whether they develop into full-scale war that pushes you and your children apart. How you handle them will determine whether the conflicts are healthy or harmful. These conflicts generally occur in two kinds of battles of will that are fought in childhood and adolescence.

Childhood Battles

Early in your children's lives, you may enter these battles of will unwittingly. It's sometimes easier to give in than to fight a battle with your children, so you might surrender and allow them to win. For example, when you and your children are in the checkout line at the supermarket and they want a candy bar that is conspicuously displayed. You say no several times, but they start screaming. Just to quiet them down and to limit your embarrassment as others look at you with disapproving expressions, you give in and buy them a candy bar. Giving in to your children and allowing them to win this battle of wills isn't in their best interests. You're surrendering because it makes life easier for you, but it will make life harder for your children because they come to learn that they can get anything they want if they scream, complain, and nag loudly and persistently enough.

You have the power to avoid or control the battles of will you engage in with your children. Battles of will require two participants. If you don't take the bait in the battles of will in response to your children's provocations, all-out and ongoing battles can never develop and no casualties will be sustained. Returning to the example of your children wanting the candy bar at the supermarket, you must clearly communicate that they will not get the candy bar no matter what they do, and especially if they continue to act badly. You can offer them the possibility of a snack when they get home if they behave. You must then stand firm in the face of continued—and sometimes loud, persistent, and embarrassing—efforts to win that battle of wills.

The problem is that children have more energy than you do and they will try to wear you down. If you are at home, they will try to divide and conquer by asking your spouse if they can have what they want. You and your spouse (if you live in a two-parent household) must provide a united front against your children's stealth attacks and manipulations. This is where your commitment and resolve must carry you through the battle of wills because it would be much easier to give in to your children's relentless demands. The peace and quiet would be so wonderful. But at what price? Only the values that encompass your family-value culture and the future of your children.

You must be resolved beforehand so that when situations like this arise you are committed to standing your ground. This prepared determination will help you weather the storm of your children's indignation at not getting what they want. When your children start to get difficult, step back for a moment and take a deep breath. This distancing alone can help you to not get drawn into the battle of wills. Remind yourself that giving in to your children's demands hurts them and weakens your resolve to act in their best interests. If you're in a public place, remember that every parent faces these challenges, and when you stand your ground, those watching will actually respect you and be envious of your strength. And nobody likes losing a battle. Once you win a battle of wills, you know how good it feels and those feelings of being value-driven, in control, and doing what's best for your children will encourage you to stand firm in the future.

Avoiding or winning the battles of will that occur early in your children's lives will teach the values of self-control, delayed gratification, and consideration of others. If children learn that they can get what they want whenever they want it, they're going to be in for a painful surprise when they enter adulthood, because the adult world just doesn't work that way. These battles should show children that they're not the only people in the world. They need to learn that others have needs too and they must be considerate of those needs. By surrendering to your children's wants, you prevent them from learning that they must consider others in attempting to meet their own needs.

You can also get pulled into battles of will when you react by lowering yourself to your children's level. It's natural for you to become frustrated or angry from time to time as your children test your limits and see what they can get away with. What should separate you from your children and what gives you the power to win these battles of will is your ability to maintain control over your emotions while they lose control of theirs. During a battle of wills, when they have a temper tantrum or sulk, you must remain cool, calm, and collected. When you react to your children's provocations by losing control (in other words, by acting like a child), you hand them a ready-made strategy for winning the battles of will. They learn that if they push and push and push, they'll ultimately tear down the veneer of mature adulthood that you wear and reduce you to their equal. As soon as you go to their level and act like a five-year-old, for example, by yelling at your children when you get angry with them, you give up your power because you're no longer the adult in the relationship. Instead, they see that they're now in a battle of wills with another five-year-old child, and that is a battle they know they can win. When you lapse into being a child, they gain the advantage because they have more energy and are more practiced at acting like a child than you and they will outlast you.

For your children's sake, you must maintain power and rule your children with a firm, but loving, hand. This power communicates to your children that you are in charge and that battles of will will not be tolerated. Your resolve also conveys that you expect them to be active and responsive members of the family. In your steadfastness, you are communicating important values that express your family-value culture. Though they may not like losing these battles of will, these losses actually help them win in the end.

Teenage Battles

A normal and healthy part of adolescence for your children is separating from you and becoming independent. Conflict is one way in which children stake out new territory and assert their independence. If you attempt to win these battles outright, you will stifle your children's journey to adulthood and they will take drastic measures to claim their independence. At the same time, if you lose all of the battles without putting up any fight, your children gain too much territory too early, and they're left to battle the world alone without the capabilities to emerge from that battle unscathed.

American popular culture encourages battles of will with your teenage children. Television shows, such as the nighttime soap opera, *The OC,* or situation comedies, like *Malcolm in the Middle,* show teenagers waging battles against their parents and usually winning. While they are distancing themselves from you, your children are drawn to the world around them, which happens to be dominated by popular culture. While you set limits for your children, popular culture gives them unbridled freedom. While you try to give your children what they need, popular culture gives them what they think they want. While being connected to you signifies immaturity and dependence to your children, connection with popular culture symbolizes maturity and independence. While acceptance by you means less and less to your children, they more and more crave acceptance by popular culture.

American popular culture's greatest ally—and your biggest enemy—in this battle of wills is peer pressure. As your children enter adolescence, they are driven by no more powerful a force than being accepted by their peers. And popular culture taps into your children's social needs in music (e.g., getting the girl or guy; finding love), television shows (e.g., reality TV's lure of fame and wealth), and advertising (by wearing and eating the "right" things, they'll be cool and popular). The two-pronged impact of separating from you and being accepted by their peers can drive a wedge between you and your children. And popular culture's influence on both of these forces encourages your children to instigate and attempt to win battles of will with you.

Your children are looking for a fight as they enter their teenage years and they will often go to great lengths to provoke you. You should expect it and prepare for it. On top of this, you're more vulnerable to being pulled into battles of will during your children's teenage years. You may fear for your children's safety as they move out into the world on their own. You may be reluctant to give up the control of your children's lives that you've held for so many years. You may question whether they're ready to go it alone and not want them to get hurt if they're not ready. You may mourn your children's impending separation from you. Your children want to separate from you, but, like most parents, a part of you wants your children to stay young and dependent on you forever.

Unfortunately, the more you cling to this fantasy, the more likely that you will not only lose your children to adulthood, but you will also lose your relationship with them. If you engage them in a battle of wills to keep them, rather than allowing your children to separate and gain independence as you should, you are sure to lose. This battle of wills can also cause your children to take extreme, and sometimes destructive, steps to win the conflict and assert their independence. Forays into drinking, drugs, and sexual activity, all of which American popular culture venerates, are a few of the dangerous ways in which your children assert their independence if they feel overly restricted. When your children take these extreme measures, both you and your children are casualties and the only victor is popular culture.

Unlike the battles of will in early childhood, you cannot and should not avoid them. But the difference is that your strategy shouldn't be to win all of these battles. Your challenge is to respond to the adolescent battles of will in a way that encourages your children's *interdependence*. The notion of interdependence involves your children first recognizing that they cannot always have their needs met immediately, must be responsive to others, and are dependent on other people. Then, as they move toward adulthood, children must shift from dependence on you to self-reliance as they separate from you and become more autonomous beings. Finally, you want your children to attain a balance between being independent in aspects of their lives and experiencing interdependence with others. In healthy interdependence, your children gain an appreciation for the connectedness between people that is necessary for healthy relationships and a meaningful life.

In adolescence, battles of will should foster increased independence and freedom while maintaining a safe environment in which your children can gain comfort in their newfound freedom. You and your children can only win the war if you allow your children to win, *but on your terms.* Only by intentionally and judiciously losing some of these battles can you ensure that both you and your children ultimately emerge as victors.

Early in your children's teenage years, you must win most of the battles to protect them from their world—increasingly dominated by American popular culture and its closest ally, peer pressure—while allowing them to win small battles that let them feel like they are gaining some control and independence. You win most by setting and enforcing reasonable limits and holding your children responsible for adhering to the boundaries. You give your children a few wins by establishing those boundaries a bit farther than you might feel completely comfortable. For example, you might want to keep your children from listening to music they like, but you find objectionable. This is a case where you recognize that you can't control what your children listen to. Though offensive in some ways, this music will probably not scar them for life. Therefore, you can allow them to buy the questionable CDs and listen to the music, thus giving them a victory that they see as their own. You have to make your own judgments on where you give your children victories. If offensive music is particularly objectionable to your family-value culture, then let them win on something that is more acceptable to you. By giving your children these small victories, they won't feel the need to go after big victories—such as alcohol and drug use, or sexual behavior—that are truly harmful.

You can use the battles of will as opportunities to talk rather than fight. You can create a dialogue with your children about finding a balance of limits and freedom, and how your children can earn more freedom by demonstrating good decision making and acting in ways that are consistent with your family-value culture. You must provide guidance and direction to your children, but you shouldn't attempt to manage, control, or coerce them too much. If your children feel excessively constrained, they will resist and push back, usually in much more destructive ways than the area that originally caused them to feel oppressed.

Establishing boundaries should be accompanied by an ongoing dialogue about why you are setting limits, the consequences of violating the boundaries, and how your children can extend those limits over time. When they want to do something that you disagree with, ask your children why they want to do it, what they get out of it, and whether there are any risks. This conversation allows you to offer your perspective in a calm and thoughtful way and encourages them to think critically about the issue before they make a decision. Allowing their input into the decision-making process and showing some flexibility in where you set the boundaries can give your children a greater sense of control and ownership of how far they choose to go.

The battlefields that you fight with your children on are, not coincidentally, the same battlefields on which they will face American popular culture: curfews, what movies they can watch, who they can socialize with and date, alcohol, drugs, and sex. In fact, the battles of will that you fight with your children often determine whether they will ultimately win the war against American popular culture. Though they will certainly not admit it, your children want and need you to help them at this point in the war against popular culture by parceling out their exposure to movies, music, television, and the like. At the same time, trying to limit their exposure to popular culture too much will actually push them toward popular culture. As your children mature, this balancing act involves ceding more and more victories and, in the end, surrendering to the inevitability of your children leaving you and becoming independent adults.

The eventual victory of independence should go to your children. Yet it is also a triumph for you because your children will be healthy and mature adults with whom you have a strong and loving relationship. In ultimately winning this battle of wills, your children develop the ability to win their ongoing, and now mostly solo, battle with American popular culture. In the end, they're going to leave whether you like it or not, so at some point you have to trust that you've instilled good values in them, given them positive perspectives, taught them sound decision-making skills, and generally done a good job in preparing them for future battles with popular culture and for life. If you have prepared them in this way, you can let them know that you're there if they need you and, with confidence—though also with some trepidation—loosen the reins and let them go.

Emerging Values

Children who have respect for themselves and others value *health and well-being*. Respectful children won't do things that might hurt them physically, emotionally, socially, or academically. For example, they won't drive recklessly, bully other children, or cheat in school because they understand that these actions would not be beneficial and would be disrespectful to themselves and others.

Children who are respectful are *kind and giving*. They are especially courteous and helpful to others. These children are warm, caring, thoughtful, and considerate. They want to share their good fortune with others and give back to the world that gave them such opportunities. Respectful children are those who tutor younger children, help the elderly, and recycle waste (because they respect the environment too). They are generous with their time, energy, and resources. In turn, these children, though perhaps not appreciated by those who have fallen under the spell of American popular culture (being nice is, sadly, not very cool in our culture) are respected and valued by their parents, teachers, friends, and others of worth in their world.

Perhaps the most notable value that comes from respect is *appreciation*. Respectful children appreciate the opportunities they have been given and understand that the best way to respect those opportunities is to take full advantage of them. These children also express gratitude to those who have given so much to them. They are willing to say how much they appreciate others' efforts on their behalf. In doing so, they not only make themselves feel good about what they do, but they also make others feel respected and valued, and provide them with a sense of gratification and joy in their efforts.

CHAPTER 6

Responsibility
(You've Got the Power)

American Popular Culture on the Offensive

In a widely publicized court case in 2003, Marjorie Knoller and Robert Noel, whose huge Presa Canario dogs viciously attacked and killed Diane Whipple, a neighbor in their San Francisco apartment building, were convicted on several charges. The attack was so savage that Ms. Whipple's clothes were entirely ripped from her body except for one sock. Two animal-control officers and three tranquilizer darts were required to subdue the dogs. During the trial, both of the defendants denied responsibility for Ms. Whipple's death. In a May 10, 2001, *Glamour* interview, Noel said, "It is totally inexplicable," insisting that neither dog had ever shown any aggressive tendencies (even though they are bred to be aggressive). "These two dogs were like my kids." Additionally, they blamed the victim, who was outweighed by each dog by thirty pounds, saying that she didn't move quickly enough to avoid the attack. In a letter to the district attorney, the couple wrote that, "Ms. Whipple may have been wearing pheromone[sic]-based cosmetic or scent or...as a serious athlete, she may have been a user of steroids, which could have triggered Bane's interest." The couple's defense attorney, Nedra Ruiz, went on to accuse the victim's partner of lying, the prosecution of kowtowing to the public, and the judge of buckling under political pressure. The jury didn't buy any of it. Said jury foreman Don Newton, "Everything she [Ruiz] said was suspect…We had a unanimous verdict throughout all of it." Neither Knoller nor Noel have ever offered a public apology to Ms. Whipple's family.

What message does the behavior of Ms. Knoller and Mr. Noel communicate? A profound disregard for human life. Absence of compassion for the life of another person. And most powerfully, an unwillingness to take responsibility for their actions. Fortunately, our judicial system maintained the value of responsibility by ensuring that they were held accountable for their reckless actions and their despicable attitudes.

Our country was built on commitment, self-initiative, and perseverance. The American Dream was about working hard, making sacrifices, and creating a better life for your children than the life you might have had. People put in their time and did what needed to be done. America was also about taking responsibility. If mistakes were made, people accepted culpability and did what they had to do to correct the situation. By accepting responsibility, people knew that they had greater control over their lives and that getting ahead was in their hands rather than being left to chance.

Times have certainly changed. America is now about avoiding responsibility. Many children these days want everything handed to them. They don't want to have to work for it or earn what they get. Many children think that life should be easy and all good things should come to them just for being who they are. Lou Holtz, who coached football for over forty years, once said, "When I first started coaching, athletes talked about accountability and responsibility. Now they talk about rights and entitlement." Children used to be grateful for the opportunities they were given. They appreciated how fortunate they were. Not any longer. Many children expect things to be given to them. It's their right to get everything they want and they're entitled to the very best of everything.

Nowhere is this more evident than in how children spend their time today. Time is one area in which parents should give their children responsibility, yet in the last decade or so, children's relationship with time has changed. In previous generations, children didn't live programmed lives. Organized sports were limited and seasonal. After school and weekends were mostly unscheduled except for family activities. Children also knew that they had to entertain themselves. "Bored? Find something to do," parents would say. Children had time that was truly free and the onus was on them to find a way to fill it. Because no one else was responsible for their stimulation, they learned to turn the mundane into the fascinating. I remember when a cardboard box or a pile of sticks could provide hours of fun for children. Or children just learned how to deal with being bored sometimes.

Yet children today are given little responsibility for their time. Children's days are structured and programmed. Children have school all day, play on organized sports teams, and take music and dance lessons. Weekends are packed with sports practices and competitions, and performing arts lessons and recitals. Parents organize, plan, and schedule their children's lives, telling them where they have to be at what time and making sure they get there. Even unstructured fun has turned into play dates!

At home, children have become passive observers rather than active participants with their time. They are absorbers of stimulation and information. Children aren't expected to be self-reliant with their time or asked to take the initiative when they don't have anything to do. When children get bored, they demand to be entertained. Instead of encouraging resourceful uses of their children's time that would foster initiative, imagination, and creativity, parents take the expedient route and turn on the television set, put in a DVD, or hand them a video game. Children's time now is filled with less meaningful social interaction, less intellectual and creative stimulation, and less physical activity, all to the detriment of their healthy development.

American popular culture doesn't want your children to be responsible. Children who don't take responsibility for their lives will look to others who are willing to assume that responsibility. Many parents abdicate this responsibility because they are too busy and too stressed, so they look to popular culture to help them. And popular culture is only too happy to oblige, offering parents music, video games, DVDs, and the Internet to take their children off their hands. And children are only too happy to become a part of the fun and stimulating world American popular culture offers. With this responsibility, popular culture has the capacity to control children's lives, shape their values and interests, and dictate the choices they make, none of which are in children's best interests.

Children who don't accept responsibility for their actions want others to be held accountable for anything they do. They don't want to be blamed for anything because then they might feel bad about themselves or look bad in the eyes of others. These children are easily influenced and manipulated because they will listen to anyone who will take responsibility away from them. They are easily led down unhealthy roads because it wouldn't be their fault if something bad happened.

There are, however, significant benefits to children taking responsibility for themselves. Children who are held accountable, though having to take on the burden of mistakes and failure, can also take responsibility for their efforts and achievements. They learn what it takes to avoid bad things from happening and what it takes to make good things happen. These children are strong, capable, and confident—in other words, the kind of children that American popular culture hates. Responsible children are not going to be so readily influenced or manipulated by popular culture. They won't just believe everything they are told. Responsible children recognize popular culture for what it is and look critically at the messages they get. Rather than accepting those messages blindly, responsible children make deliberate choices about the messages they accept and how they act on them. These children make careful decisions because they know that, whatever happens, the buck stops with them.

Responsibility Starts with Self-Esteem

Self-esteem is the most misunderstood and misused developmental factor of the past thirty years. Child-rearing experts in the early 1970s decided that all of the efforts of our society should be devoted to helping children build self-esteem. They said that the best way to develop self-esteem was to ensure that children always felt good about themselves. Parents were encouraged to love and praise and reinforce and reward their children no matter what they did. Unfortunately, this approach created children who were selfish, spoiled, and dependent on others to feel good about themselves.

Parents were also led to believe that they had to be sure that their children never felt bad about themselves because it would hurt their self-esteem. So parents did everything they could to protect their children from anything that might create bad feelings. Parents didn't scold their children when they misbehaved. Parents didn't discipline their children when they didn't give their best effort in school and sports.

Schools and communities did their part to "protect" children from feeling bad about themselves. For example, school grading systems were changed. I remember between sixth and seventh grade my middle school replaced F for failure with NI (Needs Improvement). God forbid I'd feel bad about myself for failing at something! Sports competitions eliminated scoring, winners, and losers in the belief that losing would hurt children's self-esteem. My four-year-old niece came home one day from a soccer tournament with a ribbon that said "#1-Winner" on it. When I asked her what she did to deserve such a wonderful prize, she said that everyone got one! Though Woody Allen once said that 90 percent of success is just showing up, it's the last 10 percent—the part that requires hard work, discipline, patience, and perseverance—that true success is all about. Children are being led to believe that, like Woody Allen's view, they can become successful and feel good about themselves just for showing up. But showing up is just not enough. By rewarding children in this way, they are not learning the values and skills they need to achieve real success.

In its poorly conceived attempt to protect children's self-esteem, our society caused the very thing that it took such pains to prevent— children with low self-esteem, no sense of responsibility, and the emotional and behavioral problems that go with it. The supposed benefit of the "I'm a victim" mentality is that children's self-esteem is protected. If children aren't responsible for all of the bad things that happen to them, then they can't feel bad about themselves and their self-esteem won't be hurt. But responsibility is two sides of the same coin. If children don't take responsibility for their mistakes and failures in their lives, they can't take responsibility for their successes and achievements. And without that responsibility, children really can't feel good about themselves or experience meaning, satisfaction, and joy. Also, without the willingness to take responsibility, children are truly victims; they're powerless to change the bad things that do happen to them. Because they don't take responsibility for their lives, they lack the capacity to change their circumstances. Children are at the mercy of their parents and others in their world to dictate how they feel and what they're capable of accomplishing. With a sense of responsibility, children learn that when things are not going well, they have the power to make changes in their lives for the better. This other side of the responsibility coin is what enables children to develop into mature and involved adults.

The goal is to raise children who are willing and able to take responsibility for their lives. Yes, they're going to feel bad when they make mistakes and fail. But you want your children to feel bad when they screw up! How else are they going to learn what not to do and what they need to do to do better in the future? But, contrary to popular belief, these experiences will build, not hurt, their self-esteem. By allowing them to take responsibility for their lives—achievements and missteps alike—your children gain the ability to change the bad experiences, and create and savor the good experiences.

Your challenge is to help your children understand how a valued life really comes about—by taking responsibility for their lives. Much of your parenting should be devoted to helping your children develop this sense of responsibility, the belief that their actions matter, that their actions have consequences: if they do good things, good things happen; if they do bad things, bad things happen; and, importantly, if they do nothing, nothing happens. You must allow your children to experience this connection—both success and failure—in all areas of their lives, including school, sports, the performing arts, relationships, family responsibilities, and other activities. Your children's essential need to have these experiences will require you to eschew the culture of victimization that pervades American society. You must give your children the opportunity to take responsibility for their lives, make their own decisions, take risks, and fully experience all aspects of life, including the accomplishments and joys as well as the failures and disappointments.

Teach Responsibility

Responsibility is an essential value because it connects children in the deepest and most profound way to their lives. Children who are given responsibility and accept responsibility learn that their lives are truly their own. Children feel that their involvement in their lives—school, avocations, relationships—is their own and that they have the power to express their values and shape their lives in any way they choose. Responsibility creates in children great caring about all aspects of their lives. Children who take responsibility for their lives choose the values that positively guide their lives. They participate in its many facets for no other reason than the value they place on it for themselves. Participation in, for example, their education, hobbies, and friendships, gives children with responsibility meaning, satisfaction, and joy in their lives. Their sense of responsibility—and the values that they connect with it—is the foundation of their self-esteem, how they feel about themselves, and the quality of the life they want to lead.

Children who embrace responsibility are also less vulnerable to the influences of American popular culture. They neither want nor need others to take control of their lives. These children believe that they are masters of their own universe and don't appreciate it when unwanted external forces—popular culture—attempt to take responsibility away from them. These children also don't buy into the culture of victimization because the idea of giving up responsibility is absolutely antithetical to them.

Give Responsibility

The best way to instill a sense of responsibility in your children is to give them responsibility. These responsibilities should not only teach them the value of responsibility, but they should also be couched in the larger sense of responsibility related to your family-value culture and to the values that you want your children to learn. The responsibilities that you give your children to fulfill can reflect a variety of values.

Giving responsibility can involve assigning your children jobs they must perform within your family, for example, helping with the dishes, cleaning up your home, visiting their grandparents once a week, or taking out the trash. These responsibilities highlight the value of family and the essential role your children play as contributing members of your family.

The responsibilities can be related to values beyond your family. Here are some examples:

- *Environment:* your children can be in charge of recycling for your household.
- *Community:* your children can help serve meals at a local homeless shelter.
- *Faith:* your children can organize a kids' day at your house of worship.

These responsibilities show your children that there is more to life than themselves or even their immediate family and connect them with the community in which they live.

You can also assign responsibilities that draw attention to your achievement values, for example, holding your children responsible for completing their homework, school projects, and test preparations in a thorough and timely manner. You can also teach them about achievement values by helping them to make good decisions when faced with competing interests, such as the need to finish their homework and their desire to play with their friends.

Allowances

One practical area in which children can learn the value of responsibility is with money and allowances. Teaching children the value of money and good financial responsibility is one of the most practical and important lessons children can learn. Americans, with their ravenous appetites for conspicuous—and unaffordable—consumption that is fueled by American popular culture, have never been more fiscally irresponsible. Americans, on average, carry over $8,400 in credit-card debt, 20 percent of credit cards are maxed out, only 40 percent of people pay off their credit cards each month, and personal bankruptcy is at an all-time high. How important is fiscal responsibility? Charles Dickens said it well, "Annual income twenty pounds, annual expenditure nineteen and six, result happiness. Annual income twenty pounds, annual expenditure twenty pounds ought and six, result misery."

American popular culture has connected what people have with how they feel about themselves and how they believe others will look at them. It has caused people to confuse wants with needs. Today, many people believe they need cellular telephones, big-screen televisions, and expensive clothing, when these products are simply wants rather than necessities. Popular culture has also made spending money easier than ever. Almost anyone can get one or more credit cards these days and, as the statistics above indicate, many people don't consider the ramifications of their spending until it's too late. This consumer culture is driven by the credit-card companies and producers of these goods who profit from the misery of those who are fiscally irresponsible.

According to one survey, about a half a million children in the U.S. receive a regular allowance. Advocates of early financial "literacy" recommend that children between the ages of three and five begin to understand how money works and are old enough to have an allowance. Allowances show children about the reality of spending, saving, and budgeting. For most children, they also learn the important lesson that money does not grow on trees.

The first thing you have to decide is whether your children should be given an allowance simply for being a part of the family or whether they have to fulfill specific duties. Some experts suggest that basic family responsibilities don't deserve an allowance, for example, making their beds or bringing dishes to the sink. This relationship also teaches them the value of being a contributing member of the family. Other household chores, such as mowing the lawn or raking leaves, deserve an allowance. Because these chores go beyond daily household responsibilities, they provide children with an introduction to the notions of work and the exchange of goods and services for money. An important part of giving an allowance—and teaching the value of responsibility— is that your children learn that if they don't work, they don't get paid, just like in the adult world.

Allowances can also be useful tools for teaching your children about other values. For example, requiring them to deposit a certain amount each month in a savings account teaches them about frugality and long-term planning. Having them set aside part of their allowance that they can donate to their favorite charity teaches children about the value of compassion and giving. Helping them to decide whether to wait to buy something later rather than right away shows them about the value of patience and delayed gratification.

An essential part of becoming a responsible person is learning to delay gratification. Yet American popular culture encourages—and profits from—people seeking immediate gratification. Fast-food, pre-shrunk jeans, and plug-and-play electronics all enable people to get what they want ASAP. Teaching children to delay gratification will make them more resistant to the messages of "Gotta have it now!" with which popular culture bombards them.

Micromanagement

A mistake many parents make that prevents children from taking responsibility for themselves is continuing to micromanage them long after it is necessary or healthy. For example, many parents constantly ask their children, even well into their teens, if they finished their homework, pack their athletic equipment for them, and schedule their piano lessons without consulting with them, when children are perfectly capable of taking responsibility for these activities themselves. The very act of micromanaging your children takes away responsibility from them. If you have assumed responsibility for their lives, there is no need for them to do so.

Early in your children's lives you must both manage and micromanage them because they lack the experience and tools to organize and deal with its many details. But as you micromanage your children, you should also be teaching them how to manage themselves and then progressively require them to. For example, when your children are beginning preschool, you will need to organize their school materials and lunch in the morning before they leave. Once your children become familiar with what they need, you can involve them in this process, asking them what they need and whether they have it. As they gain a grasp of their morning organization, you can give them responsibility for it while watching to make sure they have everything they need. If they forget something, you can gently remind them. At some point when your children have demonstrated the ability to organize themselves in the morning with your guidance, you can allow them to do it on their own. If you notice that your children forget something as they are leaving for school, you may consider not reminding them. When they get to school without something they needed, they will learn a valuable lesson and will be less likely to forget it in the future.

And your children will learn that they must be responsible for themselves to have everything they need.

Unfortunately, many young children will not want to assume the mantel of responsibility. Think about how good they have it. You take care of everything, so they don't have to worry about or do anything. Their lives are easier and more comfortable; they have it made. But, however much your children like it, continued micromanagement and usurping of their responsibility does them a profound disservice that will hurt them in the future because, at some point, they will be forced to take responsibility for themselves, but won't know how to. Inappropriate micromanagement may also communicate to your children that you don't believe that they're capable of taking responsibility. This perception may hurt their self-esteem because they may come to believe they are incompetent and this lack of confidence will make them reluctant to take responsibility for themselves in the future.

As your children enter their teenage years, they should have the experience and skills to organize and run much of their own lives. At this point, you have to let go of your micromanaging responsibilities and begin to reduce your management role as well. If you continue to micromanage their lives, you actually encourage your children to avoid responsibility because they will have no need to be responsible for their lives. Additionally, your children will come to resent your constant and inappropriate intrusions causing your relationship to suffer. Yet they will remain dependent on you to micromanage their lives because they won't have the capacity to take responsibility for themselves.

You may still need to manage—or help them manage—some aspects of their lives—setting limits, resisting immediate gratification, guiding their decision making. But this degree of management should diminish as your children get older and demonstrate their ability to manage themselves. Of course, you want your children to know that you are there to support and offer guidance when they are faced with new and difficult challenges in their lives, for example, choosing a college or buying a car. If you're still managing their lives as your children reach their late teens, you will keep them in a perpetual state of childhood and you'll prevent them from graduating to adulthood.

Expectations of Responsibility

You should expect a lot of your children. Set the bar high on things that you value and make it clear to your children that you expect them to live up to those standards. Expectations communicate to your children what you, well, expect of them. They are standards to which you hold your children in all aspects of their lives. Expectations act as guides for your children of what they should and shouldn't do.

Importantly, expectations should be used to instill healthy values, such as responsibility, in children. The expectations you set for your children identify how responsibility fits into your family-value culture, how responsibility connects to their behavior in their daily lives, and provide them with a threshold of responsibility above which will meet the expectation and below which will be seen as a violation of the expectation. These expectations should communicate to your children that they are responsible for their actions, will be held accountable for their behavior, and will face the consequences for bad behavior.

Sadly, American popular culture communicates to children an entirely different set of expectations based on its own values about responsibility. Popular culture expects your children to evade responsibility, blame others, avoid feeling bad about failure, and reject the consequences of their actions. These expectations are communicated by showing celebrities using their position and wealth to avoid responsibility for their bad behavior and television, movies, and video games not showing the consequences of irresponsible or harmful behavior. American popular culture encourages children to cede responsibility for their lives—what they think, feel, and do—to popular culture with the false promise of coolness, popularity, success, and happiness. These expectations create weak, powerless victims who popular culture is only too happy to care for and "protect."

Though there is a lot of talk about expectations—all parents I speak to agree that they should place expectations on their children—little thought is given to what precisely expectations are and how they influence children.

Expectations are standards of behavior grounded in your family-value culture that you insist on your children adhering to. Establishing expectations for your children communicates very clearly what you value. Expectations also act as the foundation for children taking responsibility for themselves. Expectations assume that your children have the power to fulfill your expectations.

By holding your children to certain expectations, you are implicitly teaching them the value of responsibility. For example, when you establish an expectation that your children will make their homework a priority over social interests, for example, you communicate that you're giving them the responsibility of acting accordingly. With this responsibility, they can choose to meet the expectations and reap the benefits (e.g., your approval, good grades, increased responsibility and freedom) or fail to fulfill the expectation and accept the consequences (e.g., your disapproval, poor grades, reduced responsibility and freedom).

There are several things you can do to maximize the value of expectations on your children. In establishing expectations for your children, you should be specific in the expectations and give them examples of how the expectations apply to relevant aspects of their lives, for example, how an expectation of responsibility relates to completing their schoolwork or their household chores. You should also talk to them about the value underlying the expectation and explain why you believe it is important. You can also encourage them to give their input into the expectation and consider modifying the expectation based on their feedback. The more involvement and agreement they have, the greater ownership they will feel for the expectation.

Before your children internalize and accept the expectations as their own, they must have a consequence attached to them. The consequence teaches your children about responsibility because it directly connects the expectation with their behavior; your children know the expectation, they meet or violate the expectation, they experience the good or bad consequences. Either way, they are held accountable for their actions and they learn about the value of responsibility (there will be more on consequences later).

The Right Kind of Expectations

Expectations can be indispensable tools for instilling values in your children, but only if you establish the right kind of expectations. The expectations you set should reflect the values you want to teach your children. *Value expectations* encourage children to behave in ways that are consistent with those values. Stop here and take a few moments to think about the phrase *value expectations*. It involves knowing what you value (which I discussed in chapter 2) and holding your children accountable to those values. Do you have value expectations in your family? To determine whether you're setting value expectations, ask yourself the following questions:

- Are the expectations you've set for your children consistent with your values?
- Do these expectations encourage self-esteem, responsibility, and adoption of your family-value culture?
- Do your children have control over whether they meet or go against the expectations?
- Will these expectations help your children to be happy, successful, and contributing people?

You should reality-test the expectations you have for your children against these criteria.

Value expectations are most influential if your children feel a sense of ownership toward them. You want them to feel like the expectations are theirs as well. How you word your expectations can affect their connection to them. For example, if you say, "We expect you to be kind to each other," they may rightly perceive that you (their parents) are dictating how they (your children) should behave and view the expectation as regulations that must be followed or else. However, if you say, "Our family expects you to be kind to each other," you are including them in establishing the expectation and they are, as members of the family, imposing the expectation on themselves. Having a dialogue about your expectations and having your children contribute to establishing the expectations can further encourage ownership and a sense of responsibility for the expectations.

Value expectations should also be within your children's control. As a result, they teach children about the value of responsibility explicitly, "Our family expects you to take responsibility for your actions." They also teach responsibility indirectly by placing the onus of whether your children meet the expectations in their hands. With their expectations in their control, children have complete ownership of both the choice to meet the expectations and enjoy the personal and social benefits of meeting them, and the choice to reject the expectations and face the consequences for failing to do so.

Value expectations can be general standards that reflect your values, for example, "Our family expects you to tell the truth" or "Our family expects you to be considerate of others." Though these types of expectations are a good start for establishing expectations related to your family-value culture, they are often too general, particularly for younger children, to have a direct effect on their behavior. Just as values are often seen as not being connected with your children's daily lives, value expectations can suffer the same fate. Children don't necessarily see how their everyday behavior is related to values. When, for example, your children don't share their toys with their friends, they don't see that their behavior violates an important value, namely, generosity.

After establishing the general value expectations for your children, you next want to create a set of value expectations that connect directly to their behavior, for example, "Our family expects you to work hard in school" or "Our family expects you to be attentive to your coaches." But even this isn't enough because what you see as value expectations may be seen by your children as meaningless clichés that your children learn very quickly to give the obligatory "Yes, Mom" while rolling their eyes when you're not looking. To give these specific value expectations meaning, you need to talk to your children about what they represent and explicitly connect them with the values that underlie them. Because young children have less ability to think abstractly and connect ideas with their daily lives, you should be very specific in your expectations, for example, "Our family expects you to look your teachers in the eye when they speak to you. That shows them respect and lets them know that you're paying attention." As your children get older and are able to make these connections, you can state an expectation more broadly and they will be able to apply it to their lives, for example, "Our family expects you to make good decisions when you are out with your friends," and they will know that you are talking about drinking, drug use, etc. This understanding will help your children to see the value expectations as more than the predictable admonitions that all children hear from their parents and to consider them as important and meaningful guides in their lives.

Consequences

Early in your children's lives, they won't understand the inherent value in meeting value expectations. Rather, they will or won't follow them based on the consequences that you attach to the expectations. If the benefits outweigh the costs, your children will meet the value expectations you place on them. As they mature and come to understand the meaning of the value expectations, they will internalize and follow them because they accept the values as their own. The mistakes that many parents make are:

- not establishing reasonable consequences for the expectations they place on their children; or
- not following through consistently on the consequences they do put into place.

The consequences that you should have for the value expectations can be emotional (e.g., "If you lie, we will be very disappointed in you") or explicit (e.g., "If you're mean to your sister, you'll have to do a time-out"). These consequences provide your children with the initial impetus to meet your expectations. Though I can't give you specific consequences that you should have for your children—consequences can be idiosyncratic to your family and each of your children—they should be aversive enough for them to want to adhere to your expectations, but not so severe as to cause them to become angry and resistant. Here is a hint: consequences that induce boredom or take away something that is desired are usually effective, but knowing your children and creatively putting yourself in their shoes are the best ways to come up with effective consequences. You should also allow your children to earn back with good behavior what was taken from them. This opportunity further instills the value of responsibility because, just as they chose to violate the expectation, they also have the power to meet the expectation—and reap its benefits—in the future.

Though small rewards, such as a hug or a compliment, for meeting the value expectations can encourage your children to fulfill the value expectations, it is best to keep them to a minimum. The best consequence for your children meeting the value expectations is the positive emotions that come from doing the right thing. You can help your children make this connection by pointing out the good feelings and connecting them with the good deed (you will have read more about rewards and consequences in chapter 4).

Inconsistent or nonexistent consequences are the other obstacles to your children living up to and learning the values that underlie value expectations. Failing to administer consequences that you established related to expectations will interfere with your children fulfilling your value expectations and learning the values that comprise your family-value culture. Due to time pressure, stress, fatigue, or expediency—in other words, life!—the best-laid plans of parents to enforce consequences on value expectations can slip through the cracks. But without these consequences, your children have little incentive for following the value expectations you have established for them. Without that early impetus from the consequences, your children will simply not learn the underlying lessons of your value expectations.

Inconsistent consequences send conflicting messages about value expectations to your children. One message is that the value expectations are not that important. If they were, you would enforce the consequences consistently. Another message is that, even if they are important, your children don't need to adhere to them because they won't get into trouble if they don't. The value of ever-present and regular consequences is that your children know what to expect from you so they can decide whether or not to fulfill the value expectations you've created for them.

There is no magic to following through with consequences. You must make a commitment to the consequences before you establish any expectations (expectations without consequences have no "teeth"). When a situation arises where consequences are required, you must remind yourself of how important they are to your children and, despite fatigue, stress, and other excuses, you must act on them because the consequences are in their best interests. You can also share responsibility for the consequences with your spouse (if you have a two-parent household). If you are too tired or busy to impose the consequences on your children, ask your spouse to step in and do what is needed.

A caveat here: if, for whatever reason, you do not follow through on rare occasion, don't beat yourself up about it. You will not be depriving your children of values or stunting their moral development, if it occurs infrequently. You're human and there will be days when you just don't have the time or energy to follow through. What is important is that, over time, your consistency sends the message to your children that expectations are important and that they can expect to have consequences.

Decision Making

One of the most practical ways to help instill the value of responsibility in your children is to teach them how to make good decisions and then to allow them to make their own decisions. Decision making is crucial to your children taking responsibility for their lives. If their decisions are made for your children as they grow older, they can never be held responsible for their actions because they didn't choose their actions. When your children are allowed to make their own decisions, they must accept responsibility for the consequences of their decisions because their decisions are theirs alone.

Your children may not always like this aspect of decision making because they must maintain responsibility for their poor decisions and accept the unpleasant consequences. But giving them this authority over their lives has several essential benefits. When your children make a good decision that results in a positive outcome, they can gain the greatest amount of satisfaction and fulfillment because they chose it. When your children make bad decisions that result in negative outcomes, there is still benefit. Though the results of poor decisions are often unpleasant, because your children made the choices, they have the power to learn from the experience and make better decisions in the future. Lastly, your children learn life's lessons—both pleasant and painful—because they have complete ownership of how those lessons came about.

American popular culture has very different ideas about decision making. It wants to take your children's decisions out of their hands—and yours. Popular culture wants to make your children's decisions for them, in what they think, how they feel, and how they act. More specifically, popular culture wants to decide for your children what they wear, what they eat and drink, what television and movies they watch, what video games they play, what music they listen to, and what magazines they read. In other words, popular culture wants to dictate your children's lives.

Popular culture can short-circuit your children's decision-making capabilities by tapping into their most basic needs. It influences your children's decisions by pushing their hot buttons related to peer acceptance, physical attractiveness, and stimulation. Peer pressure, whether directly from those around them or indirectly from other children or idols they see on television or in movies, exerts even more force on your children's decision making. When these hot buttons are pushed, children with poorly developed or less resolute decision-making skills are ready prey to the influence of popular culture.

Making Bad Decisions

Whenever I speak to a group of young people, I ask how many of them have ever done anything stupid in their lives. With complete unanimity and considerable enthusiasm, they all raise their hands. When I then ask how many of them will ever do anything stupid in the future, the response is equally fervent. I also ask children why they do stupid things. Their responses include:

- I didn't stop to think.
- It seemed like fun at the time.
- I was bored.
- Peer pressure.
- I didn't consider the consequences.
- To get back at my parents.

Yet when I ask them if it was usually worth doing that stupid thing, most say, "Not really."

Because children lack experience and perspective, they tend to make decisions that are rash, egocentric, short-sighted, and focused on immediate gratification. They rely on the "if it feels good now, it must be the right decision" approach to decision making. Their decisions often lack adequate deliberation. This absence of forethought can cause children to overlook the consequences of their decisions for themselves and others and to ignore the long-term ramifications of the decisions.

The fact is it's part of your children's "job" to do stupid things. Bad decision making is an essential part of their road to maturity. Making poor decisions and experiencing the consequences of their decisions helps your children learn about the decision-making process and how to make better decisions in the future. A problem arises, however, if their poor decision making continues. Because decision making is a skill, children can become very good at making bad decisions. This usually occurs when parents don't hold them responsible for their poor decisions, instead, bailing them out of the trouble their children get into. These children learn that they aren't responsible for their decisions and can continue to make bad choices and do stupid things without fear of consequences.

These children usually grow up to be irresponsible people who cannot be trusted. The long-term personal, social, and professional implications of children growing up to be poor decision makers are profound, negative, and, I think, obvious. Yet American popular culture has a vested interest in keeping your children from adulthood. Continued selfishness, impatience, impulsivity, and poor decision making means more money in the bank for popular culture's purveyors of useless and unhealthy products.

Raising Good Decision Makers

Encouraging your children to make their own decisions isn't as simple as saying, "You make the decision. You're on your own." Instead, ceding decision making to your children is an incremental process based on their age, maturity, and, most important, their history of good decision making in the recent past. It would be downright dangerous to give children complete latitude in their decision making. But you can begin to teach decision-making skills in small doses even with very young children. For example, you wouldn't want to take your children into a convenience store and tell them they can have anything they want. They would be overwhelmed with the choices and paralyzed with indecision, or they would want everything in the store. What you would do is give them a choice among jawbreakers, licorice, and bubble gum (or, better yet, sesame sticks, fruit wraps, and yogurt peanuts) and they would then decide which treat they want.

As your children get older, you can expand the number of choices you give them. You can also increase the importance of the decisions they can make, for example, what activities they choose to participate in or when they decide to go to bed. With each decision, you want them to recognize whether the consequences of their choices were good or bad and that they're responsible for whether good or bad things happened. By making this connection, they can see that they have ownership of their decisions. Also, you should retain veto power when needed, but it should be used judiciously because it takes responsibility away from your children.

Learning to Make Good Decisions

A part of helping your children gain experience with making decisions involves educating them about the decision-making process. Good decision making is a complex process that takes years of experience to master (no one ever really perfects it; even adults do stupid things occasionally).

Children are notorious for making snap judgments and acting on them without thinking; they jump into the pool without checking the temperature. Though that decision making might work for swimming, it is not the best approach to most decisions in life (like crossing a street). The first step for your children to make good decisions is simply to teach them to stop before they leap. With a few seconds of hesitation rather than impulsively jumping in feet first, your children can prevent a lot of bad decisions from being made. Of course, getting children to stop before jumping would require them to think, which is usually not part of their repertoire when they are young You can help your children by "catching them in the act," meaning when you see them about to jump without thinking, stop them and guide them through the decision-making process. Also, because you can't always be looking over their shoulder, you can use times when they do leap without thinking (and things don't turn out that well) to ask them how they could have made a different choice in hindsight. These opportunities will sensitize your children to those moments when they can stop before they act and to the benefits of making thoughtful decisions.

The next step is for your children to think before they act. There are several important questions they should ask themselves. Your children should ask, "Why do I want to do this?" You want your children to understand what motivates their decisions. A related question they should ask is, "Is this a good reason for making this decision?" The children I speak to usually know why they make decisions, at least after the deed is done, and they almost always know what the right decision is. One obstacle to good decision making is that children are often faced with conflicting motivations that influence their decisions. They may know that doing something is stupid, but they may feel peer pressure to do it anyway. Except for the most mature and value-driven children, if decisions come down to doing what is right or what is popular, the majority of children will almost always choose the latter.

The next question they should ask is: "What are my options?" Children often have several possible choices when put in any given situation. For example, when faced with the possibility of stealing candy from a store with friends, children could a) take the candy, b) not take the candy but ignore the fact that their friends are stealing, or c) try to convince their friends that stealing is wrong. Knowing their options can help your children see clearly what their decisions might be and also will make it easier for them to connect their decisions with their values. The option that is consistent with their values is the usually best decision.

Then your children need to ask, "What are the consequences of my actions?" (or in their language, "How much trouble would I get in?"). They need to judge the risks and rewards of their decisions in the short run and the long term. The challenge here is that children often underestimate the costs and overestimate the benefits of their decisions. How your children answer this question will also depend on the expectations you establish for your children, the severity of the consequences that accompany the expectations, and how good you are in enforcing the consequences. In other words, if you instill the wrath of God in your children when it comes to consequences, they're going to weigh the consequences very heavily in the decisions they make. The best way for your children to get the message about consequences is to be clear, firm, and consistent in applying them, without being overbearing or cruel.

Another question related to consequences that children can have a difficult time even considering is, "How would my decision affect others?" A complicating factor is that many decisions children make have at least short-term benefits for them (i.e., they get what they want) but may hurt others in some way. Because of their natural egocentricity when they're young, children may not even think about who else they might be affecting. A family-value culture that emphasizes concern for others can guide children in this moral conundrum and not only help them to consider others, but also to make decisions that are most beneficial to both themselves and other people.

Finally, perhaps the most important question children need to ask themselves is: "Is this decision in my best interests?" Understanding what is in their best interests in both the short and long term, having these concerns outweigh competing interests from American popular culture and peer pressure, and making a decision based on their best interests is the culmination of the decision making process. Answering this question follows from answering the previous questions correctly; if responded to in the affirmative, then your children will likely make the right decision.

Coaching Good Decision Making

You can help your children learn good decision making by coaching them through decisions. This guidance allows them to see how a decision is thought through and arrived at. During these discussions, you can help your children to identify key contributors to the decision and take thoughtful steps to the decision. After the decision, you can help them judge how good the decision was and, if the decision turned out to be a poor one, why it was a bad decision and what they can learn from it in the future. You can also present your children with hypothetical situations, such as a moral dilemma, that they are likely to face and engage them in a conversation about how they would make a decision. Of course, children won't always make such deliberate decisions, particularly when they're young, but if you can coach them and give them experience with good decision making, they'll use it more as they gain maturity.

A useful tool to help encourage your children to make good decisions is to post the questions I raised above in a noticeable place in your home, such as on your refrigerator. You can also print them on a card that they see regularly (don't expect them to pull out and review the card before they make a decision, but having it around will at least keep the questions in the front of their minds).

Part of your children learning to make good decisions is allowing them to make poor ones. If handled properly, bad decisions can play an essential role in your children becoming good decision makers. Yes, they should be held accountable for their decisions—that is the essence of responsibility—by providing them with consequences that are commensurate with their offenses. But children must also be required to explore their decisions, understand why they made a poor decision, and ensure that they "get it" so that they don't make the same bad decision again.

Teach Children to "Suck it Up"

One of the most important lessons you can teach your children is that sometimes they just have to *suck it up*! Part of being a responsible adult is accepting the fact that there are a lot of things in life that we don't care to do, but we do it anyway because we have to. How often do you do things for your children that you would really rather not do? I'll bet you just love taking your children to their music lesson at the end of a long and tiring day or to a soccer tournament two hundred miles from home on a weekend. Of course you don't, but you suck it up and do it because that's part of the job of being a parent. Your children need to learn that they too have a job to do and life often involves doing things that they don't want to do.

Unfortunately, American popular culture conveys a very different message to children about this aspect of responsibility. Through the focus on celebrity lifestyles, advertising that suggests that life should always be a party, and the reverence shown toward slackers, popular culture communicates to your children that if it's not fun, easy, or interesting, they just shouldn't have to do it. If children get tired, bored, or uncomfortable, they shouldn't even try. Popular culture also encourages children to resist their parents. The messages of rebellion in popular music, the defiance shown by professional athletes, and the disdain spoiled movie stars express toward what most people would see as normal responsibilities tells children that being responsible by listening to their parents and doing their "job" is just not cool. But I tell kids that there are going to be a lot of things that they're going to have to do before they move out of their parents' house that they really don't want to do. Children must learn that they have a job to do and, because they have to do it, why not just suck it up and do the best they can?

For example, I constantly hear children complaining that they "hate math" (or some other subject; no offense to the math teachers, but it is the subject that students most often mention). The following conversation is a common one I have with students when I speak to them individually and as a group. Though it may not convince them right away, they can never refute its logic, and they always acknowledge that it makes sense:

JT: Can you get out of math?
Students: No, we have to take it. [said with a grimace and an eye roll]
JT: But because you don't like it, you don't give much effort.

Students: Sure, why should we?

JT: What kind of grade would you get?

Students: Probably an F.

JT: How would that make you feel?

Students: Pretty bad.

JT: And how would your parents feel about an F?

Students: They would definitely not like it!

JT: Would an F help or hurt your chances of getting into a good college?

Students: It would definitely hurt them.

JT: What would happen if you just decided to suck it up, hate every minute of it, but do the best you can in the class anyway? What kind of grade would you get?

Students: An A or B.

JT: How would that make you feel?

Students: Really good.

JT: How would your parents feel about that?

Students: Duh—they would love it and they'd get off our backs.

JT: I'll bet you'd like that. Would that good grade help you achieve some other goal like getting into a good college?

Students: Yeah.

JT: What life lessons do you think you might learn from this experience?

Students: Well, like sometimes you just have to suck it up!

JT: Any other life lessons?

Students: Hard work, persistence, patience, perseverance, discipline.

JT: Another thing I've found is that many children have a surprising thing happen to them while they're sucking it up in that class that they hate. They actually come to enjoy it. Has that ever happened to you?

Students: Yeah. [with a glint of self-realization]

JT: So do you think that just sucking it up is a pretty good thing to do overall?

Students: Yeah. [said begrudgingly, knowing I'm right]

JT: Next time you're faced with a situation you don't like, but you can't get out of it, think back to our conversation and perhaps choose to suck it up.

Getting your children to suck it up is easier said than done. You start with a dialogue. Introduce the idea to them so they understand it. I should point out that some parents don't like to use the word suck with their children because it has other, less positive connotations (e.g., "That sucks"). If you feel uncomfortable with its use, substitute "tough it out." I will say that most children know the difference in their meanings and "suck it up" seems to resonate with them more. The choice is yours.

Your children can easily generate examples of having to do things they would rather not (e.g., school, household chores, music lessons). Have the same conversation with your children that I had above. Then, when "suck it up" situations arise in the future, remind them of the conversation and ask them what they should do. Your children won't immediately buy into the concept, but over time, as they see its bene-fits, they will likely start to suck it up on their own.

In teaching your children to suck it up, you give them a gift that better prepares them for the adult world. This lesson teaches your children that responsibility is a powerful and rewarding value. They will also learn to be skeptical of messages from American popular cul-ture telling them that life should always be easy and that "stepping up to the plate" is for losers. Your children learn that many aspects of life are difficult and uncomfortable, and when they choose to be respon-sible, suck it up, and do the best they can, good things will happen for them.

Emerging Values

Developing the value of responsibility in your children encourages the emergence of other essential values. Foremost among them is the value of *integrity*. Children who value responsibility understand that the "buck stops here." They know that their actions are theirs to choose and that they will be held accountable for them. Without an "out" for their behavior, responsible children understand the importance of integrity because they know that they will be judged by their actions. Integrity helps them to adhere to deeply felt values and convictions, and ensures that they act in ways for which they want to be held responsible. Integrity persuades children to make good decisions that take into account their own best interests and those of others, and the consequences of their actions. Integrity and responsibility ensure that children lead lives that reflect their commitment to their values.

Responsibility also encourages the value of *honor*. Honor signifies that children are worthy of esteem and respect because they are trustworthy, reliable, and can be counted on to act in valued ways. Honor encompasses many other fine values, including dignity, courage, virtue, conscience, and nobility. Honor ensures that children lead value-driven lives and follow their principles, even when faced with the temptation to do otherwise. Honorable children can be trusted to do the right thing, treating themselves with appropriate respect and treating others with consideration and compassion.

CHAPTER 7

Success
(Finding the Real Pot of Gold)

American Popular Culture on the Offensive

Nowhere has American popular culture's notions of success become more distorted than in the stories of corporate corruption and greed that have been making the headlines with alarming frequency in recent years. John Rigas of Adelphia Communications and Jack Welch of General Electric are just two of the most egregious examples of how, in the pursuit of wealth, power, and fame, people not only show a wanton disregard for the values of integrity and accountability, but also do irreparable harm to individuals and families who worked hard to make these companies—and these men—successful.

John Rigas, the founder and CEO of Adelphia was revered in the cable industry (Decker Anstrom, CEO of the Weather Channel, said in an article for *Fortune.com,* "If there's one person I'd like my son to grow up to be, it would be John Rigas.") and in his hometown of Coudersport, Pennsylvania ("The John Rigas they describe believed in small-town values: strong families, hard work, church on Sunday."). That is, until the discovery of alleged widespread corruption by his family, which included falsifying financial records and unapproved loans from Adelphia to buy company stock and finance of other Rigas businesses. Jack Welch, one of the best-known and most respected corporate executives in America, shocked the business world with his extravagant retirement compensation package, which included a $9 million a year pension, a $15 million Manhattan apartment, use of corporate jets, helicopters, cellular phones, satellite televisions, computers, and security service at each of his six homes, and a Mercedes and limousine service, which continues until his death. It should be noted that both of these men (and others, such as Ken Lay of now-bankrupt Enron and Richard Grasso, former chairman of the New York Stock Exchange) were already exceedingly wealthy before any of these events transpired.

It's the American Dream—success! America: Land of opportunity. The rags to riches story. The kid in the mailroom who works his way up to the boardroom. The ability of anyone willing to work to achieve success is the foundation on which our country is built. The men I describe above are, in many ways, exemplars of the American Dream; hardworking, self-made, hugely successful. Yet they also epitomize the American Dream gone bad, where more than enough is not enough, where perspective is lost and greed and excess rule. In 1887, Lord Acton observed, "Power tends to corrupt, and absolute power corrupts absolutely." His words are just as relevant today. Interestingly, few people are familiar with the conclusion to his thought, "Great men are almost always bad men."

Certainly, success is one of the most desirable and sought-after objectives in America today. Success is a powerful statement about who people are, what they value, and their commitment and hard work. It can foster a life full of meaning, satisfaction, and joy. Sadly, the pursuit of success can also lead to a life of frustration, disappointment, and unfulfilled dreams. Whether your children realize the success you envision for them or crumble under the weight of pursuing an unattainable image of success depends on the values you attach to success and the dream of success you create from your values.

During the last few decades, the drive to compete, to achieve success, and to win has been co-opted and corrupted by American popular culture. It's almost as if success has taken steroids (an appropriate metaphor here). Success has become bigger, more aggressive, more uncaring, and more desperate. This shift has become, arguably, the dominant force in American society that drives parents, children, business, and government. Unfortunately, this change has caused a myriad of societal problems, including cheating in school, white-collar crime, and political special-interest groups, all aimed at achieving success as defined by popular culture, often at the cost of healthy values.

Because of this unhealthy influence from American popular culture, many parents have lost sight of the essential meaning of success and shifted the emphasis they place on their children's achievement. So, perhaps more than ever before, they push their children to get straight A's, become star athletes, and to excel in the performing arts, chess, and other achievement activities. And children are succumbing to this assault from both popular culture and parents. A recent survey indicated that over 40 percent of teenagers equated the American Dream with wealth and material goods, and 75 percent believed that their job satisfaction would be based on their income. Why there has been this change in values is unclear. It may be due to the increased instability in the American economy and the genuine concern of parents to ensure that their children get good educations and well-paying jobs. But I would also suggest that this greater emphasis on these distorted achievement values has been driven by an American popular culture that exhorts and profits from the supposed virtues of accumulated wealth, status, and conspicuous consumption to the detriment of much more fundamental values.

The Value of Success

Children rarely choose how they define success. They internalize what success means to them from the most influential sources in their lives. In twenty-first-century America, these influences are American popular culture and parents. Unfortunately, popular culture offers children a definition of success that is both limited and limiting, offering few children any real chance of achieving success. And for those rare few who find that elusive pot of gold, they quickly learn that it is not filled with the meaning, fulfillment, and happiness that they expected. Popular culture has forsaken healthy values in a selfish and relentless pursuit of one kind of success that meets its own needs—to make more money. But that makes the achievement of success—defined by popular culture as wealth, fame, and power—for most children an impossible dream. One of America's strengths is that it is the land of endless opportunity; in theory, anyone who works hard can become successful. In reality, the American Dream offered by popular culture is, for most children, just a fantasy that can never be realized. Few children have the capabilities or resources to achieve the dream of success sold to them by popular culture.

American popular culture bombards children unrelentingly with messages about how they should define success: wealth, fame, power, popularity, materialism, and physical attractiveness. It shows children's idols and heroes living lives of material splendor and many children develop a hunger for such grandiosity. For example, *The Crib*, a television show on ESPN, highlights the extravagant lifestyles of professional athletes—mansions, fancy cars, expensive clothing, massive home-entertainment centers. Advertisers tell children that if they don't wear the right clothes, eat the right food, drink the right soda, or have the right cellular phone, they will be losers.

To attract children into seeking this pot of gold at the end of the rainbow, popular culture seduces them with evocative images of fun, excitement, respect, sexuality, beauty, riches, and conspicuous consumption—drink Pepsi and life will be a party with music, dancing, and beautiful people. A powerful example of these messages is found in the supermarket checkout line. All of the magazines, including *People*, *Us*, *TV Guide*, *Soap Opera Digest*, *Glamour*, in addition to a dozen other beauty, fashion, health, celebrity, and tabloid publications, aggrandize the very images of success pushed on children by American popular culture. Men have to be muscular, well dressed, drive an expensive car, and have money. Women have to be beautiful, thin, sexy, and rich (or use their beauty and sexuality to get rich). Children are brainwashed by movies, television, music, magazines, the Internet, fashion, advertising, and other consumer industries that a pot of gold lies at the end of the rainbow and can be had by anyone. Children don't realize that rainbows are optical illusions and that pots of gold are myths.

Or, more accurately, *American popular culture gets the pot of gold while children chase the rainbow.* For example, in 2004, Disney introduced the Cinderella's Princess Court at its flagship store in New York City, where young girls (and their mothers) can dress up and act like princesses (for only $80 plus the cost of tiaras, bracelets, and necklaces). Says an obviously excited stepmother of one six-year-old, "I already have a crown at home and a dress. I'm going to be Cinderella."

It's bad enough that children are lied to by American popular culture—you wouldn't expect anything less. But there's no excuse for parents who are seduced by the same messages, foist the same pot of gold on their children, and become unwitting accomplices of popular culture. They buy into the images of success and, rather than protecting their children from these influences, reinforce these definitions of success in their children. And children believe their parents and popular culture. Why shouldn't they? If children can't trust their parents, who can they trust? As for popular culture, how can so many rich, famous, and powerful people be wrong?

Success at Any Cost

A particularly troubling aspect of American popular culture's perspective on success is the notion that success must be achieved at any cost. This desperate need for success has created a culture of greed in which children learn that they *must* achieve success, and that they can use any and all means to attain that success. This culture of avarice has fostered a set of values that not only tolerates, but encourages, this "win at all costs" mentality, including dishonesty, cheating, manipulation, and backstabbing.

Examples of this distorted view of success abound in American popular culture. Reality TV relishes deception (e.g., *Survivor*). Corporate malfeasance and profiteering is revealing itself to be the rule rather than the exception in big business (e.g., the collapse of Enron). Sports has seen the proliferation of illegal performance-enhancing drugs, with drug violations, suspensions, and fines a regular occurrence at the highest level of sport (e.g., the professional cyclists, Jan Ullrich, Richard Virenque, and the late Mario Pantani; track star Kelli White, and the late baseball player Ken Caminiti, just to name a few on a very long list). It's worth noting that while the punishment for use of performance-enhancing drugs among Olympic athletes is severe (e.g., loss of medals, multiyear suspensions, and banishment), those meted out in American professional team sports—which are followed and watched most by your children—are comparative slaps on the wrist (mostly involving small fines and game suspensions). What messages do you think your children are getting from their sports heroes?

This win-at-all-costs attitude is painfully evident among high-school students. Two recent surveys found that 75 percent of students had cheated on a test in the previous twelve months, as compared to only 25 percent in 1963 and 50 percent in 1993. Particularly unsettling is the finding that about 50 percent of high-school students see nothing wrong with cheating. The reasons why students cheat include fear of failure, heavy workloads, insufficient time to study, and external pressures from parents and teachers. The rationales that students use to justify their cheating are disturbing:

- "I actually think cheating is good. A person who has an entirely honest life can't succeed these days."
- "We students know that the fact is we are almost completely judged on our grades. They are so important that we will sacrifice our own integrity to make a good impression."
- "I believe cheating is not wrong. People expect us to attend seven classes a day, keep a 4.0 GPA, not go crazy and turn in all of our work the next day. What are we supposed to do, fail?"

When cheating becomes the norm and children are able to rationalize it so easily, I can safely say that America is experiencing a crisis of values.

The win-at-all-costs mentality can also be life threatening. The use of illegal performance-enhancing drugs is present at all levels of sport, and is increasing among young athletes. Recent research indicates that between 4 and 12 percent of high-school male athletes—500,000 to 1 million by some estimates—said they had taken steroids. This has to be a shocking number for anyone involved with children. Why do they do this? Many young athletes feel compelled to take these drastic steps to improve their performances, relieve the pressure to win, make varsity teams, receive college scholarships, and in pursuit of pipe dreams of a career in professional sports. These athletes are heavily influenced by professional athletes who act as their role models. They see that the benefits of steroid use are significant—the research is undeniable—and the consequences of being caught are minimal. The invincibility that many teenagers feel precludes them from considering the health risks of steroid use, including infertility, high blood pressure, liver damage, and prostate cancer. Young athletes also ignore the psychological and emotional dangers of steroid use, for example, hyper-aggressiveness— what is called 'roid rage—irritability, and, upon their discontinuation, depression, lethargy, and feelings of hopelessness. At least two suicides have been attributed to steroid withdrawals in recent years, as well as an undetermined number of suicide attempts.

This win-at-all-costs attitude isn't the exclusive domain of boys. Girls express this must-win mentality in sports and dance with an increasing incidence of eating disorders aimed at maintaining or reducing body weight and physical appearance. These pressures, seen notably in swimming, gymnastics, and ballet, arise from the physical demands and the physical aesthetic of the activities. This mentality is communicated not only through typical channels of American popular culture, but by parents and coaches who have also been seduced by these distorted messages of success.

The win-at-all-costs attitude is pushed on children by a popular culture that also values an immediate-gratification, win-right-now mindset. Children not only feel extreme pressure to succeed, but also to succeed in the fastest way possible. This value encourages the easiest path to success and discourages time-honored values, such as hard work, patience, and perseverance. It also drives children to find shortcuts to success, regardless of how illegal or unethical they are. I believe that the microwave, a modern convenience if ever there was one, is the classic metaphor for our times. We want it, we want it now, and we want it without any effort. Though microwaves may work well for heating up leftovers, American popular culture convinces children that that is also the way life works.

American popular culture tells your children that success can be had quickly and easily. The emergence of reality TV has taken largely undistinguished people with no particular talents and transformed them into international stars, often by acting in selfish and mean-spirited ways.

Some of these reality TV stars, such as Richard Hatch, the winner of the first *Survivor* series, earn comfortable livings, appearing on other reality TV shows, giving talks (for up to $15,000 per appearance), and hosting other television shows.

Anyone who has ever achieved any degree of success knows that one of the most basic lessons they learned was that nothing in life worth having comes easily or quickly. Success is borne on the shoulders of commitment, discipline, and persistence. Yet American popular culture conveys a very different message to children: success doesn't have to be difficult or time consuming. Popular culture is rife with offers to get rich quick, stories about overnight successes, pills to lose weight fast, and "breakthrough" products to look ten years younger. Children see the 15-year-old soccer phenomenon, Freddie Abu, young actors, such as Hilary Duff and Haley Joel Osment, and musical prodigies like the violinist, Sarah Chang, but don't see the many years of determination, practice, and sacrifice that got them to the top of their professions. Children don't realize that overnight successes are usually ten years in the making. They also don't realize that that these exceptional young performers are the rarest of exceptions rather than the rule.

You must teach your children that life doesn't work the way popular culture says it does. There are no quick fixes or instant successes. Life isn't always easy, fun, or comfortable. If it gets difficult, your children can't get someone to make it easier. If it seems too good to be true, it probably is. You can also teach your children that they wouldn't want life to be that way anyway because it's overcoming the obstacles and adversity that give life meaning, satisfaction, and joy. Children who appreciate the value of earning their successes through commitment and hard work also develop essential life skills that further foster success, including motivation, determination, focus, and perseverance.

There may be no more powerful indication of the corruption of values in America than this arrogant and unprincipled attitude toward success. Such behavior can't be explained or justified within any value-driven framework. So the culture, and the individuals who have been seduced by it, can only act in such valueless ways by thoroughly jettisoning what most people consider to be healthy values, and by embracing a value set that serves the unquenchingly avaristic needs of American popular culture.

You need to monitor the influence of this attitude in your children. American popular culture is constantly sending messages to your children that it's okay to lie, cheat, steal, be irresponsible, and act selfishly. How can your children not come to the conclusion that such behaviors, and their underlying values, are not perfectly acceptable? When you see it on television or read about in the newspaper, you know it's wrong, but your children don't necessarily. Use examples as they present themselves as object lessons to talk to your children about why such behavior is not only bad, but truly reprehensible. When athletes are suspended for illegal drug violations, talk to your children about how cheating has not only ruined the athletes' lives, but also hurt their families, their teammates, and the fans who supported them. Connect the offending behavior with the underlying values that it represents and discuss why they are unhealthy for your children, your family, and society as a whole. Explain how illegal drug use is dishonest and unfair. Also, point out how the athletes who cheat can never feel full ownership of their successes because they are due to the athletes' drug use rather than their hard work and sustained efforts. Talk to your children about the values within your family-value culture that contrast with the negative values. Share with your children your ideas about honesty and fair play. Finally, suggest other behaviors to use in those or similar situations that are consistent with your values. If your children want to do better in sports or school, instead of cheating, they can put in more time practicing or studying and get help from teachers or coaches.

Defining Success

For the sake of your children's futures, challenge this distorted and destructive view of success and provide your children with a definition that is both value-driven and life-affirming. This starts with maintaining your perspective and seeing the definitions of success foisted on your children by American popular culture for what they are; self-serving, narrow, unreachable deceptions that can only hurt your children. You must take sides with your children and show them that the definitions of success offered by American popular culture are not ones that are consistent with your values nor are they going to make your children truly successful, happy, and contributing people. Explain to them why the definitions are grounded in unhealthy values: superficiality, materialism, social acceptance. Use examples from popular culture to illustrate your beliefs, for example, actors, musicians, and athletes who have wealth, celebrity, and physical attractiveness, but who are divorced, drug abusers, or in trouble with the law.

The only way to protect your children from these unhealthy definitions is to offer them an understanding of success that is value driven and meaningful, and that they have a good chance of achieving. I define success as achieving goals and living a life that expresses and affirms your values. Success can be further defined by the ownership, commitment, effort, and quality that your children put into their lives, and the meaning, satisfaction, and joy they get out of it. Success can also be defined in terms of how much children contribute to their families, communities, and the world at large.

Success in these broad terms fosters qualities that increase children's chances of achieving success, including motivation, confidence, courage, patience, and perseverance. These broad definitions of success open up a universe of possible ways in which your children can become successful. These definitions also place success within their control and instill ownership, and, when your children do succeed, they experience all of the personal benefits.

Imagine how your children would feel if they were pursuing success that springs from their most basic values. Imagine your children having complete ownership of their quest for success. Imagine the fulfillment they will feel. In pursuing this definition of success, your children may achieve extraordinary success in a chosen field. Or your children may not attain such lofty success, yet be no less successful. A success can be a cardiac surgeon, mathematician, concert pianist, or Olympic champion. A success can also be a great teacher, artist, carpenter, or parent. The key is to give your children a definition of success that is grounded in your values and deeply felt, and that can be realized with commitment and hard work.

The Value of Failure

There is no greater stigma in American popular culture than being labeled a loser. The expression *loser* (said in a forceful and drawn-out way) with the thumb and forefinger in the shape of an L placed on the forehead have become oft-used and enduring symbols in popular culture.

To be called a loser is, to paraphrase a well-known sports cliché, worse than death because you have to live with being a loser.

Yet failure is an inevitable—and essential—part of life. Failure teaches children important life lessons that will benefit them in all areas of their lives. Failure is necessary for responsibility, success, and happiness. Failure can foster desire and the motivation to overcome the obstacles that caused the failure. It shows children what they did wrong so they can correct the problem in the future. Failure connects children's actions with consequences, some of which are failure. By making this connection, children gain ownership of their failures—and successes—and learn that they have the power to change their actions and the ensuing consequences. Failure teaches important life skills, such as commitment, patience, determination, decision making, and problem solving. It helps children develop emotional mastery so they can respond positively to the frustration, anger, and disappointment that they will often experience as they pursue their goals. Failure teaches children humility and appreciation for the opportunities that they're given.

Of course, too much failure will discourage children. Success is also needed for its ability to bolster motivation, build confidence, reinforce effort, and increase enjoyment. As children pursue their life goals, they must experience a healthy balance of success and failure to gain the most from their efforts.

Fear of Failure

Despite the obvious importance, benefits, and inevitability of failure, fear of failure among children today is at epidemic proportions. Fear of failure occurs when children come to believe that failure is absolutely unacceptable and that failing is not just the outcome of their recent performances, but rather a statement about their value as people. Fear of failure causes children to experience debilitating anxiety before they take a test, compete in a sport, or perform in a recital. It causes them to give less than their best effort, not take risks, and, ultimately, never achieve complete success.

Where do children get such a destructive perspective on failure? American popular culture, of course. As I mentioned earlier, the enjoyment that people get from watching reality TV shows is not in sharing the excitement with the victors, but in relishing the humiliation and rejection of those who lose. On television and in the movies, the losers—nerds, unattractive people, poor athletes—are teased, bullied, and rejected. While popular culture has made its definition of success virtually unattainable for most children, it has placed them between a rock and hard place by making failure intolerable to contemplate. American popular culture defines failure as being poor, anonymous, powerless, unpopular, or physically unattractive. Being any of these things is thoroughly unacceptable, so children are driven to do anything they can—lying, cheating, stealing—to avoid failure. With this definition of failure, American popular culture has created a culture of fear and avoidance of failure; better any fifteen minutes of fame than none at all. This zeitgeist has communicated to children that failure is a reflection on their value as people and their place in society. Popular culture has conveyed to children that if they fail, they will not be worthy of love, respect, and acceptance. In other words, children who fail will be ostracized by their peers and branded as losers for life!

Though teasing and bullying, which is often directed at children who are seen as failures in the eyes of American popular culture (e.g., unpopular or unattractive), has been a part of our society for many years, children today are learning new ways to let less fortunate children know how worthless they are. Cellular telephones, email, web logs, and Instant Messaging have created a new class of "cyberbullies" that enable children to harass others away from school and from a distance. News reports indicate that this hateful use of technology is a growing problem, particularly among adolescents.

Many parents have fallen under American popular culture's spell of failure as well. They've compounded the harm that failure can inflict on children socially by also connecting their own love and approval with it. The message children get is "I won't love you if you get bad grades." These "outcome" expectations are in direct conflict with the value expectations I spoke of earlier. With these expectations, failure is unacceptable, yet, based on popular culture's definition, never more likely to occur. Children also have less ability than ever to have control over whether they succeed or fail. This double burden of failure causes children to connect their social- and self-esteem with failure. They come to see failure as a threat to their personal and social standing. This fear of failure comes to act as the driving force in their lives and most of their life's efforts are devoted to avoiding failure.

Children learn that they can avoid failure three ways. The first is that they don't engage in an activity in which they fear failure. If children don't participate, they're safe from failure. Injury, illness, damaged equipment, forgotten or lost materials, apparent lack of interest or motivation, or just plain refusal to take part are common ways in which children can avoid failure and maintain their personal and social views of themselves.

Children can also avoid failure by failing in an activity, but having an excuse so that they don't have to take responsibility for the failure. I know that two things about this sound strange. Why would children intentionally—though rarely consciously—fail even though that is what they fear most? How can children ensure failure, yet, at the same time, avoid failure and protect themselves from their fear? When children deliberately fail by, for example, giving up or blaming others, children protect themselves from their fear by having an excuse for their failure—"I would have done well, but I just didn't feel like it" or "I would have done just fine, but the teacher was totally unfair." This strategy, called self-defeating behavior in psychology jargon, actually avoids the threat underlying the failure, namely, the loss of personal and social esteem. Because their failures were not their fault, children can't be held responsible and popular culture and their parents must continue to accept and love them. Children engage in self-defeating behavior because *their fear of failure is greater than their belief that they can succeed.* Given how unattainable American popular culture has made success, self-defeating behavior is one available route children have to avoid truly failing and being labeled a loser.

Many children don't have the luxury of not taking part or coming up with excuses. For example, children can't just not go to school. So another way that children can avoid failure is to get as far away from failure as possible by becoming successful. Some children who fear failure are motivated to distance themselves from failure, thereby removing the threat. As long as children are successful, they avoid failure and can maintain their social- and self-esteem. This strategy seems like a good one because these children avoid failure and achieve some degree of success. But children who engage in self-defeating behavior are stuck in limbo between failure and success. Avoiding failure protects children's social- and self-esteem, but their inability to give their fullest effort and achieve real success leaves them frustrated and unfulfilled. I call this the "safety zone," in which the threat of failure is removed because they are far from it and they cannot be faulted because they achieve some success. At the same time, these children are not motivated to pursue greater success because intensifying their efforts, though increasing the chances of more success, also increases the chances of failure.

Defining Failure

To protect your children from these destructive definitions of failure, you must take the same approach as you do in redefining success. Show your children why American popular culture's definition of failure is not healthy; it's narrow, limiting, superficial, and valueless. Give them a positive definition of failure that connects its meaning with values that are important to you. For example, you can tell them about the relationship between failure, perseverance, and ultimate success. Provide them with examples of people in your family's life, as well as individuals in the popular culture, who bought into its definition of failure and found neither ultimate success nor happiness. For example, Mike Tyson, the former heavyweight boxing champion, for a time achieved popular culture's definition of success—wealth and fame—but was also convicted and imprisoned for sexual assault, has had numerous run-ins with the law, has been married and divorced, saw his boxing career flounder, and is now bankrupt. Also, describe well-known examples of others who were not seduced by popular culture's definitions and found both success and happiness. Pat Tillman, the former NFL player, exemplifies the rejection of popular culture's definition of success. In the middle of a successful football career in which he gained both wealth and fame, Pat abruptly retired from football and forsook his multimillion-dollar salary to join the military. Most people thought he was crazy, but he felt a higher calling, following his most fundamental values and his own definition of success. He earned a place in the Army Rangers and was sent to fight in Afghanistan. Sadly, Pat was killed in battle in April of 2004. He gave up success and happiness in the traditional sense to seek both in a way that was consistent with his values. In making this choice, Pat inspired others in positive ways that he could never have done as a football player.

I define failure in several ways that encourage children to value and take ownership of failure, rather than fear it. Failure can be defined as children not living in accordance with their values. When children cheat, lie, treat others poorly, focus too much on results, or don't take responsibility for themselves, then they fail. It can also mean children being successful in other people's eyes, but not in their own eyes. When children buy into popular culture's definition of success, for example, being overly concerned with popularity or appearance, then they fail. Failure involves children not giving their best effort, making poor decisions, and not doing what is in their best interest. When children look for the easy way out, are influenced by peer pressure, and act in ways that can hurt them, then they fail. It also means treating others poorly and not giving back to their families, communities, and the world as a whole. When children are selfish, uncaring, and disrespectful of the world in which they live, then they fail.

Giving your children a definition of failure that takes away the fear liberates them from that fear. It also frees them to strive for success without reservation, to explore, take risks, and vigorously pursue their dreams. Your children will know in their hearts that some failure is okay and in no way a negative reflection on themselves as people. Finally, failure will ultimately enable them to achieve success, however they define it.

Total Failure Is Total Success

Children who buy into the definition of failure offered by American popular culture are most fearful of what I call total failure, which I define as children giving their best effort and doing everything they possibly can to succeed, but still failing (usually their definition of failing is right out of popular culture, for example, not getting a 100 percent on a test or not being #1 on their team). This is a total failure because, having given their all, there is nothing else they can do. Total failure is so threatening because children have no excuse for their failure and they can't do anything to change the outcome. They can't blame things about themselves they can change, such as lack of effort, because they gave their best effort. They can't blame things outside of themselves, such as the test was unfair. Children must admit to themselves and others that they simply didn't have what it takes to meet that definition of success. Herein lies the threat. With this admission, they know that there is nothing they can do to succeed and gain acceptance from popular culture and love from their parents. Children will do anything to avoid being in this uncontrollable and untenable position, and will go to great lengths to experience anything but total failure. To avoid total failure, they do one of the three things I described earlier: not participate, engage in self-defeating behavior, or achieve a moderate, but not fully satisfying, level of success.

I define total success as children giving their best effort and doing everything they possibly can to achieve goals that are consistent with their values. What children—and parents—don't realize is that without being willing to accept the possibility of total failure, children can never experience total success. Let me repeat this idea because it is one of the most important lessons your children need to learn to become value-driven, successful, and happy people: *To achieve total success, your children must be willing to risk total failure.*

You can help your children let go of their fear of failure. Instead of something to fear, total failure should be your children's goal. Now you probably think I'm crazy for suggesting that your children should aim for total failure, but let me explain. Except for those few people who reach the absolute pinnacle in their chosen activity (for example, an Olympic gold medalist, the prima ballerina for the Bolshoi Ballet, or the recipient of the Nobel Prize), everyone, at some point, will fail to achieve their goals if they set the bar high at all. But some people fail without giving everything they have. They will experience regret and have to ask themselves, "I wonder what could have been?" These people haven't achieved total failure and will never be completely satisfied with whatever level they attained. The lucky ones—besides those who are fortunate enough to reach the acme of their field—are those who gave it their all and didn't achieve their goals. Of course, they will feel disappointment that some of their goals went unfulfilled. But they will know that there wasn't anything else they could have done to reach their goals. The lesson for your children is that all they can do is give everything they can. If you hadn't already noticed, total success is total failure because both involve your children giving everything they have to reach their goals.

Teaching your children about total success and total failure begins with introducing them to positive definitions of success and failure I spoke of earlier before they learn less healthy definitions from American popular culture. If you can offer your children definitions that are empowering and within their control, that enable them to feel good about their successes and rebound from their failures, they will be more resistant to those offered by popular culture.

As your children grow and become immersed in the popular "success" culture of school, sports, the performing arts, and other achievement activities, they will nonetheless feel a pull toward unhealthy definitions of success and failure. Continuing to highlight your definitions by establishing and rewarding positive success expectations and goals that focus on effort, patience, perseverance, and other relevant values and skills can help your children maintain a good perspective and stay focused on striving toward total success.

Hopefully, as you keep your children's "eye on the prize," they will learn another valuable lesson. By staying focused on giving their best effort, your children actually have a better chance of achieving total success. Because total failure is no longer to be feared and total success is entirely within their control, your children have what it takes to become successful.

Gifted vs. Hardworking

American popular culture reveres giftedness. It believes giftedness is a guarantee of success in life. Popular culture tells children this inborn talent—whether intellectual, athletic, or artistic—ensures that they will be successful and that life will be easy for them. Parents buy into this message from popular culture and hope beyond hope that their children are gifted. Many parents, in their anxiety, have their children tested at an early age to find out how gifted they are. This overwhelming desire to have gifted children comes from parents believing in the supposed advantages of being gifted. Having gifted children is also complimentary to parents because they passed gifted genes to their children, so they must be gifted as well. These benefits can cause parents to delude themselves into believing that their children are "special" and that their children's giftedness will ensure that they'll be successful.

When I speak to parent groups, it seems that every parent thinks their child is the most intelligent, athletically gifted, and artistically talented child in school. In fact, in a survey of parents of elementary school children, 80 percent thought their children were above average. Unfortunately, this belief is a statistical impossibility, as only 50 percent of children can be above average (the other half are, of course, below average). Yet parents buy into this mentality and raise their children emphasizing their giftedness whether they actually are or not—"You are so smart," "You are the best out there"—with the belief that their giftedness (or their children's belief that they are gifted) will assure them of success in their lives. Just once, I would like someone to tell me that their children are not particularly bright, athletic, or creative, but they are really good kids.

This perspective on giftedness comes from American popular culture, which reveres innate talent and communicates to parents and children that the way to be successful is to be gifted; athletes who are successful are talented, scientists are geniuses, and singers have a gifted ear. The notion of giftedness has even been adopted by the American educational system. Argues Dr. Jeff Howard, President of The Efficacy Institute, an organization dedicated to fostering development in children, "A simple belief has structured American education for most of this century: intelligence is an innate endowment, fixed at birth and unequally distributed, setting the upper limits on a child's prospects for learning." If children are gifted, parents and children are told, they get a free pass to success. Popular culture conveys the message that if children are gifted, they don't have to work hard to succeed—they just will be—and children who have to work hard are obviously not as talented and simply can't go as far. How many times have you heard "Tiger Woods was born to play golf" or "Sarah Chang was destined to be a brilliant violinist"? Well, let me clear something up: No one is born to do anything, certainly not to swing a golf club or play a violin. The only thing that can be reasonably said is that some children are born with certain abilities that can help them excel if they choose to pursue a particular activity. However, giftedness is no guarantee of success; the world is full of gifted failures, of can't-miss kids who missed.

Problems with Giftedness

The result of this delusion is that children have bought into the value of giftedness. Whenever I speak to children, I ask them whether they would rather be gifted or hardworking. With almost complete unanimity, children say they would rather be gifted. When you're gifted, they say, everything is easy. Parents and children don't realize that giftedness can be as much a cross to bear as, well, a gift. In fact, giftedness can be a curse that haunts children throughout their lives and actually hinders their ability to become successful.

Perhaps the worst part about being labeled as gifted, fairly or otherwise, is that natural ability is not something that children can control. Gifted children didn't do anything to deserve or earn their giftedness. They were just lucky in that their parents gave them good genes. In fact, if your children aren't intelligent or talented enough, don't blame them; it's your fault that you didn't give them gifted genes!

Because gifted children succeed at an early age with little practice or preparation—they can't connect their efforts with success ("I got an A, but I didn't even study."). Without ownership, gifted children don't learn the connection between their efforts and their outcomes. They can't say, "I did well because I worked hard." They may also develop the belief that they will always succeed in the future without effort.

Gifted children also have no sense of control over their successes. They didn't do anything to succeed, so they don't know what to do to succeed in the future. When they succeed—and they do early and often—they have to attribute to their success to their ability. Unfortunately, if gifted children attribute their successes to their ability, when they fail—which they inevitably will sooner or later—they must attribute their failures to their lack of ability; they must be unintelligent or lack talent. The problem is children can't change their ability. They can gain more knowledge, but they can't become more intelligent. They can develop new skills, but they can't become more athletically or artistically talented. Without ownership and the belief in their ability to control their achievements, gifted children can only conclude that they are incapable and, as a result, have no reason to try in the future.

To illustrate the problems with being gifted children, let's look at some of the challenges they face as they grow up. Because they're gifted, these children experience early success and little or no failure.

These children get straight A's, compete above their age group in their sport, or take advanced classes in the performing arts. But sooner or later, at some point in their development, they reach a level where everyone is gifted (e.g., when they go to Harvard, the U.S. Olympic Training Center, or Julliard). At this point, giftedness isn't what makes these children special, because they're all gifted. And their giftedness isn't what ultimately determines who becomes truly successful. What separates those children who are simply gifted from those who are gifted *and* successful is whether they possess the skills to maximize their gifts.

Unfortunately, because everything comes so easily to gifted children at a early age, many never learn the skills—hard work, persistence, focus, patience, perseverance, discipline, and emotional control—that will enable them to overcome the inevitable obstacles they will face as they perform at higher levels. At some point, these children will find that their inborn talent is no longer sufficient to be successful. Yet they will get stuck because they won't have developed the tools to take their natural ability to the next level. For children to fully realize their ability, gifted or otherwise, they must develop healthy attitudes about mistakes, failure, and setbacks that will enable them to respond positively to these common difficulties. Children must also learn skills I just mentioned that will allow them to meet these challenges. These attributes, which can only be learned through experiencing both success and failure, are often lacking in gifted children early in their lives.

Redefining Giftedness
You might be getting the impression that I think that giftedness is a bad thing. That's not true—giftedness is neither good nor bad. But its value to children—or the harm it causes—depends the perspective that they develop about it. If children (and parents) buy into American popular culture's view of giftedness, then, yes, I believe that giftedness will be as much of a burden as a boon for them. At the same time, with the right perspective, giftedness can be a wonderful opportunity for children to accomplish great things.

Whether giftedness is a benefit or a hindrance depends on how you define it and the attitude you have about your children's giftedness. Here's what I recommend. If you think your children might be gifted, have them tested by objective and impartial experts—parents are, of course, biased and partial, and, as a result, notoriously poor judges of their children's ability. If your children have been evaluated to be gifted, don't tell them. There's no point. They don't need to be told by you that they have a special talent. They'll figure it out on their own and then they'll be more likely to gain ownership and a healthy perspective on their abilities without your help. Whether they're gifted or not is not within their control, so there is nothing they can do about it one way or the other. And labeling children as gifted places unnecessary pressure on them to live up to their talents, when giftedness is only one ingredient for success. If they find out that they're gifted, sit down and talk to them about what it means. If you want giftedness to be a gift for your children, you should tell them that they're fortunate to have this talent, but it's only a starting point. You can give them ownership of their giftedness by convincing them that what they choose to do with their talent and whether it is ever fully realized is entirely up to them.

At what point you speak to your children about giftedness depends less on their age than on their maturity. You should gauge for yourself when they can understand the concept of giftedness and you can have a meaningful dialogue with them. I do encourage you to begin this discussion with your children before American popular culture starts to impose its view on giftedness on them. The following thoughts with give you a framework on what to say to your children.

I see giftedness as providing children with an early advantage. It places them at the front of the line, but it is no guarantee of success. Where children start in life says little about where they will finish. There is so much time and distance between that start and finish, and giftedness becomes less and less important as children develop. I would suggest that, whether your children know they're gifted or not, that you erase the word gifted from your vocabulary. It serves no purpose and holds no value for your children. Instead of emphasizing your children's giftedness, you should talk to them about the attitudes and skills— those that are within their control—that they will need to fully realize their giftedness and achieve their goals. If they develop those tools, then their giftedness might mean something. Innate ability, as I have just suggested, is only one piece of the success puzzle. Gifted children will only achieve true success if they enjoy the area of their natural talent, choose to pursue their talent, develop the skills necessary to maximize their gifts, and make every effort to fully realize their abilities. If your children aren't gifted, that's fine too, because they may have talents that haven't been discovered yet and, regardless of what abilities they have, they can still do their best and achieve some level of success. For these "less gifted" children, just skip the first part of the discussion about being gifted and talk to them about the attitudes and skills necessary to become successful.

Potential Is a Pipe Dream

Another word that is closely linked to giftedness is potential. I regularly hear parents, teachers, and coaches extolling the talents of gifted children by saying, "She has unlimited potential" or "With his potential, the sky's the limit." But, as a basketball coach once said, "All potential means is that you haven't done a darned thing yet." When children are labeled as having potential, they're being told that they have something that they might not have and are being saddled with an expectation that they may not be able to fulfill.

Saying children have potential is saying that we can predict who will become successful with great certainty. Yet to call predicting success an inexact science is to be exceedingly generous. It's below tarot-card reading in predicting the future! The fact is that we're lousy at predicting who becomes successful in school, sports, the arts, or any other achievement area.

Think of all of the "can't miss" kids who missed, all of the phenoms that became phenomenally unsuccessful, or the prodigies who became prodigious failures. For example, National Football League teams spend millions of dollars each year in an effort to identify which college players will become superstars, yet these efforts often go for naught. Terrell Davis was a sixth-round draft pick by the Denver Broncos—meaning he was not expected to be a very good football player—yet he became the preeminent running back of the late 1990s. In contrast, Ryan Leaf was the number-two pick in the 1998 draft by the San Diego Chargers and was considered "a sure thing," yet he was a flop from the start and is now out of professional football. The 1994 documentary, *Hoop Dreams*, chronicles the lives of Arthur Agee and William Gates, two 14-year-old basketball players with immense "potential" from Chicago. The film follows them for four and a half years as they strive to find success in the high school, collegiate, and professional ranks, and, ultimately, never realize the potential they were purported to have had.

I recommend that you erase the word *potential* from your vocabulary as well. Like giftedness, it offers nothing to your children and only burdens them with an expectation that they might not be able to meet out of no fault of their own. Instead of talking about potential, I use the phrase "fully realize their ability." This means that whatever ability they were born with—and no one knows with certainty how much ability any child has—the goal is to help your children do everything they can to fully realize that ability. If they take full advantage of whatever ability you gave them, can there be any greater form of success?

It's about Hard Work

Contrary to what American popular culture says, giftedness is actually overrated as a contributor to success. Dr. Anders Ericcson, a professor at Florida State University, has studied expert performance for years. He has examined experts in sports, music, and mathematics, as well as in activities as mundane as typing. He found that so-called innate ability was unnecessary to predict who would become most successful. The two greatest predictors of who would be become successful were how early a child started and how many hours they devoted to the activity. In a nutshell, the more they practiced, the better they were.

People may think that Venus and Serena Williams were born with tennis racquets in their hands. But most people don't realize that racquets were put in their hands by their father, Richard, and they were drilled and coached, at a very young age. By the time they were 10, they probably had hit more tennis balls than most high-level players twice their age. Do you think Richard Williams was the first parent to raise his daughters to be superstars? Hardly! But these girls had the right combination of ability—even Dr. Ericcson admits that innate talent plays a role—and desire and work ethic to be successful at the world-class level. There are probably thousands of other parents who tried, but their children either didn't have the natural ability or the necessary physical attributes ("You can't teach height," said a basketball coach), they stopped enjoying the activity and chose other pursuits, or they rebelled and quit because their parents pushed them too hard.

As Dr. Ericcson's work demonstrates, success comes from hard work. For children, hard work means committing themselves to an activity, putting in the necessary time, sticking with it when it's not always fun, persevering in the face of obstacles and setbacks, and being patient enough for whatever ability they do have to be realized. Unfortunately, American popular culture doesn't want your children to hear this message. Popular culture tells your children that they shouldn't have to work hard and that success should come easily to them. This view reinforces popular culture's emphasis on immediate gratification and lack of responsibility. Of course, that's a message that children want to hear because easy is better than hard.

I used to work with a junior sports program in Colorado. There was one athlete on the team, I'll call him Rick, who was really terrible. Everyone knew it, including Rick himself. Yet Rick was my poster child for the value of hard work. He was the first one at training in the morning and the last one to finish at the end of the day. Rick put in more time in the weight room than anyone else, took care of his equipment better, and watched videos, read about, and talked to coaches about his sport more than any other athlete on the team. At competitions, Rick was consistently one of the worst finishers on the team. He was never going to be successful in the sport. American popular culture would call him a loser. "What a waste of time for Rick," it would say, "Why do something that you stink at?" Thankfully, Rick was raised in a very different family-value culture and a different way of looking at his sports participation. No matter how poorly he did, Rick was always a happy guy who loved his sport with every ounce of his being. Can you imagine working so hard and never seeing tangible results from your efforts? But Rick didn't care about results. He just loved training and competing.

Though Rick would never have success in his sport, he was learning essential life skills that would serve him well later in life. Sooner or later, Rick was going to find something for which he had an aptitude and, combined with these life skills, he was going to be incredibly successful. After high school, Rick went to a good college, applied everything he learned from his sport to his academics, did extremely well, and is currently finishing medical school with an eye on sports medicine for a career. Rick, who was the antithesis of gifted in his sport, is what I call a success in every sense of the word.

Perfectionism

We live in a "perfect" culture. Bo Derek was proclaimed a perfect ten (though clearly very attractive, perfect she was not, as evidenced by the quality of her acting). The automaker Lexus's advertising slogan is: "The passionate pursuit of perfection." Though Lexus is certainly a great car, it is far from perfect. Even a Lexus gets dirty, you still need to put gas in it, and it still needs maintenance. American popular culture offers children images of perfect people with perfect bodies, perfect faces, perfect hair, and perfect teeth. Perfection is in our daily vocabulary: "That was perfect," "It's a perfect day." Every parent wants a perfect child: top student, star athlete, saving the world in their free time. Yet perfectionism is one of the most insidious and destructive diseases among American children today. American popular culture has elevated success to such absurd heights that, for many children, only the attainment of perfection can be truly considered a success. Yet, like giftedness, perfection places a burden on children that is ultimately far more destructive than beneficial.

Perfectionism is a double-edged sword (I use the metaphor of a sword deliberately because children use their perfectionism as both a weapon to protect themselves and to inflict pain on themselves). One edge of the sword drives children maniacally to be perfect. These children push themselves to do better and better, and do often achieve a high degree of success. The other edge of the sword is that I have never met a happy perfectionist. Happiness and perfectionism are mutually exclusive. They simply cannot coexist. Why? Because what do perfectionists have to be happy about? Even when they succeed by most people's standards, they're not satisfied. An A-, finishing third in a competition is not good enough—they always find some flaw, however minute. Success as seen by most people is just not good enough for perfectionists. They try and try and try to be perfect, but they never are! There is no peace, no contentment, certainly no happiness, only a never-ending struggle to achieve something that they never will.

What exactly is perfectionism and why is it so unhealthy for children? Perfectionism involves children setting unrealistically high standards of behavior and performance in some area of their lives that they—and their parents—care deeply about; they must get straight A's, be the first-chair violin in the school orchestra, be the most popular, etc. Perfectionist children strive for a goal that they will never, ever achieve. Let me emphasize this point again: never, ever achieve. Yet they believe that anything less than perfection is unacceptable. Any perceived mistake or failure can cause perfectionistic children to berate themselves unmercifully, punishing themselves for not being perfect. These children are never satisfied with their efforts no matter how good they may appear to the objective observer. Contrary to popular belief, people don't have to be perfectionistic in every part of their lives to be considered perfectionists. They only have to be perfect in areas of their lives that they care about. That's why you see perfectionists in school who have messy rooms or perfectionistic athletes who have little concern for the quality of their schoolwork.

At the heart of perfectionism lies a threat: if children aren't perfect, their parents won't love them. When I say this to parents, they find it hard to believe that their children could possibly think that they wouldn't love them if they weren't perfect. Yet that is the most common perception of perfectionistic children I work with. The price these children believe they will pay if they are not perfect is immense—the withdrawal of love by their parents—and that too is unacceptable. Perfectionism has been found to be associated with a variety of psychological problems, including procrastination, depression, anxiety, poor stress coping, social phobia, eating disorders, substance abuse, and suicide.

Imagine what it's like for your children to pursue a goal that is unattainable: frustrating, discouraging, disappointing, devastating? After I spoke to a group of students at a school near Boston, a girl from the audience approached me and told me that she felt that I was speaking directly to her about perfectionism. She described how she had scored a 100 on a recent test that also gave ten additional extra-credit points. But she only got seven out of the ten points for a total of a 107 out of 100. Yet missing those three extra-credit points had been eating her alive ever since the test, and she couldn't let go of it!

Perfectionism and Failure

Though it appears that perfectionistic children are driven to succeed, being successful is not what motivates them. In fact, these children have little interest in success. For perfectionistic children, there is nothing more terrifying than failure and, because they connect failure with feelings of worthlessness and loss of love, their singular motivation in life is to avoid failure.

These dire consequences cause perfectionistic children to view failure as a voracious and unrelenting beast that stalks them every moment of every day. If these children stop for even a moment's rest, they will be devoured. The baseball legend, Satchel Paige, once said, "Don't look back. Something might be gaining on you." For perfectionistic children, when they look back, they see failure catching up with them. So they strive and strive and strive to keep failure at bay. Imagine how tiring that must be. Perfectionistic children live in a constant state of fear of not being valued and being unworthy of love. Every morning waking up and needing to prove to themselves and the world that they are deserving of love and respect—that is no way to go through life!

Because perfectionistic children have a profound fear of failure, they never truly achieve success and fully realize their ability. As I discussed earlier, the only way to attain total success is to be willing to risk total failure, and perfectionistic children are unwilling to take that risk. The problem for these children is that, though the chances of success increase when they take risks, the chances of failure also increase and the rapid approach of that insatiable beast must be avoided at all costs. So perfectionistic children hover in the "safety zone" that I referred to earlier in which they remain safely at a distance from failure, but are also stuck at a frustrating distance from total success.

Perfectionism and Emotions

Consider perfectionistic children who, despite their desperate efforts, inevitably fail to meet the absurdly high standards that have been ingrained in them. What emotion would they experience when they fail? Most people I ask say, "Disappointment." But disappointment is far too kind an emotion for perfectionists to feel. Nonperfectionistic children experience disappointment when they fail. It's a normal reaction to not achieving a goal that is important to them. Children should be disappointed when they fail because it says that they care about doing their best and it should inspire them to do better. Perfectionists experience an emotion much more intense and painful when they fail to live up to their impossibly high expectations—devastation. A perceived failure is not just a disappointment at failing to achieve a goal, but rather it is a negative judgment of their value as people and a personal attack on their worth to receive love. Rather than inspiring them, devastation is a severe blow to their very being.

Now consider perfectionistic children who, because of their extreme efforts, actually reach a level of success that meets their severely high standards. What emotion do you think they experience? Excitement, elation, joy? Those emotions are far too normal and healthy for perfectionistic children to feel after a success. The strongest emotion perfectionistic children can muster is relief! Can you imagine working so hard to be successful and the best emotion these children can come up with is relief? What is the relief for? They dodged another bullet of failure. They feel that they're okay for the moment.

How long do you think that relief lasts, though? Not long ago, I was speaking to a group of students at a school near Philadelphia and I asked that very question, which was intended to be rhetorical. Well, as soon as I asked that question, a girl threw up her hand and said, "Till the next exam!" As this girl suggested, the relief lasts only a short time because that relentless and ravenous beast called failure continues to pursue them and they can't allow it to catch them.

Where Does Perfectionism Come From?

After almost every parent talk I've given in which I speak about perfectionism, a parent comes up to me and says, "I'm sure that my child was born a perfectionist." Let me make something very clear: there is absolutely no scientific evidence that perfectionism is inborn. All of the evidence suggests that children learn their perfectionism from their parents, most often from their same-sex parent (i.e., sons from fathers, daughters from mothers). Through their parents' words, emotions, and actions, children come to connect being perfect with being loved. And being perfect becomes children's *raison d'etre*, the all-consuming purpose in their lives subordinating all other needs, wants, or goals. This finding doesn't mean that there are no inborn influences on whether children develop into perfectionists. Some attributes that are inborn, for example, temperament, may cause children to be more vulnerable to perfectionism, but, at this point in our understanding of perfectionism, the consensus is that what you say, feel, and do determines whether your children become perfectionists.

Parents pass on perfectionism to their children in three ways. Some parents were raised as perfectionists themselves and are now passing their perfectionism on to their children—such a wonderful gift! These parents abhor failure, cannot accept their own perceived imperfections, and show great upset when they're unable to live up to their own impossible standards. These perfectionistic parents raise their children to become perfectionists by actively and obviously praising and rewarding success, and punishing failure. These parents set expectations focused on results—"We expect you to get straight A's"—and then offer or withdraw their love based on whether their children meet the expectations. At a very early age, children of these parents get the message loud and clear that if they want their parents' love, they'd better be perfect. Thankfully, in my twenty years of practice, I have only come across a few parents who were this overtly perfectionistic. Sadly, the prognosis for their children was not good.

Another type of parents unintentionally instills perfectionism in their children in less conscious and more subtle ways. These parents, who were also raised as perfectionists, convey perfectionism simply in being who they are—what they say, how they express emotions, and in the way they behave. These parents act as powerful—and harmful—role models to their children. Parents' perfectionism is expressed in how they talk about success and failure, their efforts to be perfect in their own lives, and the frustration, anger, and devastation they feel when they're unable to be perfect and in control. Examples of how perfectionism is communicated by these parents include having to have the house look a certain way, needing to have just the right hairstyle and clothing, their competitiveness in sports and games, their career efforts, and how they respond when things don't go their way. Children see the incredibly high standards that their parents hold themselves to and how their parents treat themselves when they aren't perfect and come to believe that this is the way they have to treat themselves as well. These parents unwittingly communicate to their children that anything less than perfection is unacceptable and won't be tolerated in the family. These parents also unintentionally convey perfectionism to their children subtly in their emotional reactions to their children's successes and failures. For example, when their children do poorly in a sports competition, though attempting to be positive and upbeat, their facial expressions and voice intonations communicate sadness and disappointment in their children's performances, which the children interpret as their failure causing their parents unhappiness.

The final type of parents that convey perfectionism are the antithesis of anything approaching perfection. They are, in fact, deeply flawed. But, by gosh, they're going to make darned sure that their children are perfect! They project their flaws on their children and then try to fix those flaws by giving love when their children don't show the flaws and withdrawing love when they do. Unfortunately, instead of creating perfect children, thereby absolving themselves of the "sin" of being imperfect, they pass their imperfections—anger, insecurity, laziness, unhappiness—on to their children and stay tragically flawed themselves.

American popular culture also encourages perfectionism in children. Especially when it comes to physical appearance, children, particularly girls, are told through advertising, fashion magazines, television shows, and movies, that they have to have perfect faces, perfect bodies, perfect clothes, and perfect hair. The growth of cosmetic surgery and the popularity of reality TV shows, such as *Extreme Makeover,* also illustrates how popular culture worships at the altar of physical perfection.

The influence of American popular culture on perfectionism is not exclusive to physical appearance. Children are taught that they must grow up to have the perfect house, the perfect car, and live in the perfect neighborhood. Even more substantial parts of our culture are infected with perfectionism. The reverence shown to elite colleges, such as the Ivy Leagues, and the difficulty of gaining a coveted acceptance pressures children to be perfect students and perfect college applicants. Straight A's and high SAT scores are no longer sufficient for admission—those are routine these days. Children must also have extensive "résumés" that help them stand out from the crowd, for example, excelling in sports or the arts, doing charitable work, or contributing to the world in an unusual way.

Excellence: The Antidote to Perfection

I encourage you to erase the word *perfect* from your vocabulary, too. It serves absolutely no constructive purpose in raising your children and its use does far more harm than good. You should replace perfection with excellence. I define excellence as *doing good most of the time* (I use poor grammar intentionally because that's how most children talk—and I'm not perfect either). Excellence takes all of the good aspects of perfection (e.g., effort, high standards, quality work) and leaves out its unhealthy parts (e.g., unrealistic expectations, fear of failure, being overly self-critical). Excellence still sets the bar high. Excellence is not okay, mediocre, good, or even very good. It's excellent! But, importantly, excellence allows for failure and never connects failure with the love you give your children. Because children don't associate failure with the loss of their parents' love, they aren't afraid of it or preoccupied by it. Rather than being that menacing beast that pursues them unrelentingly, children who strive for excellence see failure as an annoyance at worst and a challenge at best, but never a threat. Without their fear of failure, they can turn their gaze toward success and pursue it with commitment and gusto while knowing you will love them no matter what they do.

You Don't Have to Be a Perfect Parent

There's even a book called *Perfect Parenting*. When I first heard that title, I almost fainted. You mean parents have to be perfect? What an impossible standard you have to live up to! Talk about setting the bar high. But here's a hint: You don't need to be a perfect parent. You just need to be an excellent parent. (I can hear the collective sigh of relief from every parent in America.)

Here's a bit of news that should relieve some of your worry about parenting: you can actually make mistakes with your children. Being an excellent parent means you only have to be good with your children most of the time. If you screw up on occasion, you won't scar your children for life. You can lose your temper. You can be disappointed when they get a poor grade in school. You can occasionally act like a soccer—or tennis or stage or chess or spelling bee—parent. Children are remarkably resilient creatures. They can take a lot and still come out just fine. My point is that you need to cut yourself some slack about being a perfect parent. Make sure you and your children do the right thing most of the time. When any of you make an occasional mistake, don't beat yourself up about it. Instead, hold yourself and your children responsible so you both learn from it and it is less likely to occur in the future.

Expectations of Success

In chapter 6, I wrote about the importance of establishing and enforcing expectations for your children. In that chapter, I discussed the essential importance of value expectations in raising children. Setting expectations to foster your children's achievement efforts is equally important. Unfortunately, the culture of success that has been promulgated by American popular culture has convinced many parents to set the wrong kind of expectations for their children's efforts at achieving success.

Unhealthy Success Expectations

There are two types of expectations that you shouldn't set for your children: ability and outcome expectations. *Ability expectations* are those in which children are expected to achieve a certain result because of their natural ability, "We expect you to get straight A's because you're so smart" or "We expect you to win because you're the best athlete out there." As I mentioned earlier in the chapter, children have no control over their ability. Children are born with a certain amount of ability and all they can do is maximize whatever ability they are given. The fact is that if your children aren't meeting your ability expectations, you have no one to blame but yourself, because you didn't give them good enough genes to meet your expectations.

Another problem with ability expectations is that there is always going to be someone who is more intelligent, athletically talented, or creatively gifted. When you set ability expectations, you are automatically setting your children up to compare themselves to others. And comparison with others is another area over which your children have no control and which will do them no good. American popular culture wants your children to compare themselves with others. Social comparison fosters jealousy, envy, and greed—"I want what they have." Popular culture tells children to "Be like Mike" and tells you to "Keep up with the Joneses." In doing so, children fall prey to the culture of consumption that is the reason for being of American popular culture. Sadly, comparing themselves to others offers children little benefit and considerable misery because the models that popular culture holds up to compare to are largely unattainable for most children.

American popular culture also worships at the altar of results and encourages parents and children to pursue outcomes without regard for their meaning or value. As a result, parents establish *outcome expectations* in which their children are expected to produce a certain outcome— "We expect you to win this game" or "We know you'll be the first-chair violin in the orchestra." The problem is that, once again, children are asked to meet an expectation over which they may not have control. They might perform to the best of their ability but still not meet your outcome expectation because another child just happened to do better than they did, so they would have to consider themselves as having failed despite their good performance. Setting outcome expectations also communicates to your children that you value results over everything else, so they'll come to judge themselves by the same standards. And when you do anything that causes your children to focus on the outcome, you're actually interfering with meeting the expectation because they're not paying attention to what they need to do to achieve that outcome.

Many parents believe that, by establishing ability and outcome expectations, they're encouraging their children to strive for success, building their self-esteem, and furthering their development as people. To the contrary, these expectations stress values that will hinder their healthy growth and interfere with them fulfilling whatever aspirations you have for them. These expectations can cause your children to feel unloved, insecure, and unsuccessful. Ability and outcome expectations can be so defeating because they may establish a standard that children have little control over attaining and when they do meet your expectations, they have no sense of ownership in those successes. Ability and outcome expectations create feelings of frustration, anger, disappointment, and sadness at their failures. They can also hurt their confidence in their ability to succeed and reduce their motivation to strive to meet expectations in the future.

Expectations in the Real World

Like many parents who hear my views about expectations, you might be thinking, "Wait a minute! I can't push my kids to get good grades and do their best in sports? Then they'll just be couch potatoes! No way I'm buying this one." Before you jump all over me, give me a little time to bring all these ideas back to the real world.

Here is a simple reality that we all recognize in twenty-first-century America: results matter! No two ways about it, in most parts of our society, people are judged on the results they produce: grades, sales, victories, earnings. Though it would be great if everyone got paid for their good intentions or efforts, that is not the way the world works. Our society is based on a market-driven system in which those who produce the best results are rewarded. Unfortunately, this societal focus can cause you, like many parents, to lose sight of your values and place your desire for your children to succeed—as defined by American popular culture—ahead of doing the right thing for your children, your family, and your community. So there is no further confusion on this issue, let me also say that I want your children to be as successful as they can be. The challenge for you is to set expectations that will help your children grow up to be value-driven people who can resist popular culture and who can also be successful in whatever endeavors they choose to pursue.

A problem with expectations is that they're often established by parents and placed in front of their children without their consultation or "buy in," and parents then push them toward the expectations. Children have no ownership of the expectation and little motivation, outside an implied threat from their parents, to fulfill the expectations. Without understanding the rationale behind the expectations or having a sense that the expectations are reasonable and achievable, children will often need to be dragged to the expectations for them to be fulfilled. For example, when I speak to kids about the expectations their parents place on them, they usually describe ability and outcome expectations and feel that they are often unfair and unattainable. Children seeing expectations as such bad things causes them to feel undue pressure at needing to meet the expectations, yet feel profound fear that they can't. These expectations may also encourage children to decide to resist them to avoid the pressure.

Work-Ethic Expectations

If you want your children to be successful, instead of setting ability and outcome expectations, you should establish expectations over which they have control and that actually encourage them to do what it takes to achieve the outcomes you want. Most important, these expectations should be established in collaboration with your children. This cooperative approach ensures that your children have ownership of expectations rather than feeling that you have forced the expectations on them. These expectations should, as I have said repeatedly, also be within your children's control. If your children feel that they have the tools to achieve the expectations, they are much more likely to embrace and pursue them. Think about what your children need to do to become successful and create what I call *work-ethic expectations:* commitment, hard work, discipline, patience, focus, persistence, perseverance, positive attitude. "Our family expects you to give your best effort" or "Our family expects you to make your studies a priority" These expectations are worthwhile whether someone is striving to be a scientist, teacher, professional athlete, writer, musician, spouse, or parent. Regardless of the abilities they inherited from you or with whom they might be compared, children have the capacity to use work-ethic expectations and the values associated with them to be the best they can be in whatever area they choose to pursue.

Establishing work-ethic expectations with your children should be a collaborative effort. You can talk to your children about the value of a work ethic, how it will help them achieve their goals, and that they have complete control over their work ethic. You can share examples with your children of how notable people used the skills associated with a work ethic to become successful. Most important, you want to help them make the connection between their work ethic and success.

If your children meet these reasonable effort-based expectations, they will, in all likelihood, fully realize whatever ability they have and gain satisfaction in their efforts. Your children will achieve some level of success (how successful they become will depend on what abilities they were born with). They will also reap the benefits of your approval, good grades, and improved performance in other achievement activities. If your children don't meet the work-ethic expectations, your children may not succeed and must face the consequences, including your disapproval, poor grades, etc. They will also be disappointed (they should be), but they won't be devastated. Rather than being crushed by the failure, they will know that they have the power to fulfill the expectations in the future. Meeting their work-ethic expectations will encourage your children to set even higher effort expectations.

My recommendation to only set value and work-ethic expectations would work great in an ideal world. But we don't live in utopia and, let's face it, most parents are going to establish outcome expectations for their children—remember, results do matter!—whether it is good for their children or not. If you feel compelled to set outcome expectations for your children, I can live with that and your children probably can too. But after you have given them outcome expectations, remind yourself how they will best meet those expectations. Having received outcome expectations from you, they're focused on the results they will need to gain your love and approval. Both the attention on the results and the pressure to meet your expectations will actually interfere with your children achieving the results you want.

Now you must help your children to achieve those outcome expectations by shifting their focus onto what will enable them to get the results you expect of them. The way you do this is to give them work-ethic expectations that will lead to those desired results. Ask yourself what your children need to do to meet the outcome expectations you set for them—commit to the activity, work hard, be disciplined, manage their time well—and establish work-ethic expectations over which they have control. These expectations give them something to focus on that they won't perceive as pressure and will also give them the tools they need to meet your outcome expectations, thereby making those expectations less threatening to them. Your children will also feel more supported by you because you're not just telling them that they have to achieve a certain standard, but you're also showing them how to do it. Thus, they will feel like you're with them rather than against them.

The chances are that you will bring up your outcome expectations with some regularity. Each time you do, your children will feel a little jolt from the cattle prod that are those expectations. Reminding them of your outcome expectations isn't inherently bad, though they can become downright annoying to your children, making them angry, and perhaps causing them to resist your expectations. When you do bring up your outcome expectations—and, for your children's sake, don't make it a daily activity—always follow them up with a reminder of their work-ethic expectations.

Goals Instead of Expectations

An even better suggestion is for you to give up outcome expectations all together, but still give your children outcome "somethings." Those somethings I refer to are outcome goals. Goals are very different from expectations. When I ask children about expectations, they usually grimace and say things like, "That's when my parents get really serious and I know they're gonna put pressure on me" or "They're telling me what to do and I better do it or I'll get into trouble." Not exactly "feel-good" parenting! But when I ask about goals, they respond much differently. Their faces perk up and they say things like, "It means I decide to do something and I really work hard to do it" or "I feel like my parents are really behind me and I'm psyched to do it."

A big difference between expectations and goals is that the former are all-or-nothing—they're either reached or they're not—so anything less than complete fulfillment of the expectations is a failure. This black-and-white aspect of expectations also sets your children up for failure because it means that children have only a small zone of success, anything at or above the expectation, and a large area for failure, everything below the expectation.

Goals, by contrast, are yardsticks that children—with their parents' guidance—can set for themselves, take ownership of, and strive toward by their own choice. Rather than being all or nothing, goals have gradations of attainment that give children a large zone of success and reduce their area of failure. Children won't achieve every goal—that is impossible—but children will show improvement toward almost every goal they set and put effort into. For example, a child's parents established an outcome expectation of raising her math grade from an 80 to a 95 during the school year. If she only improved her grade to an 89, then she would have failed to meet the outcome expectation. But, if she set an outcome goal, even though the goal of a 95 wasn't fully realized, she would still see the 89 as a success—as well she should.

Many parents believe that results at a young age are important, so they emphasize results and place outcome expectations on their children.

Yet success in early childhood is not highly predictive of success later in life. Childhood is about learning, improving, developing, and gaining the values, attitudes, and skills necessary for later success. Using goals rather than expectations is one of the best ways to foster this growth.

Outcome goals have a similar problem as outcome expectations in that both cause children to be focused on the result of their efforts. To maximize the value of outcome goals once they are set, you should shift your children's focus away from the outcome and onto what they need to do to achieve that outcome. In other words, you should help them set process goals. Ask your children what steps they need to take to achieve their outcome goals, for example, how much time they will need to devote, what resources they will need to access, whose help they might need. By having them focus on the process, the pressure that comes from the outcome is relieved. Also, because your children are paying attention to the process, they're more likely to do what is needed to do their best. And if they do their best, they have a better chance of achieving their outcome goals.

You can also ease the burden of outcome goals by helping your children set smaller outcome goals that lead to a big outcome goal. For example, if you want your son to improve his reading-class grade, he could set outcome goals for the four quizzes that he will be taking throughout the term. Short-term outcome goals give your children something more immediate to focus on and toward which to direct their efforts. Their success in achieving these outcome goals can also provide them with feedback about how well they are fulfilling their work-ethic expectations and can suggest changes that they may need to make to achieve their long-term outcome goal.

An outcome goal produces an entirely different mindset than an outcome expectation. Even though children may not fully reach a goal, if they do everything they can in its pursuit, they can feel satisfaction and pride in the progress they make. The improvement they demonstrate should also reward their efforts, boost their confidence, and motivate them to continue to set outcome goals and work hard to achieve them in the future.

Emerging Values

Because of the unhealthy perspective American popular culture offers children about success, the pursuit of success can be a frustrating, demoralizing, and unsatisfying experience. Children can develop an aversion to achievement because it is associated with so many unpleasant pressures, experiences, and emotions. In contrast, developing a healthy *value of achievement* encourages children to pursue success, however they choose to define it. In wanting to set goals and strive to do their best, children receive a gift that offers many benefits. Achievement is by definition about producing and contributing to the world, thus children learn to create and give back to a world that has given them so much. One of the great joys in life is setting, working toward, and achieving goals, thus embracing achievement provides great meaning, fulfillment, and pride to children. Having the value of achievement also prepares children for an adult life that is both productive and satisfying.

By grounding success in a work ethic, children come to appreciate the connection between their efforts and their outcomes. They see that the more they put into something, the more they get out of it. This relationship teaches children about the *value of commitment.* Commitment plays an important role not only in school, but also in families, friendships, careers, and virtually every aspect of people's lives. Commitment acts as the glue that holds our lives together. It ensures diligence, trust, responsibility, and follow-through. In a culture that encourages children to quit when things get hard (as evidenced by the "slacker" mentality, the growing high-school dropout rate, and the high divorce rate) the value of commitment shows children the value and rewards of sticking with something even when things get difficult.

This healthy perspective on success that emphasizes values, attitudes, and skills over which children have control instills the *value of confidence* in their ability to achieve the goals they set for themselves. This confidence in their capacity for success grows from commitment, hard work, persistence, patience, overcoming obstacles and setbacks, and daily successes. These experiences create in children a strong belief that they can accomplish anything that they set their minds to. At the same time, the appreciation of a work ethic also teaches children the *value of humility* and an appreciation for the opportunities they have been given.

CHAPTER 8

Happiness
(No, Money Can't Buy It)

American Popular Culture on the Offensive

In a recent segment of *All Things Considered* on National Public Radio, a 17-year-old girl, Shakima Swain, offered a commentary, "The Importance of Fashion to One Brooklyn Teenager and Her Peers." The following are some excerpts:

> SWAIN: When I used to live on 91st Street in Brooklyn with my mother's boyfriend Steve, I was the poster girl for Guess. Everything matched. One day I'd be decked out in a Guess skirt, Guess jumper, and, yes, Guess sneakers, or another day, I'd be Miss Jordache. I remember this neighbor thinking I was too dressed up just to be sitting on a porch. But my mom wanted us to stand out. She sat out all the time, so I had to be the bomb... I like to look like a princess, a Diana or a Grace Kelly.
>
> SWAIN: [to her younger sister]: Do you wear name brands?
> TAMIKA: No.
> SWAIN: Why not?

TAMIKA: 'Cause I can't afford it.

SWAIN: How do you feel about that?

TAMIKA: I feel embarrassed.

SWAIN: So do I. I feel like we're at the bottom now, rock bottom...

SWAIN: Sometimes I really wish B [her stepfather] could use his money and buy my mother a car rather than buy Ghetto shoes or even that Louis Vuitton bag I forced him to buy me. He needs to take a step back and look at the big picture.... A car would enable my mom to drop the baby off at the sitter's, go schooling in Long Island and hold a part-time job.

SWAIN: When I get to school...the girls size you up from head to toe in quick peeks, as if they're going to break their necks from turning their heads too fast...

SWAIN: I am smart. With my powers to mix and match, I will find a way to keep wearing a few long-lasting name brands and still be able to buy my own car when I get older. That's when I'm going to have bills to pay. I see how it is with my mother. *But right now clothing is what makes me smile.* [italics added]

Shakima Swain is a victim of American popular culture. She—and her family and friends—has been led to believe that designer clothing is the answer to all of her problems. By wearing the right clothes and shoes, she believes that she'll find self-esteem, status, popularity, and happiness. But Shakima is actually acting against her own best interests. Nice clothes won't enable her to find those elusive good feelings. Shakima and her family also can't afford them. Not only is she pursuing an unrealizable dream, but Shakima is also preparing herself for future financial hardship.

But is Shakima's dream of finding happiness that different from anyone else's? Is there anything more decidedly American than the pursuit of happiness? It's even in the Declaration of Independence. Is there anything that we devote more time, effort, and money to than attempting to achieve that elusive goal? And is there anything that we pursue with such vigor and yet with such poor results than our pursuit of happiness?

Happiness is, at the same time, the most desired of human conditions, yet one that is neither understood nor fully valued by most members of American society. One would assume that the increase in wealth and all of the advances that have been made over the last fifty years would have made people happier. But that assumption is painfully incorrect. If the growing rates of depression, divorce, and suicide are any indication, Americans are less happy than any time in our past.

One of the most frequent comments I get from parents is "I just want my kid to be happy." Though an admirable and common objective, happiness is one of the most neglected family values in twenty-first-century America. Many parents I speak to pay lip service to the importance of happiness in their children's lives. Few parents, though, grasp the essential meaning of happiness for their children and fewer still have given serious thought to what happiness is and how they can help their children to find it. At the many parent workshops I give, parents are very good at giving the "right answers" about happiness, but, if my clientele is any indication, very few parents know what the true answers are about happiness. More often than you'd expect, parents unwittingly act in ways that actually cause their children's unhappiness.

Parents' efforts at helping their children gain happiness are undermined by the distorted messages that American popular culture communicates to parents about happiness. Mark Kingwell, the author of *In Pursuit of Happiness*, suggests that "...the problem might be that we are most of the time looking in the wrong places and, worse, seeking the wrong things.... The fundamental issue is the lack of clarity in our conceptions of happiness, combined with the fact that those notions of happiness we do have at our fingertips are created and molded by obscure social forces." As with other values, many parents are seduced by these appealing messages from American popular culture—despite the fact that it is the single greatest obstacle to your children's happiness—instill them in their children, and send them through childhood and into adulthood on a road that ultimately takes them far from happiness.

What Happiness Is Not

Like everything else it does, American popular culture lies to your children about what happiness is. One lie it foists on them is to mistake *pleasure* for happiness. I see pleasure as a temporary state of good feelings caused by experiences outside of ourselves that we enjoy. We can gain pleasure from many sources depending on what we value, for example, food, conversation, exercise, entertainment, shopping, travel, etc. Happiness, by contrast, is a much deeper, longer lasting experience that comes from within. It does not come from what we do, but rather from who we are and what we value. Happiness can never be provided to us, but we can only find it ourselves. Yet Starbucks, the ubiquitous purveyor of all things coffee, suggests otherwise. The tag line of one of their magazine ads reads, "Sometimes the coffee stirs you" and the ad copy continues, "A completed sentence ends with a small black dot, but that's how epiphanies begin...A tiny, good thing from the earth. But the best ones have something locked inside: an exotic destination, a spirited conversation." As if drinking a cup of coffee—even a double decaf, low-fat, mocha latte—could bring inspiration, stir passion, and trigger epiphanies—in other words, create happiness.

We undoubtedly live in the most hedonistic, self-indulgent, immediate gratification, "gotta feel good" time in American history. Children have been led to believe that the sensations of pleasure that they experience are actually happiness. American popular culture sends messages to children about happiness, like McDonald's Happy Meal and Ben and Jerry's Euphoria To Go! ice cream. The great selling point of this perspective is that pleasure is easy to find for children, so according to popular culture, happiness is easy to achieve as well.

American popular culture lies to your children in telling them that they should always feel good: excited, elated, HAPPY!—in the "big smile on their face constantly" sort of way. With the popularity and prevalence of drug use on television, film, and in music and sports, children are led to believe that they should always feel, well, high. Popular culture equates anything that is not this emotional high as being unhappiness, so when children are bored or just plain neutral, they think they're unhappy.

American popular culture also lies to your children by communicating to them that happiness is not their own responsibility. If they're not happy, someone else should make them happy. Many children today have lost the initiative and creativity to create happiness for themselves. They look most often to their parents to entertain them—they equate being entertained with being happy—and most parents look to American popular culture—television, movies, music, video games—to get their children feeling good, which parents also mistake for happiness.

The problem is that pleasure is a superficial and temporary sensation. Therefore, it must continually be sought out. Children constantly look for pleasure, are never satisfied, and continue to look elsewhere. Children seek fun, pleasure, excitement, and, more generally, the absence of boredom—thinking it is happiness—by accumulating toys, surrounding themselves with "cool" peers, playing video games, and watching movies. As children move into adolescence, their sources of pleasure take on potentially more dangerous forms, such as alcohol and drug use, sexual gratification, driving fast, and extreme sports. But, contrary to their argued purpose, these activities drive children away from happiness because children stay occupied and feeling pretty good on the surface, which prevents them from even considering, much less understanding or exploring, what real happiness is.

Another unhealthy side effect of children's pursuit of pleasure is that it creates narcissistic and hedonistic children. Because of their constant quest for pleasure, their focus is predominantly selfish and directed toward immediate gratification. These children show minimal concern for others, have little patience, are easily bored, and are demanding of others to provide them with sources of pleasure.

The most telling, ironic, and painful aspect of children pursuing American popular culture's manipulation of the relationship between happiness and pleasure is that their search will never be rewarded. Whatever good feelings that children feel are never fully satisfying and they never last. Children's pursuit of this distorted form of happiness becomes like a drug for which they need their fix. Children who get hooked on pleasure need more and more of it to satisfy them, if only temporarily. This ongoing and insatiable hunger is exactly what American popular culture wants because these children continue to consume its offerings in the fruitless pursuit of happiness. And, sadly, the longer they stay "addicted," the farther away these children get from ever finding happiness. It's not surprising that many children turn to video games, television, movies, and the Internet, or worse, to alcohol, drugs, and sex to make them feel "happy," when they have no understanding or way to gain real happiness themselves.

Where Happiness Doesn't Come From

To an unprecedented degree, Americans now have the time and resources go to psychotherapy, read self-help books, meditate, and seek spiritual awakening, all in pursuit of happiness. But despite our best efforts, America has never been a more unhappy place. The reason is that pursuing happiness not only doesn't bring happiness but, in fact, can actually *cause* unhappiness. Research has shown that people are often wrong in identifying what will make them happy (e.g., wealth, materialism, status), with the inevitable result being that they pursue something that, in reality, won't make them happy. Other research has reported that the active pursuit of happiness actually reduces happiness. Ironically, trying to find happiness keeps people from finding happiness. In addition, the simple monitoring of happiness—"How happy am I feeling now?"—also lowers happiness.

Yet American popular culture creates a profound hope in people that they can find happiness. They're getting close. It's just around the corner. People just need to find, do, or buy one more thing. Suggests David Brooks, the author and the *New York Times* columnist, "Just beyond the next ridge, just with the next entrepreneurial scheme or diet plan; just with the next political hero, the next credit card purchase or the next true love, there is a spot you can get to where all tensions will melt, all time pressures are relieved, and all contentment can be realized…" This lure acts as the carrot that keeps people hopeful of realizing happiness, yet, sadly, pulls them inexorably down a road that takes them farther and farther away from happiness.

Money

American popular culture tells your children that if they achieve "success"—become wealthy, powerful, and famous—happiness will be the result. What popular culture doesn't tell you and your children is that the happiness will be gained not by your children, but by the purveyors of popular culture—the television, film, music, fashion, magazine, advertising, and related industries—who are laughing at you and your children all the way to the bank. And people fall for this lie. Two of the most commonly cited sources of happiness in our society, wealth and popularity, were found to be mostly unrelated to happiness. In fact, wealth and popularity had, in some situations, a negative effect on happiness.

The reality is that the pursuit of American popular culture's notion that money can buy happiness will not only not lead to your children's happiness, it can actually make them unhappy. This view of happiness is an insatiable beast. In pursuit of happiness, nothing is ever enough. As J. D. Rockefeller once observed, "How much money is enough? Just a little bit more." This hunger creates an constant need for more, more, more, and offers no peace or contentment with what a person has. It also produces a variety of emotions—greed, envy, jealousy—that are absolutely antithetical to happiness and that foster even more unhealthy emotions, such as frustration and resentment. These emotions can partly explain the epidemic of corporate corruption that has arisen in the U.S. in recent years. The business executives who are responsible for this avarice were already wealthy, but that didn't quench their thirst for more. Research suggests that young people have bought into this notion of happiness. One study reported that the number of college students who said that being financially well off was very important to them rose from 40 percent to 75 percent between 1970 and 1993. Moreover, making money led their list of long-term aspirations. What these people don't realize is that by devoting so much time and energy in their pursuit of wealth, they sacrifice family, friends, and other meaningful activities, the very things that actually bring happiness.

"Stuff"

American popular culture also tells children that "stuff" will make them happy. If they buy the right toys, clothing, or electronics, they'll be happier. Advertising on television and in print portrays happy children wearing particular clothing and shoes, drinking beverages and eating food, and using MP3 players, video games, and the like. Your children make the connection that these products are the source of the happiness and they want to feel that way too. Products can certainly entertain children and make them feel good for a while. And they might make you feel better because your children are no longer nagging you and they're out of your hair. But stuff will definitely not make your children happy. How many times have your children clamored for a new toy? You bought it for them, and they were so happy and played with it constantly for a week or two, then lost interest in it completely and wanted another toy they saw on television just as badly? I'm not saying that well-placed consumption is a bad thing. Buying something that your family values, for example, a new stereo on which to better enjoy music or new skis that make skiing more fun, can create very good feelings and bring happiness by enhancing your children's experiences in some area. But the simple act of possessing a product will never increase your children's happiness unless it is connected to your family's values.

Considerable research supports this perspective. For example, researchers have coined the phrase, "materialistic value orientation" (MVO), to refer to the notion that the acquisition of money, possessions, status, and the "right image" will bring people happiness. Their research indicates that people who adopt an MVO actually report lower levels of quality of life and happiness, have poor relationships, suffer from substance abuse problems, and contribute less to their communities. They also found that when the value of wealth, influence, and luxury takes precedence over other values, people report lower levels of well-being and increased behavioral problems. These findings begin to emerge in children, such that teenagers with an MVO have higher incidences of depression and anxiety, and college students with an MVO are more narcissistic, have lower self-esteem, have difficulty with relationships, and are more likely to abuse drugs.

I had a client, Carl, a real-estate developer who became a wealthy man. When he came to me, he said that he felt like he was stuck on a treadmill that he couldn't get off. When Carl was young, he bought into the idea that money would bring him happiness, so he set a goal of making a million dollars in the belief that when he reached that threshold, he would find happiness. Well, Carl made his first million—and had a big house and fancy cars—but still wasn't happy. He figured that one million dollars just wasn't enough, so he set his sights on five million. In this latest pursuit of happiness, Carl said that he would dwell on others he knew who had more money and possessions and how happy they seemed, and these ruminations would make him angry and frustrated. When Carl reached that threshold—and had even more stuff—to his surprise, he still wasn't happy. Carl continued on this vicious cycle in the fruitless pursuit of happiness, accumulating more and more money until, at age 52, it finally hit him; perhaps money doesn't bring happiness and he needed to look elsewhere for peace and contentment. That's when he called me and began to reassess his perspective on what really brings happiness.

Physical Attractiveness

American popular culture tells children that physical attractiveness will make them happy. Children, particularly girls, are overwhelmed by images of beautiful people who are wealthy, powerful, popular, and having fun. Popular culture sends these messages, in fashion magazines, in celebrity-driven television shows such as *Entertainment Tonight,* and in advertising, because it wants children to buy products that will make them attractive and, by extension, happy. Especially influential on girls, the fashion industry pushes them to wear makeup, to diet, color their hair, and to wear the latest fashions.

This pressure to find happiness through physical attractiveness has moved to a new level recently with the reality TV show *Extreme Makeover.* As described on the abc.com website: "Following nationwide open casting calls and over ten thousand written applications, the lucky individuals are chosen for a once-in-a-lifetime chance to participate in *Extreme Makeover.*" The large number of applicants for the show's few slots is a telling indication of how important physical appearance is to people. Continues the description, "These men and women are given a truly Cinderella-like experience: A real-life fairy tale in which their wishes come true, not just to change their looks, but their lives and destinies." American popular culture has led people to believe that life is a fairy tale with a happy ending and that changing their appearance will change their lives. Concludes the website, "This magic is conjured through the skills of an 'Extreme Team,' including the nation's top plastic surgeons, eye surgeons, and cosmetic dentists, along with a talented team of hair and makeup artists, stylists, and personal trainers." As Dr. Mark Andrejevic, an assistant professor of communications studies at the University of Iowa in Iowa City, notes, *Extreme Makeover* offers "to rebuild 'real' people via plastic surgery so that they can physically close the gap between themselves and the contrived aesthetic of celebrity they have been taught to revere." What people who are seduced by this illusory pot of gold don't realize is that happiness doesn't come from how they look, but rather from what they think, how they feel, and what they value. The world is full of beautiful, but profoundly unhappy, people, for example, the actor Ben Affleck, who has been in alcohol rehabilitation, the supermodel, Kate Moss, who has undergone treatment for drug and alcohol addiction, and the actress and diva, Elizabeth Taylor, who has been married—and divorced—nine times (I'm assuming that people who have these kinds of problems are not very happy).

Many parents become victims of this same manipulation and then become enablers of American popular culture by falling for its false promises about physical beauty. How often do you hear parents saying to their children, "You are the most beautiful [or handsome] child?" Remember that, early in children's lives, parents decide how their hair is cut and what they are allowed to wear. An early emphasis on physical appearance by parents only encourages children to believe the messages they later receive from popular culture. It is sad to see young girls who are already preoccupied with their appearance; primping, preening, and having to look just so. And yet, to a large degree, this focus by young girls has been around since well before the first Barbie doll, so we don't notice it as much. But lately I've encountered more and more boys as young as 5 or 6 years old who won't leave the house without their hair moussed and combed in a certain style, and wearing the right T-shirt and baggy pants. The fashion culture has truly invaded childhood. I'm sorry, but part of being children is having uncombed hair and not having the least concern for what they wear. And where did these children first get their ideas about physical appearance? From their parents, of course.

If your children connect their happiness to any "false idol," whether wealth, fame, power, popularity, materialism, or physical attractiveness, the ultimate result of this misguided quest for happiness is the exact opposite of that which they covet so much. The more time children spend pursuing American popular culture's definition of happiness, the more unhappy they will become for two reasons:

- They are chasing after pots of gold that will actually cause them to be unhappy.
- They are also putting so much time and energy into these pursuits that they're not experiencing the things that will actually make them happy.

These children, if they remain on this road for too long, will grow up to be people who are truly unhappy and may never be capable of experiencing real happiness.

What Is Happiness?

The fact that so many people search for happiness with such commitment and fervor and with so little success should lead us to conclude that, whatever these people are pursuing, it is obviously not happiness. This fact should also cause us to reconsider what we believe happiness is and how we can attain it.

The first question to ask, then, is: what is happiness? Though few people hear about it, the subject of happiness has been studied extensively for over thirty years. Most researchers don't even use the term happiness, preferring subjective phrases such as well-being and life satisfaction, because happiness means so many things to so many people (e.g., joy, excitement, contentment, or inner peace). Because the term "happiness" is so much a part of the American lexicon, I will use it for the purposes of this discussion. At the same time, because it holds so many different meanings, I want to offer my perspective on happiness in children based on the extant research as well as my own professional and personal experiences. The emphasis in my entire discussion of happiness is on developing an intuitive and sensible definition of happiness in children and offering you a practical approach to helping your children find happiness. I also want to place it in the context of not just being a desired condition, but rather seeing happiness as an essential value that you want to instill in your children for them to have a rich and fulfilling life. This understanding of happiness includes the values, attitudes, and qualities related to happiness that you can actively help your children to develop.

This view of happiness also builds on the other values and ideas I share with you throughout this book.

I think of happiness as an intuitive experience that all children are capable of feeling. In other words, given a real understanding of what happiness is and how they can develop it, all children can come to know and feel happiness. I see happiness as an ongoing experience of good feelings and contentment. It is a long-term, persistent "condition" that, though there are ups and downs caused by life events, always returns to that steady baseline of happiness. Happy children feel at ease, confident, and comfortable. Importantly, there is an absence of persistent anxiety, worry, or negative feelings. Happy children feel like they're in a good place in their lives and approach life with a positive attitude, enthusiasm, and appreciation. Though happy children periodically experience feelings of excitement and elation, they realize that experiencing such intense feelings regularly is not possible or even desirable. As happy children mature, they learn what makes them truly happy, recognize that their happiness is their own responsibility, and they develop the means to actively maintain and regain their happiness when it is temporarily lost.

Happy children aren't Pollyannas, either. They realize that happiness is not a 24/7 experience. It is not about your children being in nirvana or experiencing eternal bliss. They can't always be feeling good and carefree. Part of being human is that life is difficult sometimes. Your children will frequently experience setbacks, failures, and losses. They will have stresses, doubts, and fears. These realities, common among all people, are especially evident in childhood, which, by its very nature, is uncertain, scary, and turbulent, and children have limited experience with which to face these challenges. Happiness can be thought of, not as feeling great all of the time as American popular culture tells children, but rather feeling contented and angst-free most of the time and possessing the tools to successfully return to that good feeling following the normal highs and lows of life.

The difficult nature of childhood—many ups and downs with few tools to deal with them—makes it particularly incumbent on parents to instill the healthy value and feeling of happiness in their children as a defense against and antidote to American popular culture. This grounded sense of happiness places children in a position of strength from which they will be less vulnerable to the assaults from popular culture and better equipped to respond to the challenges they will face as they progress through adolescence on their way to adulthood.

Raising Happy Children

You can't make your children happy. In fact, the more you try, the more unhappy they're likely to become. Children need to come to their own understanding of happiness and how they can best pursue it. What you can do is create a family-value culture in which happiness is an important part. You must provide your children with the values, perspectives, and tools from which true happiness is more likely to emerge and remain. Instilling the value of happiness, much like teaching your children other values that I speak about in this book, involves walking the walk, talking the talk, and living the life that encourages both an understanding of what happiness is and how your children can find it. I'll get into the specifics of how to do this a little later. But before I do, you must understand how happiness fits into your family-value culture.

Happiness as a Part of Your Family-Value Culture

Without even formally addressing happiness with your children, you can start them on the right road by immersing them in a family-value culture like the one I describe in this book. All of the values that I discuss—respect, responsibility, success, happiness, family, and compassion, in addition to the many emerging values—guide your children toward a life that can be rich in happiness. In building happiness into your family's culture, along with the other beneficial values, you also add to their potential for happiness because you are teaching them the perspectives and tools that allow for happiness to emerge. This foundation enables you to then build on the meaning and value of happiness in their lives in a more active way.

Because American popular culture is the single greatest obstacle to your children's happiness, you must envelop them in a family culture that values and understands happiness. This gives them the ability to resist popular culture's influence and frees them to find their own happiness. Making happiness a family value also protects your children from the unhealthy messages that American popular culture communicates to them about happiness. The simple process of surrounding your children with a family-value culture and instilling values that counter those that popular culture tries to impose on your children is the most important thing you can do to foster their happiness.

Be Happy!

In addition to the value culture that underlies your family, you also communicate an overriding emotional tone that permeates your family life. The quality of the emotional climate will have a great influence on the happiness of your children. An atmosphere that is positive, joyful, and contented will likely rub off on your children to their benefit. A family mood that is angry, pessimistic, or sad will likely hurt your children.

This emotional zeitgeist of your family comes from you. The best way to raise happy children is for you to be happy yourself. Being happy is not always easy, as we all carry "baggage" from our past and stresses in our present that can keep us from being happy. But accepting happiness as an essential part of your family-value culture and committing to happiness both as an individual and as a family will benefit both your children and you. If you realize that your children's happiness is in large part in your hands, is there is a more powerful impetus for you to make changes in your own life to find happiness? And, despite any difficulties that you may have faced in your life and any unhappiness you now feel, wouldn't it be wonderful to unload your baggage—or at least lighten the load—and, at long last, find some happiness yourself?

In my work with families in which unhappiness dominated their landscape, the best predictor of the long-term happiness of the children is the willingness of their parents to face their own unhappiness and find some measure of peace for themselves. The journey toward happiness by the parents slowly alters the emotional climate of the family, lifts the pall of unhappiness that may hang over the family, and, metaphorically, brings a much needed appearance of sunshine to the children.

The search for happiness—or at least a reduction in unhappiness—can occur in many ways. Happiness can be found in self-exploration, through reading, discussions with family and friends, or counseling with a trained psychotherapist. It can also be discovered outside of yourself, with new activities and people. Happiness can be uncovered with small changes in your life, for example, beginning an exercise program or helping at a home for the elderly, or with major life changes, such as starting a new career or moving to a new city. You can even learn from and follow some of the ideas aimed at your children in this chapter. The important thing is that, for your future and that of your children, you need to begin the journey soon.

Teach Happiness to Your Children

A recurring theme throughout this book is that a part of instilling healthy values in your children involves educating them about those values and their meaning to you. This approach is no less important for teaching your children the value and meaning of happiness. If you don't talk to your children about happiness at an early age, they might get their ideas about happiness from American popular culture. By educating your children about happiness, you lay the foundation upon which they can experience happiness with an accuracy and depth of understanding that will allow them to make clear decisions about what will bring them happiness. This happiness "curriculum" should provide you with ongoing opportunities to share your views on the value and meaning of happiness with your children, including what it is and how it can be gained. You can use the ideas I offer in this chapter as well as those you have from your own life experiences. This education should also teach your children about American popular culture's view of happiness, provide them with examples that illustrate its perspective, and give a thoughtful explanation of why its perspective will not bring happiness at all. Teaching your children about happiness should also offer your children chances to discuss how they feel about happiness and what experiences they believe bring them happiness. A continuing dialogue that highlights the importance of happiness in your family-value culture and enables your children to learn about and experience happiness will ensure that they head down a road that will ultimately allow happiness to emerge.

Everything I write about in this chapter—and related topics in other chapters—is fodder for your happiness curriculum. You can discuss issues related to happiness in more structured settings, such as at dinner or in family meetings. Or you can bring them to light when

an opportunity for your children to learn more about happiness arises in the course of their daily lives, for example, when something
causes you or your children to be happy or unhappy. Pointing out the
reasons for their happiness or unhappiness as they happen, and how
they can maintain or change their feelings provides your children
with direct experience coupled with an invaluable learning opportunity. A powerful way in which you can educate your children about
happiness is by sharing your happiness with them. When you're excited about something that happened at work, share with it with them.
When you feel joy at having a wonderful family, bring them into it.
When you feel contented with your life, tell them why.

It's the Journey *and* the Destination

Happiness is like sleep; the harder you try to get your children to fall
asleep, the less likely it will occur. To help them fall asleep, you need to
put them in a situation in which they allow sleep to come; give them a
warm glass of milk, read them a story. The same holds true for happiness. Often, the harder people try to find happiness—especially if
they're looking in the wrong places—the farther away they get from
happiness. Rather than trying so hard to attain happiness, if you put
your children in situations that will encourage their happiness, then
happiness will more likely come to them. This is where many parents
have been seduced by American popular culture's view of happiness
and fail their children. Parents try to make their children happy by
avoiding expectations, pushing experiences on them, and buying toys
that they believe will make their children happy. In doing so, parents
create lives that provide children with a lot of "feel good" experiences,
but few if any that actually foster happiness.

Dr. Richard S. Lazarus, the noted University of California–Berkeley
researcher, and the co-author of *Passion and Reason*, believes that happiness is not an outcome (e.g., wealth, fame), as American popular culture asserts. He teaches that happiness cannot be pursued and achieved,
but rather emerges out of the process of life—family, social, cultural,
religious, intellectual, athletic activities. Happiness, says Dr. Lazarus, is
not a goal toward which we strive, but rather it is "a by-product of the
continuing process being personally involved and committed…in what
we are doing." Dr. Lazarus is saying that most people are going about

experiencing happiness the wrong way. They are so intent on achieving happiness by pursuing it relentlessly that they don't allow themselves to experience happiness in their daily lives. His understanding of happiness demonstrates two reasons why children are led down an unhappy road. Children who buy into American popular culture are searching for Shangri-La—which we all know doesn't exist. They are also so focused on getting to this magical destination that they miss out on real happiness that is simply woven into their daily lives.

Having talked to your children about what happiness is and how they can encourage it, you can highlight in your own experiences the times that you are happy. For example, you can point out that it makes you happy to spend time with your family in the park. Or you can tell your children how happy you feel when you're exercising outdoors. In doing so, you show your children that happiness is not about the end result, but about the experiences along the way. When you do accomplish something important, for example, finishing a big project at work, you can share with them that getting the job done felt good, but what really made you happy was your commitment to the goal and the steps you took along the way.

This perspective is not to say that the outcome has only a negative effect on happiness. The problem arises when children see the destination as the only valuable part of the journey. When that happens, children miss out on all of the good feelings they can experience along the way and, because they can't always control whether they arrive at the destination of their choosing, children may be disappointed, hurt, and unhappy when they get to an endpoint that wasn't what they expected.

Another difficulty with your children focusing on the destination is that there are relatively few of them in life. Think of a cross-country train trip in which there are vast amounts of miles and time and few stops between the coasts. Because stops are few and far between, if your children are just looking forward to the arrivals at the infrequent way stations, they'll be bored during the long segments in between and they will miss a lot of beautiful scenery along the way.

Remember, though, that the destination is part of the journey too. As such, the destination can be as much of a contributor to happiness as any other point of the trip. Successes that are found at the end of the journey can be a source of profound satisfaction and joy, both of which can contribute to happiness as long as the destination is meaningful to your children. The benefits of seeing the destination as only one piece of the journey rather than its only point is that if children do not arrive at their desired destination, though they may feel badly about it, they can nonetheless feel happiness from positive aspects of the journey, thus reducing the effect of the poor outcome on their evaluation of the journey and on their overall happiness

Contributors to Happiness

By understanding how happiness develops, you can offer your children perspectives and experiences that will encourage their happiness. Recent research provides us with some insights into what enables people to be happy. What makes these factors so important is that they are all within your children's control so they can actively engage in experiences that foster their own happiness.

For all the different areas to follow, teach your children how to experience happiness by using the strategies I've discussed throughout this book; talking to them, being a good role model, establishing value expectations, highlighting examples of these areas from your family's lives as well as from others your children know, rewarding good behavior and having consequences for bad behavior.

Self-Esteem

One powerful contributor to happiness is self-esteem. Children who feel loved, safe, and capable tend to be happy people. Self-esteem is important to happiness because it gives children a sense of security that establishes a position of strength from which they can engage the world. This attitude enables children to approach life with confidence and with few doubts, worries, or fears. Self-esteem also offers children a strong sense of competence, in which they view themselves not only as generally able people, but as having specific skills to master important aspects of their lives. This faith in their abilities can facilitate success, which can cultivate happiness. It also reduces uncertainty and anxiety, which can detract from happiness.

American popular culture doesn't want your children to have self-esteem. It foists lies about how to build self-esteem in your children. Popular culture tells children that they'll feel good about themselves if they are more attractive or wear the right clothing. Reality TV shows, such as *The Swan* and *Extreme Makeover,* convey these messages through powerful images and treacly testimonials. Children who lack self-esteem don't feel loved or valued, so they look to others for validation. They also lack self-respect, thus making themselves vulnerable to persuasive messages that tell them how they can feel good about themselves. Without self-esteem, children don't see themselves as capable people, so they're more likely to be passive recipients rather than active participants in their lives. They will also be more likely to rely on others—such as popular culture—to tell them what they should think, feel, and do.

Autonomy, a key quality associated with self-esteem, is another positive influence on happiness. Children who feel that they possess the ability to make decisions and choose the direction that their lives will take tend to be happy. This self-determination provides children with the belief that they have power over their lives and can change things they don't like about it. This sense of independence encourages happiness because children learn what makes them happy and unhappy, and they can choose to follow the road to happiness. American popular culture doesn't want your children to be autonomous people either. In fact, it wants them to be dependent and needy. This inability to act decisively and to make choices on their own makes children highly impressionable and causes them to be "sitting ducks" for messages from popular culture, including advertising, video games, and peer pressure.

Positive Attitude

American popular culture wants your children to have bad attitudes. It wants your children to be unhappy and pessimistic. The very name BratzPack dolls (mentioned in chapter 1) suggests to children that being a brat—spoiled, demanding, critical—is to be aspired to. The angry, rebellious, and negative language of punk, hip-hop, and metal music tells children that it's cool to have a bad attitude. With this negative attitude, children search desperately for anything that will make them feel happier. Popular culture is only too happy to bring a little cheer to their lives, for example, through buying new clothes, eating fast-food, or playing a video game. But there is a price to pay for this good cheer, both literally and metaphorically.

We've all seen children who just have a great attitude about things. They're positive, optimistic, and hopeful. They see a world filled with sunlight and warmth rather than clouds and cold. These children tend to be happy because they see the "glass half-full," meaning they expect good things to happen to them. "What's not to be happy about?" is their view of life.

Children with positive attitudes are more likely to express gratitude, which has been found to be strongly related to happiness. Children who are grateful for the opportunities they're given and convey genuine gratitude to those who help them have been found to be happy people. When was the last time your children showed true gratitude to you? I don't mean the perfunctory "Thanks, Mom (or Dad)" that comes out of children in rote and with little conviction. I mean the deliberate, thoughtful, and earnest expression of appreciation: "Dad (or Mom), I really appreciate everything you do for me." Sadly, American popular culture tells your children that it's uncool for them to thank you. "Why should I thank my parents? They're just doing what they're supposed to do and anyway, I deserve it." That type of statement comes from an unhappy child, I assure you.

Ownership

Children don't just gain happiness from any journey on which they embark. We all know children—perhaps those with an early talent in school, sports, or the performing arts—who are on a journey to achievement, but their parents are the ones driving and they're forced to sit in the backseat and go along for the ride. Instead, happiness comes from children having ownership of their journey. Ownership comes from the journey having personal meaning to children based on it being consistent with and affirming of their deeply held values. Ownership is found in children who love the activities in which they are involved. With this strong connection, children choose for themselves the road they take and the destination at which they wish to arrive. By engaging in activities that coincide with their most basic values and for which they have a great love, children feel that they own their journey, that it is truly theirs. They feel confident with the road they have chosen. These children feel great fulfillment and joy in each step of the journey. They also experience greater equanimity, regardless of the destination at which they arrive. Finally, they find happiness on the road they have taken.

American popular culture doesn't want your children to have ownership of their lives. It doesn't want them to feel personally connected with the journey they are taking. Children without ownership will be constantly looking for road signs to tell them where to go and billboards to tell them what they want along the way. And popular culture has the biggest, brightest, and most enticing signs and billboards on your children's journey.

Passion

Another essential contributor to your children's happiness is a passion for something in their lives, be it writing, history, music, soccer, or some other avenue. Passionate children are happy children because there is something in their lives that they absolutely love to do. Children's passions engage, absorb, and thrill them. They appreciate the minutiae of what they do. These children can get lost for hours in their passions. For example, the reader who savors every word of every book she pours through. The cellist who listens to Yo Yo Ma for hours on end. The astronomer of the future who gazes at and catalogs the stars every evening. Just being involved in any way in the activities for which they have a passion makes these children happy.

American popular culture doesn't want your children to be passionate about their lives. It doesn't value passion and doesn't encourage your children to seek out such a deep connection. Popular culture wants your children to make shallow connections with things that make it more money, for example, the aforementioned passion for video games and shopping. In a short time, children get bored with their purchases and need to buy more stuff in the misguided belief they will feel passion for them. Popular culture pushes children to pursue activities that meet its own needs, for example, listening to music and watching movies. Without passion, children are easily bored and lack initiative and creativity to relieve their boredom. They are dependent on external sources for excitement and fun. And there is no more immediate and powerful source of stimulation for children than popular culture. Parents exacerbate this dependence by choosing the expedient route for entertaining their children—handing them over to popular culture—

rather than finding activities that engage their children, from which they might find a passion. The result is that many children believe they are passionate when, in reality, they are simply readily entertained by a stimulating form of popular culture. When I ask kids whether they have a passion for something, about half of them raise their hands. The activities that they have a passion for range from the predictable (e.g., sports, music, dance) to the professional (e.g., writing, science, reading) to the absurd (e.g., video games, shopping). I tell kids that video games can't be a passion…unless they create the video game!

Children without a passion are easy prey for the messages from popular culture because they are in search of interest, stimulation, and a bond with anything. Because the attractions of popular culture are so readily available and give the brief and superficial feeling of passion, passionless children welcome the opportunity to feel anything that approximates a connection with an activity. In contrast, children who care deeply about something will usually think twice when faced with a temptation from popular culture to go down a bad road and will choose the road down which their passion leads them.

Given all of the alluring enticements offered by American popular culture, for example, conspicuous consumption, alcohol, illegal drugs, and sex, a passion for an activity acts as a shield from American popular culture and can literally save your children's lives.

The wonderful thing about children having a passion in their lives is that it provides them with so many sources of happiness. If one area of their lives isn't going well, the others keep them inspired. Sure, these children love to be successful and gain all of the external benefits, including good grades, awards, trophies, but these are not the overriding reasons for why they do what they have a passion for. Learning new things, being challenged, becoming more skilled, sharing their passion with others, and feeling inspired are all tremendous sources of happiness. What I learned from happy children is that they are entranced by and revel in so many aspects of their lives and it is this total absorption in their involvement that makes them both successful and happy.

Mattie J. T. Stepanek was born with a rare neuromuscular disease called dysautonomic mitochondrial myopathy. From birth, Mattie was bound to a wheelchair and required constant medical attention. It sounds overwhelming for a child, but Mattie had a immense passion for life. From an early age, Mattie used writing to help him cope with his physical challenges. He wrote his first poetry at 5 years old, and at age 11 his first book of poetry made the *New York Times* bestseller list. Mattie also became a spokesperson for the Muscular Dystrophy Association and spoke to children and adults alike around the country about his illness as well as about global tolerance and peace. Despite his difficulties and his knowledge that those with his disease do not live long, Mattie pursued his life with gusto and saw every day as a gift. Mattie died on June 22, 2004, at age 13, of complications from his disease.

Of course, it's impossible for children to be passionate about everything they do. There will be many things that children simply don't like to do. At the same time, I've found that passionate children hate fewer things and are less resistant to experiences for which they have no particular affinity. They are more willing to do their best, even in areas in which they have little interest. In other words, passionate children are more willing to "suck it up." Passionate children value commitment and quality in all of their endeavors, and take pride in a job well done in whatever they do. Because children with a passion find interest, satisfaction, and joy in the minutiae of the activities which they care deeply about, they're able to find small nuggets of these qualities in the most disliked of activities. They're able to find enough good in things to keep them engaged and motivated to do their best when most children would give up or give as little effort as is necessary.

The challenge for parents is to help children develop a deep connection with life. The foundation of children becoming passionate comes from you, including passion in your family-value culture. Making the pursuit of a passion a value that you incorporate into your life and the lives of your family members will ensure that your children come to see its value and make it a priority of their own.

Teaching the value of passion begins with your living a life of passion. Having activities in your life that you care deeply about shows your children that passion is something that you value. You can also talk to your children about the meaning of passion and how it can enrich their lives. Sharing your passions allows your children to see and experience the inspiration, excitement, and joy of activities that mean a great deal to you and encourages them to develop a passion on their own.

Exposing your children to many diverse activities gives them the opportunity to find one with which they feel a deep connection.

Meaningful Goals

Children with ownership in their lives and passion are on a journey in which they have chosen the route and the destination. Their "road map" is based on goals they set for themselves that are grounded in their ownership of and passion for particular areas of their lives. These goals have profound meaning to children because they are connected to their most basic values and to their ownership and passions. These meaningful goals are a powerful source of happiness because children are engaging in activities that they love; setting, working toward, and achieving those goals give them immense satisfaction and joy.

American popular culture doesn't want your children to have meaningful goals. It doesn't want your children to learn about the value and satisfaction of setting and achieving goals. Popular culture wants your children to be slackers who don't care about anything and don't want to do anything of value in their lives. Fad diets, get-rich-quick spam, and game shows that rocket people to fame and fortune are just a few of the ways that popular culture discourages your children from striving for meaningful goals. Children with no meaningful goals are prime candidates for indoctrination by popular culture because their lives are devoid of meaning, purpose, or direction and they lack the desire to be proactive in any part of their lives. Popular culture is happy to provide these children with the appearance of meaning and direction—watching television, listening to music, playing video games, spending money on stuff—however shallow and valueless it is.

You can help your children develop meaningful goals by first educating them about their importance. Giving them examples from your own life and from people they know can bring the idea of goals to life. You can then guide them in setting goals for themselves. The emphasis should be on goals that reflect your family-value culture and encourage success and happiness. As your children achieve their goals, you can point out what enabled them to reach those goals and to help them adjust future goals as needed. You can also help your children to connect positive emotions (such as pride and inspiration) with their goals by sharing similar experiences you have had and by asking them how they feel when they have worked hard and achieved a goal.

Balance

American popular culture has communicated to parents that if their children are to be successful—as it defines success, of course—they must specialize at a very early age. We see children who only play golf, chess, or the flute, or who are forced to study constantly to the exclusion of other activities that they might enjoy, that would be healthy for them, and that might make them happy. Parents say that children must make sacrifices if they want to be successful. But is your children's happiness a sacrifice worth making?

The unhappiest children I work with are those who lead unbalanced lives. They spend most of their time in one activity. Their self-esteem—and the self-esteem of their parents—becomes based on how they perform in that one activity. Though deep immersion in one area can be a source of great happiness, it also has its dangers. The problem is that things will not always go well in that one activity. There will be times when children will experience setbacks and failures. They will experience boredom, disenchantment, and frustration. If the one activity is all that your children have, you will have some very unhappy children on your hands.

Balanced children derive happiness from many outlets. Most of these children are involved in several activities that give them great fulfillment, for example, sports or fitness participation, involvement in spiritual or cultural activities, reading, going to movies, spending time with family and friends. Children who have balance in their lives will still have those negative feelings when things don't go well in the area they are committed to. But, because their self-esteem is not based solely on one activity and other parts of their lives bring them happiness, they're still able to maintain their happiness. Difficulties in one part of the lives of balanced children have a much less detrimental effect because there are so many other sources of happiness to which they can turn to remain happy.

Commitment to one activity, though potentially harmful, is also inevitable in our achievement-oriented culture. This singular devotion can be a source of meaning and growth and a positive influence on children's lives. It will also create significant imbalance. The ultimate impact of this imbalance will depend on whether children can find *balance in the imbalance*. What this means is that, even when their general lives are unbalanced, children find ways to fit small doses of balance into their busy lives. For the serious student, it's contributing to student government. For the committed athlete, it's his religious devotion and church activities. For the devoted musician, it's time spent with her grandmother. These experiences expand the otherwise narrow focus in the lives they lead and provide a healthy perspective on its place in their lives. These outlets are their opportunity to escape from the intensity of their lives and to find happiness by engaging in "meaningless fun" or "meaningful experiences." Many otherwise imbalanced and happy children comment that it is this balance time that "keeps me sane."

American popular culture wants your children to be imbalanced. Children see young stars, like the NBA player, LeBron James, or the actress, Hilary Duff, who achieved stardom at young ages. Or children are told by popular culture that they must sacrifice balance and, for example, join "all-star" traveling sports teams or take piano or dance classes five days a week to become superstars. Children who are out of balance are at risk of falling over—metaphorically—and will look anywhere they can for a helping hand to keep them propped up. When things aren't going well in that singular part of their lives and they have no other ways to find happiness, imbalanced children will look for the most immediate and readily accessible means to feel less unhappy. As usual, popular culture is more than willing to lend a hand and offer children things that will make them feel good and take their mind off their unhappiness, but, in the long run, will only add to their unhappiness.

You have the most influence over how much balance your children have in their lives. At a young age, you choose what activities your children participate in. As your children become more involved in a particular activity, you often decide their level of involvement. Because your children aren't mature enough to understand how balance affects them, it is up to you to monitor their lives—and your family's—and make deliberate decisions about how to maintain balance in your family's lives.

Be a Human Being

American popular culture doesn't want you to raise human beings. Instead, it wants to create "human consumings" whose primary purpose in life is to spend, devour, and accumulate. Human consumings buy, buy, buy in the mistaken belief that it will bring them happiness. When human consumings aren't sated by their latest purchase, they assume that they just didn't buy the right thing or they haven't bought enough of it to make them happy. They just need to buy the bigger, more expensive thing and then they'll be happy. You can observe ravenous young human consumings every day in the malls, buying clothes and shoes "they absolutely must have!" You can find this common species of animal at Best Buy and Circuit City salivating over the newest home-entertainment products. You can see the human consumings with the biggest appetites at car dealerships eyeing their prey and ready to make the kill.

Happy children don't find happiness in consumption. Their happiness comes from being *human beings*, not human consumings. *Being* involves children finding happiness not in things, but in experiences, relationships, and activities that offer meaning, satisfaction, and joy. The ability to just be grounds happy children in who they are rather than what they own, and gives them control over what brings them happiness. Children who are human beings, rather than human consumings, gain little value from the "stuff" itself. Instead, they only buy products that enrich the experiences, activities, and relationships in which they invest themselves.

Whether your children become human consumings or human beings is entirely up to you. The values you live by that act as the foundation for your family-value culture will dictate how your children value themselves. If consumption is part of your family-value culture— if you are a human consuming—your children will undoubtedly become human consumings who are "ripe for the picking" by American popular culture and its messages of conspicuous consumption. If, however, you value being over consuming—and you are a human being—your children will develop into human beings with little interest in what popular culture has to offer.

Relationships

One of the most robust findings in the research on happiness is that people who have strong relationships—feeling close to and connected with others—tend to be the happiest people. The opportunity to give and receive love, friendship, and support from family, friends, classmates, coworkers, and others is essential to happiness. Happy people, as a rule, are closer to their families, have more close friends, have larger social networks, join more organizations, and are generally more sociable than unhappy people.

The reasons why this relationship exists is unclear. It may be that this connection is hardwired into us. As beings who are dependent on extended social groups—families, communities, countries—for our safety, well-being, and prosperity, this relationship may persuade us to seek out others, which benefits us individually and collectively. Perhaps positive feedback from others—love, respect, encouragement—is the most readily available source of happiness, compared to, for example, grades in school or results in sports, which require considerable effort and can't always be counted on to bring us happiness. Social relationships may also reduce stress, increase feelings of security, foster better problem solving, and generate other positive emotions, all of which help create an environment more conducive to happiness. Regardless of the reasons, helping your children surround themselves with healthy relationships is an essential contributor to their happiness.

American popular culture doesn't want your children to have healthy social relationships because they act as a buffer against popular culture's incursions into their lives. Children who are overscheduled don't have time to play with their friends. Home entertainment centers and portable and car DVD players inhibit meaningful interaction even when children are present. The Internet culture encourages "virtual" relationships at the expense of real human contact. Popular culture preys on isolated, lonely, and disenfranchised children who are desperate for any kind of connection with others, even if that connection is temporary, distant, or virtual. Popular culture also wants to control the relationships that your children do have, ensuring that they are friends with its allies, that is, other children who have been brainwashed by popular culture. Children who have good relationships with family, friends, teachers, and others have less of a need for attention, stimulation, and acceptance, so they're less vulnerable to appeals from popular culture that may make them feel important, excited, or popular.

Giving to Others

Americans, in their pursuit of the happiness that American popular culture promises them, often look in the wrong directions. We're preoccupied with looking inside ourselves to find happiness. To that end, we engage in psychotherapy, meditate, and read self-help books to uncover our internal obstacles to happiness. Or people look for happiness outside of themselves in the form of wealth, fame, materialism, drug and alcohol use, and other forms of gratification. But happiness can't be found down either of these roads.

I believe that your children will ultimately find happiness outside of themselves, by giving of themselves to others. Have you ever met a selfish, spoiled, needy child who is also happy? No, I haven't either, Why, you ask? Because being spoiled and selfish are entirely incompatible with being happy. And have you ever met a caring, unselfish child who gives as much as he or she gets? Happy or unhappy? Happy, of course. Why?

There is something profoundly nourishing about putting others needs ahead of our own and helping others find happiness. Giving to others somehow touches us in a very deep way and provides a feeling of meaning, satisfaction, and joy that can't be found elsewhere. Teachers, nurses, social workers, and others in the helping professions, are some of the happiest people I know. I believe it is because, in putting their own needs aside to help others, their own deepest needs are met.

Let me have a former client, a 14-year-old girl whom I will call Kristi, who learned this lesson, tell you. "Remember how I told you that I used to be a really selfish kid? It was all about me. I wanted the world to revolve around me and I didn't want to do anything that I didn't feel like doing. Then my mom got sick and I had to take care of her after school and on weekends. At first I hated it because it was taking time away from my friends. But after a while I realized how much I loved her and without even thinking about it, I just threw out all of the junk in my life, including some of my friends who were just as selfish as I was. I just loved being with my mom and I was so grateful and happy, even though I was also sad that she was sick. Once she got better (thankfully), I started babysitting and tutoring little kids at my church every week. Then I had this big epiphany the other day when I was with them (I just learned that word and I'm using it all the time now!) that taking care of my mom and my work at my church was totally not about me. I would get so wrapped up in them that I just felt this amazing peace inside of me. When I'm with the kids, they are my total focus and it makes me so happy to help them that I feel like I'm gonna explode. I just realized that I feel that same way when I'm with my family and friends, but it's not as strong. I see now that I'm happiest when it's not all about me."

What Kristi is saying is that your children will experience happiness when they're not focused on themselves, trying to get their needs met, or trying to feel good. Instead, they'll be happiest when they're connected to and invested in others, when they're totally absorbed in something that isn't about them. Children who are raised in a healthy family-value culture are happiest when they're giving of themselves to others, yet without realizing it, they're getting so much in return.

Emerging Values

Emotions, such as happiness, are one of the most neglected aspects of children's development. Emotions play an essential role in your children's happiness, relationships, and achievement efforts. Despite this importance, your children have few opportunities to develop what I call *emotional mastery*; the ability to understand, experience, and express emotions in a healthy way. Emotional mastery gives your children the perspective and the tools they need to respond positively to challenges they will face throughout their lives.

In fact, most of the messages that your children get prevent them from learning anything about emotions. American popular culture certainly doesn't offer your children examples of healthy emotions. On television and in the movies, children either see people who are totally out of control emotionally (e.g., violent rages or out-of-proportion sobbing) or who are totally repressed emotionally (e.g., seething inside but not showing it). Popular culture encourages boys to express only "manly" emotions, such as anger and aggressiveness. At the same time, it has largely made it taboo for boys (and men) to express any form of emotional vulnerability, such as hurt or sadness. Popular culture teaches girls to use their emotions as tools of affectation and manipulation. There are few healthy role models in popular culture for children to learn from about how to develop emotional mastery.

American popular culture also presents children with a myriad of contradictions about emotions. Many television shows, for example, reality TV, game shows, and soap operas, highlight unhealthy emotions, such as greed, envy, and humiliation. At the same time, much of advertising directed toward children is aimed at evoking intensely positive emotions, for example, feelings of fun, excitement, and joy (usually associated with drinking a certain beverage, eating a particular food, or wearing the right clothing). Also, as I mentioned previously, popular culture tells children that they should always feel good emotions. Popular culture offers children few chances to learn about what emotions are, how to recognize what they're feeling, or how emotions affect their lives.

Yet emotional mastery is a necessary part of becoming a vital, mature adult. Emotional mastery is an essential emerging value that can evolve as your children learn about and experience happiness. The ability for children to recognize, understand, and express happiness is part and parcel to gaining mastery over all of their emotions. But children's lives can't just be filled with pleasant emotions, such excitement, joy, contentment, and happiness. They'll also experience difficult emotions, including fear, frustration, anger, disappointment, and sadness. That's just the way life is. These emotions certainly don't feel good, but they are an important part of learning how to deal with life's inevitable ups and downs. They're also necessary if children want to feel all of the good emotions. Emotions are two sides of the same coin. Children can't feel good emotions unless they also allow themselves to feel so-called bad emotions. What makes emotions healthy or not is not whether children feel them, but rather whether they understand what causes their emotions and how they express and resolve them. By making emotional mastery a value in your family-value culture, you create an environment in which the experience, expression, and discussion of emotions are not only acceptable, but encouraged.

Gaining emotional mastery will serve your children well in their battle against American popular culture. Children who have emotional mastery will be better prepared to resist its unhealthy emotional messages because, as sophisticated emotional beings, they will recognize the emotional messages for what they are—blatant attempts at manipulation. Because children with emotional mastery have an active and rewarding emotional life, they have little need to gain emotional sustenance from other sources, particularly those that are exploitive, shallow, and short lived.

Emotional mastery can be taught to your children in much the same way that you teach other values. You can talk to them about what emotions are, their meaning in your life, and the kinds of emotions that we all feel. You can model healthy emotional expression when you feel frustration, anger, or sadness. You can coach your children through their emotional experiences, helping them to recognize the emotions they're feeling, why they're feeling those emotions, how they can express them in a positive way, and, if needed, how they can resolve the emotions to their benefit. What's important is that this education is a clear part of your family-value culture and is incorporated into your daily lives.

Another value that emerges from happiness (as well as the other values I talk about) is just plain *goodness*. Happy children are nice, thoughtful, caring, decent people. Though a bit amorphous I suppose, the value of basic goodness is much neglected in our society. American popular culture certainly doesn't honor goodness. It venerates badness, glorifying athletes who behave immorally or break the law, and giving second (and third and fourth) chances to celebrities who offer little reason to deserve such consideration. Popular culture tells your children that if they want to be accepted, they have to be "bad," "cool," and have a 'tude (attitude). What a profound compliment it is when the first thing parents tell me about their child is that he or she is just a good kid. And what a joy it is when I meet children (particularly teenagers, who are most vulnerable to the pressures to be cool) who are open, kind, and giving people.

CHAPTER 9

Family
(Make the Joneses Jealous)

American Popular Culture on the Offensive

The women's professional tennis tour is a breeding ground for parents who have lost perspective and hurt their children in pursuit of wealth and fame. In 1990, Jennifer Capriati, at age 13, became the youngest player ever to reach a Grand Slam semifinal. Guided by her father, Stefano, who many believed was using Jennifer as a meal ticket, she rose quickly in the rankings. But, in late 1993, at age 18, Jennifer burned out, left the game, and was arrested for shoplifting and possession of marijuana. Her police mug shot became an enduring image of youthful promise and success gone bad. Only after a long break from the game and a slow comeback as a more mature and somewhat world-weary young woman was Jennifer able to gain the achievements—and peace of mind—that she was unprepared for as a young teenager. Mary Pierce, another tennis prodigy who went on to win a Grand Slam tournament, was also guided by her father, Jim. Having verbally abused Mary's opponents and physically abused Mary, Jim was banned from attending tour events and the Women's Tennis Association established the "Jim Pierce Rule," which prohibits abusive behavior by players, coaches, and relatives. Other tennis parents who have been accused of overinvolvement and potentially abusive behavior include: Melanie Molitor, mother of former number one, Martina Hingis; Peter Graf, father of Grand Slam winner, Steffi; Richard Williams, father of Venus and Serena; and Damir Dokic, father of Jelena.

These parents, and many others in other sports, dance, music, education, and chess, start with the best of intentions: to help their children realize their potential. But then they cross a line. They lose sight of why they're involved and their children's welfare is no longer their primary concern. What causes parents to make such a monumental shift in their approach to their children? For many parents, it's because of problems of their own, such as emotional, career, or marriage difficulties. These problems create a need for fulfillment that they can't find in their own lives, so they place this burden on their children's shoulders. In this vulnerable position, they're easily seduced by the powerful messages of wealth and fame offered by American popular culture. Once these parents "sell out," they head down a road that rarely has a happy ending for the children, the parents themselves, or their families.

Another reason is that American popular culture wants to destroy your family. With your family in ruins, it can more easily shape your children in a form of its own choosing that fulfills its own needs rather than your children's or your family's. Popular culture can take over as the dominant force in your children's lives and instill in them the values that it wants them to have, not ones that are best for them.

So American popular culture convinces you to push your children maniacally to excel in every aspect of their lives, to overschedule them, to participate in weekend sports tournaments in distant cities, to eat fast-food dinners between activities, to give children unfettered access to video games, DVDs, and television, and to have no free time for your family. Is this road good for you and your family? Rarely. Does it feel like this road has no exits? Probably so. So who benefits from such an unhealthy family? Isn't it obvious? American popular culture. The busier and more stressed out you and your family are, the more you'll turn to popular culture for convenience and relief. And for American popular culture, it's all money in the bank—at your expense!

The Runaway Train

Most families were different fifty years ago. During the week, fathers would work hard, mothers would take care of the children and tend to the house, and children would go to school, come home, do their homework, and play. Families would sit down every evening for dinner together and then, as a treat, would watch a few select shows on television. Kids also played musical instruments, took dance lessons, and families played games together. On weekends, the children would play pick-up games with other kids in the neighborhood, the parents would visit with friends, or the family would take a trip together periodically.

Times have changed. Now, both you and your spouse may have careers and both of you are probably responsible for tending to your children. If you're divorced, your family is fragmented, and you may not even get support from your spouse. Your days are spent working and your late afternoons and evenings are spent shuttling your children from school to sports practice to performing-arts lessons. Your children have school all day, followed by extracurricular activities (often more than one per day), homework, and perhaps some time with friends squeezed in somewhere, usually by phone or over the Internet. They often stay up late to try to get everything done for the next day. Breakfast and dinner are usually eaten on the run to and from work or school, and meals together are more the exception than the rule. Weekends involve taking your children to sports competitions or artistic practices or performances, often far from home. Despite all of the time- and energy-saving amenities at your disposal, life seems so much more complicated than it used to be.

You probably feel huge societal pressure to give your children every possible opportunity to achieve and succeed—all at once! You're afraid that if you don't give your children "essential" educational, athletic, or creative experiences at an early age, their development will be stunted somehow. You worry that your children will fall behind their peers. You don't want to be seen as a bad parent. You absolutely must "keep up with the Joneses!"

So you put your children in Gymboree and baby music classes, you have them watch and listen to "Brainy Baby—Right Brain," "Bee Smart Baby Multilingual Vocabulary Builder," and "Baby Genius— Mozart and Friends." Says one mother, "You want to make sure you're doing everything you can for your child, and you know everyone else uses 'Baby Einstein,' so you feel guilty if you don't."

But here's some news for you: None of this accelerates your children's development. American popular culture has marketed child-development products by preying on your fears of permanently stunting your children's growth. These companies get rich while your children gain no benefit! Early childhood experts agree that emotional and social skills act as the foundation of more sophisticated cognitive development. They suggest more basic and natural activities to help stimulate your children's intellectual development, for example, reading and talking with them, holding them, and playing with them. In other words, children's daily lives offer them plenty of what's needed for them to develop at a normal and healthy pace.

This compulsion to "fast forward" your children's development hurts them, you, and your family. Your children feel pressure to achieve and are overwhelmed, stressed out, and unhappy. You never seem to have enough time or energy, and you have little opportunity to meet your own needs. You feel exhausted, resentful, and frustrated. Your family suffers because everyone is moving in different directions, constantly rushing from one place to another. There is little time to spend together, and every family member is too tired and stressed to enjoy themselves or the family. You feel like your family is on a runaway train that you can't stop and you can't jump off of.

The Professionalization of Youth Sports

Nowhere is this phenomenon more evident than in changes in youth sports over the last twenty-five years (though these same ideas, you will see, can easily be applied to other achievement activities, such as dance, music, chess, and spelling bees). Youth sports used to be about play, fun, and fitness. Neighborhood children would get together on their own and organize pick-up games, set rules, keep score, and self-referee. Parents were nowhere to be found. Yes, there was Little League baseball and other organized sports, but they were mostly local and seasonal, and few parents had any great ambitions for their children beyond the fun of being on a team.

Youth sports are no longer about children these days. Says Ashley Hammond, a leading soccer coach and league organizer in Montclair, New Jersey, "It is too embedded in what is a highly competitive culture. The baby boomer parents generally have been very motivated, very successful people in life, and they want to transfer all that to their kids. People talk about youth sports and say, 'This is only for fun.' If you talk to parents, they might say that, but they don't mean it. They want to their kid to get ahead." With the emphasis on winning and the potential riches that can now come with success in professional sports, parents have fallen for the messages of American popular culture that their children can become Olympic or professional athletes, and rich and famous, if only they start their children early enough and push them hard enough. As the *New York Times* writer, Bill Pennington, puts it, "To many people, this is yet another example of the modern American compulsion to overdo everything. It is a cross between a 1950's keeping-up-with-the-Joneses sensibility and a 1990's chase for the very best of everything."

Perhaps the most blatant and painful example of this change in the objectives of youth sports is the proliferation of traveling teams and clubs among baseball, basketball, soccer, gymnastics, figure skating, and other sports for ever-younger children. Children as young as 7 and 8 years old are now specializing in one sport, practicing daily, have private coaches, are sent away from home for better training, and travel hundreds and thousands of miles to competitions, all with the goal of raising athletic superstars. In most cases, this track is not only a waste of parents' time and money, it's a disservice to your children and an abuse of their childhood. The chances of your children earning an athletic scholarship, much less becoming professional or Olympic athletes, is miniscule. One study conducted by the National Collegiate Athletic Association found that about 6 percent of high-school football, baseball, basketball, hockey, and soccer players receive college scholarships and, of that group, fewer than 1 in 10,000 play professionally. For those lucky few who reach the professional ranks, the average career span of baseball, basketball, and football players is four to five years. In other words, the chances of your children becoming professional athletes is almost zero. Your children have a much better chance of becoming doctors or lawyers.

The fact is that there are only two sports in which children need to focus at such an early age: girls' figure skating and girls' gymnastics. This is because girls often reach their competitive peaks before they fully mature physically, although the performances of the world champions, Michelle Kwan (24-year-old figure skater) and Svetlana Khorkina (25-year-old gymnast), would suggest otherwise. There is no need to specialize until 12 or 13 years old—at the earliest—because athletes in most sports, for example, football, baseball, basketball, tennis, golf, and most other sports, don't reach their prime until well into their twenties.

A powerful indication of the problems with this change in youth sports is the 70 percent drop-out rate from organized sports of children between ages 10 and 13, often because the singular devotion to a sport and pressure from parents takes away the fun, makes the sport work rather than play, and causes children to have to sacrifice other valued parts of their lives. In recent years, children have also been moving in droves to so-called alternative sports, such as skateboarding and snowboarding, because they're less organized and far away from parents. But American popular culture is corrupting these sports as well. The cover story of the September 21, 2003 issue of the *New York Times Magazine* about a sponsored 5-year-old skateboarder with professional contracts shows how popular culture is always on the prowl for new avenues into the hearts and souls of children. Professional skateboarders now make hundreds of thousands of dollars a year from sponsors and competitions. Alternative-sport events, such as the X Games and Gravity Games, have gone mainstream, with major corporate sponsorships, network television coverage, and big-money purses. Alternative-sport video games and equipment and fashion merchandising have made the likes of Tony Hawk, a skateboarding icon, a multimillionaire. Your children can run to other sports, but they can't hide. If there's money to be made, American popular culture will find and exploit them.

Stop That Train!

You can easily get caught on this runaway train of activity. You can be seduced by society's messages that say that you will be a bad parent if you don't get your kids on the fast track as soon as possible. Your challenge is to recognize how this lifestyle is affecting your family. Ask yourself whether it's worth it. Despite feeling that you're on a runaway train, you actually can stop it if you want. But the train won't stop just because you wish it to. Look at your family life with a critical eye. Examine and reconnect with your values (or change them). Make some deliberate choices about the kind of family life you want to have. In this process, you'll be able to find the brakes for that runaway train, and, perhaps for the first time ever, create a family life that is consistent with your values and in the best interests of you, your children, and your family.

At the heart of this process, you must regain the balance that has been lost in your family. Of course, you should consider the importance of giving your children opportunities to experience new activities and to achieve their goals. But you must also keep their participation in those activities in long-term perspective and weigh their involvement against the cost to each member of your family as well as to your family as a whole. This balance means that you must reassert your commitment to family as a part of your family-value culture and make family a priority. You must then make some difficult, yet necessary, choices in establishing a reasonable schedule of your family's activities based on your newly minted commitment to his value-driven balance.

Ironically, this balance will create a family life that will not only make everyone in your family happier and more relaxed, but it will also *make the Joneses jealous!* While the Jones parents are driving their children all over town to practices and lessons, stopping at fast-food on the way, you'll be at home sitting down to family dinner with, reading to, playing with, and talking to your children. While the Jones parents are driving five hours on Friday night to take their soccer-playing child to a tournament (and dragging along their less-fortunate children kicking and screaming), your family can have a picnic at the park on Saturday, your children can play pick-up soccer with other kids in the neighborhood, and you can read a really good book that afternoon. Your family can watch a movie together, go to your house of worship on Sunday morning, visit a museum, and, as a new family tradition, the entire family can help make dinner Sunday night. Gosh, which weekend plans would you rather to have? Let's look at how to make this happen for your family.

Regain Perspective

The first step to stopping the runaway train is to regain perspective. There are so many examples of parents losing perspective with their children, most notably in sports.

- The tragic and fatal beating of a hockey father by another hockey father in Massachusetts.
- Fathers attacking coaches and umpires in Florida and Wisconsin.
- A brawl between more than a dozen parents during a youth soccer game in New Jersey over where a coach was allowed to stand.
- In Houston, parents of a young baseball player sued his school district because his coaches weren't playing him enough to give him a chance at a college scholarship.
- And just so you don't think that women are immune, two mothers assaulted another mother after a youth baseball game in Salt Lake City.

There are probably many egregious examples from the world of music, dance, and chess as well, though not as publicized and perhaps not quite as violent.

The first step toward stopping your runaway train and making the Joneses jealous is to maintain perspective on why your children are involved in activities—such as sports, music, dance, chess, or other achievement activities—and not be seduced by American popular culture's messages of fame and fortune through athletic success. This can be difficult when you're bombarded daily with reality TV talent shows, children's beauty pageants, and young performers, such as Britney Spears and Jessica Simpson, and young athletes, like Maria Sharapova and Carmelo Anthony, making millions of dollars. But if you fall for this pot of gold, you will not only be sorely disappointed, but you will be doing possibly irreparable harm to your children. Let me say this as loudly and clearly as I can: whatever American popular culture tells you about your children's impending superstardom, *it's not going to happen!* Your expectations for your children with regard to activities should be limited to:

- having fun;
- fostering their healthy development;
- love of a lifetime activity;
- appreciation for physical health (if it's a physical activity); and
- the development of life skills that will benefit them later in life.

Everything else—a place on their high-school varsity team, an athletic or music scholarship, or a professional athletic or performing-arts career—is icing on the cake. If you buy into these, and only these, expectations, your children will be as successful as they can be and they will also likely be happy. If you're looking for a bigger return on your investment, you're most likely going to be very disappointed and make your children miserable.

That doesn't mean that it's impossible for your children to achieve greatness—someone has to win the Olympic medals, perform at Carnegie Hall, or become a Grand Master—it's just not very likely. If your children have greatness in them, trying to rush them to the top will actually interfere with them getting there. By accepting the assumption that your children will never achieve superstar status in some area of their lives, two important things happen. You're able to stop the runaway train and put some sanity back into your family's lives because you won't be chasing a pipe dream. You also lift the weight of that expectation off your children's shoulders, so that if they happen to have the inborn talent and the desire to pursue greatness, then they'll be free to do so without you on their backs.

Clarify Your Family Values and Priorities

The next step in stopping the runaway train is to clarify your family values and priorities. A problem with having your family life on a runaway train is that life flies by, you forget what's important to you, and a disconnect occurs between your values and your life. Now is the time to look closely at your family-value culture and see if you're living your daily lives in accordance with it. Here's a helpful exercise. On one side of a piece of paper, list some of the activities that are consistent with your family-value culture. They might include shared family activities, travel, religious or cultural experiences, or being outdoors. Then on the other side of the sheet of paper, list your actual weekly schedule. If yours is like most families' schedules, you will be amazed—and troubled—by how incongruent they are.

Having clarified the activities that are in line with your values, you should now establish and apply the priorities that will guide your family's choices. The priority that most parents mention as the first to fall to the wayside is family dinners. A 2000 study reported a significant relationship between regular family meals and higher school performance, better mental health, reduced drug use, and lower rates of early sexual behavior among teenagers. You don't have to have dinners together every night—that's probably not realistic—but reserving several nights is reasonable. You can also establish some rules for these evenings, such as no telephone calls, television, surfing the Internet, video games, or Instant Messaging, and everyone must help prepare the meal. You can encourage your children's participation by having a rotation of who chooses the meal, so everyone gets to have their favorite meal regularly.

Another neglected priority that many parents speak of is weekend activities together, for example, hiking, visiting museums, or attending their house of worship. These events not only affirm your values about family, but they also expose your children to another important part of your family-value culture and enable your family to share activities that you enjoy. One of the most common, yet objectionable, parts of being on the runaway train is family trips and vacations that are planned around sports or other events in which your children participate. These trips are rarely enjoyable because they often are in locations that are less than desirable, other siblings don't want to be there, and the focus on the event takes so much time and energy that the vacation isn't much of a vacation and your family is exhausted and in need of a vacation after the trip.

Now it's time to make the Joneses really jealous! You should set a time each week when your family does nothing—yes, you heard me, nothing. Perhaps the greatest casualty of this runaway train is family time. Families have so many things going on in their lives that family time has become almost nonexistent. Parents have less time than ever for themselves or to enjoy their children. Children become disengaged from their parents and siblings, and parents lose their influence over their children simply for lack of meaningful contact. So at least once a week just hang out around the house, go to the park, play games. It doesn't matter what you do as long as it is together and has no other purpose beyond enjoying each other as a family.

Limit Your Child's Activities

Now things get a bit more challenging. It's one thing to say that you want to make family a priority and to want to do more things together. It's an entirely more difficult thing to tell your children that they can't do something that they want to do, for example, take skating lessons or go to dance class, or to limit their participation. You must decide what activities your children participate in, how many at one time, and the depth of their involvement. Too often parents allow their children to get involved in an activity simply because their friends do it or it's a popular activity in the neighborhood. Or parents push their children into an activity because they're worried they won't make the Olympics if they don't. Some parents create the problem because they're afraid that if they don't, other parents will look down on them. All of these are bad, knee-jerk reasons for your children being involved in activities.

Setting limits on the number and frequency of activities in which you allow your children to participate is essential to stopping the runaway train your family may be on. I recommend that you restrict your children to two activities during any season and no more than one extracurricular activity per day. With this stricture, you won't be driving from soccer to a snack to dance to dinner to karate and getting home at nine o'clock at night exhausted. I can't tell you what activities you should allow your children to participate in or the depth of their involvement. What I will tell you, though, is to make sure that they're involved for the right reasons, that their participation is consistent with your family values, and that their involvement doesn't interfere with your family as the priority. The important thing is that you approach organizing your family's lives in a thoughtful way. You should understand the benefits and costs of their participation, the benefits and costs to the family (to you and all of your children), and then make deliberate choices that take into account the best interests of your children, of you and your spouse, and of your family as a whole.

I'm not saying that children shouldn't commit themselves to an activity if they enjoy it, or that you shouldn't support that commitment

(I hope it is clear to you how much I value achievement). What I am saying is that you as a family should make that commitment because it will benefit their long-term development and your family won't suffer because of it.

Maintain Balance

Because of the extreme quality of American popular culture and the seemingly limitless options available to children today, it's difficult for children to understand, much less live, the value of balance. Yet a hallmark of a value-driven family is its clear sense of balance. Children gain an appreciation of the value of balance from a family that explores the benefits and costs of various aspects of their lives, sets priorities based on their values, and makes deliberate choices about the lives they lead. Children also experience the value of balance in their lives as part of a family that lives a balanced life. These benefits include satisfaction of most of their needs most of the time, manageable levels of stress, opportunities for both breadth and depth in their experiences, and a healthy level of comfort in their lives. Children learn this process, come to value balance, and begin to create balance in their own lives.

Despite its obvious importance, balance is one of the first values that is lost when your family's life turns into a runaway train. You must make great efforts to find and maintain some semblance of balance in your hectic, multi-activity lives. You want to encourage your children in their activities, but you also want to maintain your family's sanity. Balance is an essential ingredient to family sanity, particularly yours as a parent. Your family life can be thought of as a tightrope walker who carries the long pole to maintain his balance. If the pole has too much weight on one side, the tightrope walker is pulled off the wire and falls to the ground (at least he or she has a safety net). For the tightrope walker to make it across the wire, he or she must keep the pole equally weighted. Similarly, you must make sure your family maintains its balance, otherwise it will also come crashing to the ground.

Striking this balance involves acknowledging and appreciating that your family can't get everything they want, as much as they want, when they want it, all of the time. It also means recognizing that some aspects of your family-value culture may conflict and that these differences must be reconciled. For example, your family might value both cultural growth (which occurs with regular trips to museums) and athletic achievement (which is realized through time-consuming commitment to a sport). When these conflicting values clash, something has to give. Your ability to make deliberate choices and find a balance that meets the overall needs of your children and your family-value culture will determine whether your family is able to maintain control of the train that is your life.

Set Priorities

Every family is unique in its member's personalities, needs, and goals, family relationships, family-value culture, and the activities in which they participate. At the same time, the world in which most families live in twenty-first-century America is not so different regardless of whether you live in a big city or a small town, the Pacific Northwest or the Deep South, because popular culture is so omnipresent and homogenous. Though I can't tell you what values and priorities you should have as you organize your family's lives, I can offer you some food for thought—based on years of exploring this issue with thousands of families—on areas you will want to consider as you decide for yourself how you want to emphasize the value of family in your family.

Physical Health

The health of children in America has reached a crisis point. Studies have found that about one in five children are overweight, more than double the number from twenty years ago. Childhood obesity is responsible for the rise in Type-2 diabetes, high cholesterol and blood pressure. And 70 percent of overweight children become overweight adults, creating even more healthy problems.

Because of this threat, your children's physical health should be a priority in your family-value culture. American popular culture doesn't care about your children's health. In fact, it does everything it can to hurt their health. Fattening foods, candy, and soft drinks cause children to gain weight. Television, DVDs, and video games keep them sedentary. Your children's lives should never interfere with them eating three healthy meals a day—fast-food dinners in the car going from one activity to another doesn't qualify! Your children should have regular opportunities for exercise. Your children should always be able to get to bed at a reasonable hour and should be able to get a good night's sleep on a regular basis (experts say a minimum of eight hours is necessary for children). And your children's physical health should be a priority above of all else because, without their health, all other aspects of their lives will be moot.

Education

Considerable research has demonstrated the value of education in children's lives. Children whose families value education have fewer emotional problems, are less likely to drink alcohol or take drugs, and have lower rates of sexual activity, sexually transmitted diseases, and pregnancy. As adults, they have better-paying jobs, fewer health problems, and lower rates of divorce.

Because of this widespread influence, education is another value that should take precedence in your children's lives. They should have whatever resources are necessary for them to do their best in school, for example, school supplies, computers, and Internet access. Your children should always have time to complete all of their homework assignments as thoroughly as they can. You must stay particularly vigilant about the effects of your children's social lives and their extracurricular activities, such as sports and the performing arts, on their efforts in school. You should establish clear expectations that communicate the value of education to your children, and be ready to follow through with appropriate consequences when they start to place something other than their education as a priority. You must recognize when you too place other activities over education. Your children should also be given opportunities each week to immerse themselves in unstructured educational activities, such as reading, discussing current events, and playing educational games.

Play

Play is becoming a dinosaur in the lives of today's children. According to studies, school-age children's playtime decreased by 25 percent and older children's playtime by 45 percent between 1981 and 1997. Unstructured outdoor activities also declined by 50 percent. Children are just too busy to play these days and many seem to have lost the ability to play. Instead, too often children's play involves sitting in front of a video-game console, television, or computer, which isn't play at all. In allowing their children to engage in this substitute for play, many parents are acting out of sheer expediency; it's just easier letting them be entertained by an electronic box than having to help their children to learn how to really play.

One of the saddest developments in twenty-first-century family life is the play date, in which parents schedule a time during the week in which a group of children are brought together to play. I can just see one kid saying to another, "Wanna get together later this week to play? I'll have my people call your people." This phenomenon is a horrible symptom of the runaway-train life in which so many families are trapped. It probably also reflects the disintegration of neighborhoods, as well as the concern for children's safety, as playgrounds and parks are often deserted out of fear of predatory adults, or are simply being replaced with malls and housing developments.

Another unfortunate development has been the growing popularity of home-entertainment centers. In previous generations, families had a den with a television or a rec room. Backyards were the real entertainment centers, where children climbed on monkey bars, played whiffle ball and tag, and just ran around having fun. But today, a television and stereo are simply not enough. Thirty-two percent of households now have home-theater systems and these entertainment centers have become the center of the family. They have also taken away any incentive for children to play and entertain themselves.

Remember that home-entertainment centers didn't just appear out of nowhere and children didn't buy them for the house. Rather, parents buy them out of their own interests, without consideration of how these often-extravagant systems will affect their children. Most of these parents would be resistant to getting rid of the systems themselves. And they are terrified of their children's reactions if they get rid of them. Because many children have lost the ability to play, they won't know what to do with themselves, and they will let their parents know of their displeasure in the loudest way possible. There is hope for your children, though. Children can be effectively weaned off of television and DVD watching. A recent study found that children who were given alternatives to watching television, who were encouraged to read, and whose parents turned the television set off during dinner reduced their television viewing by 25 percent.

Parents also lose sight of the value of play, seeing it as a distraction from their children's efforts in school. They don't understand how playtime can help their children achieve good grades and get into the best colleges. Schools also contribute to the problem by reducing the amount of free time at school and increasing class and study time. For example, the Atlanta school system dropped recess altogether from its school day, despite the fact that play has been shown to be an essential part of children's development. Play has been found to foster creativity and imagination. It encourages cognitive, emotional, and social skills. Play requires initiative and independence in which children are left to their own devices to entertain themselves. Play helps children with problem solving and decision making. It teaches them how to overcome frustration. Children also learn to play and cooperate with others. And, of course, active play develops motor coordination, enhances physical health, and fights obesity. Contrary to the views held by many schools, breaks actually help children's academic efforts. Breaks relieve stress, refresh and stimulate the mind, release pent-up energy, increase interest, and improve attention.

A nice balance to the value of education is the value of play, in which your children should have time several days a week to experience unstructured play with friends outside during the day and inside in the evenings. The play your children engage in should be thoughtfully considered in terms of how it encourages your children's cognitive, emotional, social, and physical development. Ideally, they should be left to their own devices with little input from you or American popular culture, and be able to play with their friends. And don't forget the main reason children should have plenty of playtime: fun! Though it may be unavoidable, I would recommend that you do everything you can to create an environment that allows your children to play with their friends spontaneously and freely.

Family

As I mentioned earlier in this chapter, the value of family should always be at the forefront of your family-value culture. This value can be expressed in your family sitting down and eating dinner together more times than not each week. The value of family meals cannot be over-stated. One study found that regular family dinners were the strongest predictor of greater academic achievement and reduced behavioral problems, including decreased rates of drug and alcohol use, less sexual activity, and lower risk of suicide. At least several times a week your family should have "hang out" time during which you do something—or nothing—together. Your family should share an activity at least twice a month, such as going for a day hike, visiting a museum, or attending a dance concert. Weekends should involve sharing quality family time. I suggest that at least one weekend each month be open and unplanned, but with the focus on your family sharing experiences.

Creating enduring traditions is a powerful way to strengthen your family and make it a priority. Traditions are commonly seen as activities that hold particular significance to a family that occur on an ongoing basis. Traditions can be major yearly events, such as Thanksgiving or a family vacation, or they can be seemingly minor occasions, for example, Sunday dinners and movie nights. What makes traditions so valuable is that they reflect and reinforce some aspect of your family-value culture, every member of the family values them, and they take precedence over other activities that might interfere with them. Traditions provide families with a sense of familiarity, consistency, cohesiveness, and continuity to their lives. Research supports the value of traditions in raising children. Family traditions have been found to be positively related to childhood behavior, academic achievement, adjustment, and general health.

You can build traditions in your family by selecting a few aspects of life that you would like to honor and preserve, for example, a family camping trip each summer that fosters fun, an appreciation for the outdoors, and "roughing it." If your children are old enough to contribute, include them in your decision making. You may need to explain your rationale for the tradition to your children, particularly if they're older and not initially open to establishing a new family tradition. You must recognize from the outset that traditions can't be created overnight, but rather take hold over time and with shared experience and enjoyment. Essential to creating family traditions is your commitment to making them a priority, particularly in the face of scheduling conflicts that will inevitably arise, for example, a sporting event scheduled during the same period or an invitation from one of your children's friends.

What ultimately make family traditions enduring and rewarding are the positive emotions that each member of your family connects with them, providing warm memories of past traditions and anticipation of future traditions. A good way to keep your family traditions alive is by recording them in some way. Whether with photographs, videos, memorabilia, or storytelling, these reminders make your family traditions more tangible and lasting, and keep the memories and feelings associated with them fresh in your family's minds. They also provide your family with a living history of your lives that can become cherished connections across generations.

Your Family's Mental Health

Creating a family life that's consistent with your family-value culture is not a one-time thing. Rather, it's an ongoing process that involves frequent observation, exploration, and reevaluation of your family's status. To have a healthy and balanced family, you must act like a doctor—both a physician and a psychologist—and give your family regular "check-ups" to ensure everyone is maintaining their health and their sanity. Periodically look at whether your family is overly stressed (recognizing that twenty-first-century American life is inherently stressful). Symptoms of too much stress include frequent illness, difficulty sleeping, loss of appetite, irritability, loss of interest and motivation in previously engaging activities, a decline in school or work performance, social withdrawal, and family conflict.

You can also monitor your family's general level of happiness. Are your children their usual cheery selves? Have you become a crabby, volatile parent? Every member of your family is going to experience ups and downs; that's just life. But when you, your spouse, or one of your children remain down for a long period of time, you should take notice. Whether regularly frustrated, angry, or sad, you can assume that life isn't going as well as it could and a change may need to be made. You want to uncover the cause of the unhappiness and find a solution. Being sensitive to your family's happiness can enable you to nip problems in the bud before they get out of hand.

One thing that you should value immensely is your own sanity. You will not be able to meet the needs of your family and keep everyone sane if you are neglecting your own needs and losing your own sanity. If you're stressed out, tired, or frustrated, you won't be at your best and your entire family will suffer for it. Your ability to stay positive, calm, and relaxed in the chaos that can be family life will affect everyone in your family, so pay attention to your sanity and do what you need to maintain it. Set aside personal time for you and your spouse, perhaps when your children are doing their homework, playing, or asleep, in which you can have some of your own needs met. Take time to read a newspaper or a book, watch something you enjoy on television or a DVD, or share a relaxed, non-family-related conversation with your spouse every week. Because your physical health is paramount to the overall functioning of your family, reserve time for exercise and recreation. Have a social life of your own if that is something you value. Get together with friends away from your children and engage in adult activities—movies, theater, concerts, golf, wine tasting—that you enjoy.

You should also occasionally reassess your family life. It's easy for you to get so caught up in the busyness of life that you don't realize that it has turned back into that runaway train. Ask yourself whether life has taken control of your family or whether your family is still in control of its life. By monitoring your family life periodically, you can be sure that it remains true to your family-value culture and you are doing what needs to be done to ensure that each member of your family is heading down a positive and healthy road.

These recommendations are obviously quite general and open to adaptation. Your family-value culture, the activities in which your children are engaged, and the overall lifestyle your family leads will determine what specific steps you take to make the value of family a priority. Ultimately, you must decide what is best for your children and your family as a whole. I believe that you know when your family has crossed the line. It's up to you to let your values direct you and to make the tough choices that are in your family's best interests. When you let your family-value culture guide you, you will know you're doing the right thing because your family will be happy and you can get some satisfaction knowing that you're making the Joneses jealous!

Emerging Values

Because family is the value our lives are founded upon, it has the ability to teach your children other values that will benefit them in their lives. The most powerful value that emerges from family is the *value of relationships*. As I discussed in chapter 8, the quality of relationships is one of the most significant contributors to happiness and an essential part of helping your children to become vital and contributing adults. By valuing family, you implicitly value relationships of all kinds and your children will internalize this value in their own lives. Just as important, in emphasizing a strong family value, you give your children the experience and tools to develop healthy relationships with others. As an essential value in your family, you show your children how to love others, communicate effectively, express emotions, resolve conflict, share, assume relationship responsibilities, among many other fundamental tools that will enable them to develop good relationships with friends, teachers, coworkers, and others. This emphasis will also demonstrate to your children the benefits of relationships and encourage them to seek out relationships in all parts of their lives.

CHAPTER 10

Compassion
(It's Not All About You)

American Popular Culture on the Offensive

The female pop duo Daphne & Celeste recorded a song called "U.G.L.Y.," which appeared on the *Bring It On* motion picture soundtrack. The song is inspired by an actual cheer, and centers around the chorus "U-G-L-Y, you ain't got no alibi, you ugly, eh-eh, you ugly, eh-eh." The lyrics of the song are disturbing to say the least, with lines such as "I don't mean to insult you, oh wait, yes I do./Your teeth are yellow, they're covered in mold,/You're only fourteen, you look a hundred years old." The entire song, in fact, is a litany of insults ("In the Miss Ugly Pageant, you win first prize.") that are hurtful beyond belief, and are delivered with an attitude that says tearing down someone else is not only okay, but is a sign of strength and popularity. And in case the listener should miss the point, the song climaxes with a spew of slurs:

Quasimodo! Camel breath! Squarehead! Ugly!
Chicken legs! Pig face! Chin like Bubba! Ugly!
Fish lips! Toad licker! Poindexter! Ugly!
Spaghetti arms! Limp butt! Freak show! Ugly!

Can you imagine being so insensitive and mean-spirited? Can you imagine being the recipient of such vitriol? Yet these types of attacks are commonplace in schools across America. As the lyrics of the song above indicate, those who are considered unattractive—or unpopular, poor, or unacceptable in other ways—must face cold, cruel, and heartless attacks from those who are fortunate enough to meet the standards as defined by American popular culture.

What drives children to act so shamefully? Where do they learn that such behavior is appropriate? Children who are this self-centered and callous are often driven by low self-esteem. Despite an air of confidence and bravado, they are insecure and unhappy. The only way they can feel good about themselves—even if only temporarily—is to build themselves up by tearing others down, particularly those who threaten them. For example, in the 2004 film, *Mean Girls* (based on the best-selling book, *Queen Bees and Wannabees*, by Rosalind Wiseman), a high school's queen bee is threatened by a new girl who is both beautiful and intelligent, and goes on a mission to vanquish her through lying, manipulation, and backstabbing. The film's website encourages viewers to become mean girls and offers tips on the "art of sabotage" to help girls rise through the ranks or maintain their mean-girl status, including sabotaging cosmetics, destroying clothes, spreading vicious rumors, and helping other girls to get fat. Whatever happened to kindness and compassion? Where did dignity or just plain civility go?

American popular culture wants your children to be malicious and unfeeling creatures who don't care about anyone or anything but themselves. It wants children to be insensitive to those who are less fortunate than they are, whether that means less physically attractive, affluent, educated, intelligent, social, or some other way. According to popular culture, if others don't measure up, they are thoroughly undeserving of compassion, consideration, or respect. Uncaring children need popular culture to maintain their air of superiority because its messages are often the only things that create the advantage. The beauty, cosmetics, and fashion, in the case of girls, and the macho and muscular world of sports, for boys, are used by these children as shields against their own insecurities and as weapons against those they deem inferior. These children must continue to use popular culture (and buy its products) to maintain their superiority and their victims often succumb to its pressures in order to be accepted.

There is no more powerful example of this message of selfishness than the widespread popularity of the expression, "It's all about me." This expression means that everyone and everything in children's lives should be directed toward meeting their needs. It also tells children that the needs and wishes of others are irrelevant and giving to others is "oh so uncool." What a great marketing slogan for a culture that really wants it to be all about them!

From the simple act of not sharing toys on the playground to bullying by boys and girls alike to widespread corruption in the boardrooms of corporate America to police brutality, there is an epidemic of coldness in America today. For a variety of reasons ranging from economic need ("I gotta get mine while I can") to a decay in values ("Nobody cares about anything anymore") to a decline of the nuclear family ("What do you mean you're getting divorced?") to the migration away from the communities in which we were raised ("My pot of gold is at the end of the rainbow"), an increasing segment of America seems to be driven overwhelmingly by selfishness and callousness, as opposed to social interest. This increased emphasis on our own needs being somehow primary and disconnected from others' needs has resulted in a discounting of the necessary connection we have with others, the value of the communities in which we live, and a lack of interest in the world we inhabit. This wanton disregard for others has caused many in our society to lose their compassion for others.

Some observers thought that the events of September 11, 2001, would change all that. The tragic attacks, they argued, would have a sobering effect on people, pull America together, put life in perspective, and elicit a never-before-seen concern for others. And there was change for a while. American flags were flying everywhere. People were helping each other cope with the national grief. Attendance at houses of worship rose dramatically. Charitable donations for the victims poured in in staggering amounts. Even America's political parties set aside partisan bickering and pulled together to pass laws that were intended to help all Americans. Sadly, that new-found compassion was short-lived. Since the terrorist attacks, life in America has returned to business as usual. American flags, like other popular trends, are rarely seen now. Religious observance has returned to previous levels. More examples of corporate greed emerge weekly. And, of course, it's politics as usual in our nation's capitol.

Even a crisis as profound as no other in history couldn't stop the tidal waves of selfishness and uncaring that have been drowning our country and the values that brought us to this point in time. And it is fed by a popular culture that idolizes and popularizes selfishness for its own selfish purposes.

How the Other Half Lives

This egocentric orientation may appear to be necessary for our own survival. After all, if we want to survive, we have to look out for ourselves first, don't we? Yet a lack of appreciation for our place in our local communities, our country, and the world at large has never been more important. Our world, with its rapid advancements in communication, appears to be shrinking. The influence that people can have on others, both good and bad, has never been greater. Yet so many children are being taught to look no further than the narrow world in which they live. Many children today, because of private education, homogenous neighborhoods, and gated communities, have little exposure to people and cultures different from their own. This limited view of the world has created a myopia that has morphed into an ignorance of and a general disregard for how others live. Because of this restricted upbringing, many children today have no appreciation for how fortunate they are and, instead, have a strong sense of entitlement without any sense of gratitude for what they have been given. Without a broader perspective for their place in the world or how others in the world live, children are not given the opportunity to develop empathy and compassion for those less fortunate than themselves.

What Is Compassion?

Compassion is a word that is bandied around often these days as a "value du jour" in our big-talk, little-action culture of values. Yet, as with most values that are co-opted for a particular agenda, compassion has lost its fundamental meaning and value to people. It isn't explored for its deepest significance or placed in the context of daily life. Thus, the importance of compassion in our lives is not fully appreciated nor expressed in our daily lives.

To better understand compassion, it's helpful for you to consider its alternatives: hatred and indifference. Can you imagine being consumed by hatred for another person or group? People with hatred wish the worst for others. Not only will those fueled by hatred not feel for or help someone in need, but they will often inflict the pain on them. People with hatred lack empathy or concern for others. A person who is indifferent doesn't care and has no feelings toward another person or group. An indifferent person is also someone who won't reach out to or help others. An indifferent person is someone who lacks meaningful values, is void of deep relationships, and is truly alone on an island in a sea of humanity. Whether hatred or indifference, just imagining the feeling of rage or disconnection makes me shudder!

Developing compassion begins with several realizations about our individual place in the world. It starts with the recognition that we are not isolated creatures, but rather individuals who are a part of many groups—communities, races, religions, nationalities, and citizens of planet Earth—that must coexist to survive. This realization leads to an awareness of others; who they are, the culture in which they live, what they believe, how they live their lives, and the challenges they face. Compassion provides us with a context in which we can place ourselves in relation to others. In doing so, we realize that people are more alike than they are different. We all want to be healthy and happy, safe and secure, and feel connected; we work, we play, we raise families. In recognizing the similarities between the most disparate people and cultures, we gain our first sense of compassion with feelings of empathy, that we all feel much the same: love, sadness, joy, pain, hope, despair, inspiration, frustration. From empathy, we develop a concern for others and a wish to put others' needs ahead of our own when necessary. What makes compassion so important is not just that it elicits feelings and concern for others, but rather it spurs people to want to alleviate the suffering of those they feel empathy toward. At the heart of compassion is a thought ("I am not alone in this world"), an emotion ("I feel for others and others feel for me"), and an action ("How can I help others?") that propel children to want to give of themselves to others.

Why Is Compassion Important?

Your challenge is to help your children understand their place in the world and to encourage them to open their minds and hearts in a culture that increasingly turns its back on those who are different from they are or lie outside of its immediate borders. You must actively expose your children to perspectives and experiences that challenge much of popular culture's limited and uncaring view of the world. Only by doing so will your children learn the value of compassion and how it benefits both themselves and others.

With the challenges we face in the twenty-first century, the value of your children developing compassion for others is as important as ever. Compassion can enable your children to understand others who are different from themselves and will allow them to see that there are perspectives different from their own. Compassion will open the door to your children being able to contemplate ideas and experiences that will enrich their lives and expand their view of the world. It shows children the joy of reaching out to others and contributing to making the world a better place. Compassion gives children an appreciation and caring for others and a deep connection with the world in which they live. Children learn that acting compassionately is also in their best interests. Compassion encourages others to act compassionately toward them, providing them with support and assistance when they are in need. An important lesson that compassionate children learn is that compassion begets compassion and that everyone benefits from its expression.

In the chapter 8, I wrote about how children will find true happiness outside of themselves by giving of themselves and connecting with others. This notion has broader and even more powerful implications in relation to compassion. Children will learn that compassion can bring them meaning, satisfaction, and joy that they could never experience living in the insular and disconnected world that American popular culture offers them. This meaning comes from compassion eliciting other essential life-affirming values, including empathy, kindness, and generosity.

Compassion has also been shown to be beneficial to people in other ways. Research has found that compassion acts as armor against American popular culture. People who value compassion, helping, and contributing to the world are less likely to be seduced by popular culture's values related to wealth, materialism, superficiality, and popularity. These studies found that compassionate people are happier and better adjusted than those who hold common popular cultural values. They also have more energy, fewer behavioral problems, and a lower incidence of depression and anxiety than people who have bought into popular culture's values.

Raising Compassionate Children

Because of the messages of selfishness and disregard for others that American popular culture communicates to children, they're not likely to learn compassion on their own. You must nurture the ability to care about others in their early years. Compassion, though grounded in values about the world and our role in it, must be woven into the very fabric of your family life. If you're unable to express your concerns for others in your daily lives, your children will be unlikely to develop compassion and will ultimately become emotionally, intellectually, and socially disconnected from the larger world in which they live. If you want your children to be compassionate, you must be compassionate yourself. You must talk to your children about what compassion means and why it is important. You must surround your children with compassionate people and regularly seek out opportunities for them to have socially relevant experiences that cultivate compassion for others. Only then will children come to see the value of compassion and embrace it as their own. Let's take a look at how to do this.

Live a Compassionate Life

A common theme through this book is that you can best instill healthy values in your children by expressing those values in your own life. This influence is no less important in teaching compassion. If you lead a compassionate life, your children will naturally see its importance to you and will likely assume its importance for themselves. You will also be placing the value of compassion within the context of your overall family-value culture. Many of the other values you espouse will co-mingle with and reinforce the messages that you send about compassion.

Leading a compassionate life is communicated to your children in both obvious and subtle ways. Your children, particularly when they're young, will most notice the larger compassionate acts you engage in, for example, volunteering your time for worthy causes or traveling a long distance to support a family member in need. As your children get older and begin to grasp the concept of compassion, they will also see the smaller expressions of compassion you make, such as comforting them when they scrape their knees, assuming dinner duties when your spouse is stressed out from work, or helping a neighbor with a home project. Small acts of compassion, for example, being kind to a waiter or giving spare change to a homeless person, show your children how compassion is expressed in daily life. A meaningful lesson from these examples is that compassion doesn't discriminate; acts of compassion can be small or large, given to friends or strangers, or be empathic or substantial.

Talk to Your Children about Compassion

As with all of the values I discuss, you can encourage the value of compassion by talking to your children about it. Tell them what compassion is and why it is important to them, your family, and the world as a whole. Because compassion is, at its core, an emotion, you should describe what it feels like to feel compassion (an urge to do good for someone else) and how it feels to act compassionately (satisfying, joyful, inspiring). For example, you may volunteer one day a month at a nursing home, where you spend time with its elderly residents, talking and playing games with them. You can tell your children that these people led good lives, but may now be ill, lonely, or isolated. Spending time with the residents gives them the opportunity to talk, laugh, and tell stories, and lifts their spirits. They deserve respect, compassion, and caring. You also want to share with your children what you feel from these visits. You might tell them that you love hearing their stories and you leave your visit inspired and uplifted, knowing that you made someone else's life a little bit better. As your children learn more about compassion and ingrain the emotional connection, they will sense it from you directly.

To help show your children why compassion is so important, you can talk to them about the consequences of compassion: connectedness and meaning, or the lack of compassion: hatred (anger and fear) and indifference (alienation and insignificance). The way to really make this discussion hit home is to give your children examples of compassion in the world at large, as well as examples of hatred and indifference. Point out ways in which your children can express compassion in your family, for example, being kind to their siblings. You can also highlight ways they can show compassion toward their community, such as donating old clothes to charity. To give them a much broader perspective on compassion in the larger world, you can show them events in the news, such as relief efforts in a poor country. Finally, you want to establish expectations about compassion in your family. These expectations should clarify what compassionate behavior you expect and attach appropriate consequences for violations of the expectations. These discussions lay the groundwork of knowledge, understanding, and appreciation for creating a family-value culture in which compassion is an essential component and where your children get to learn to live the life of a compassionate person.

Explore Compassion

Educating your children about the value of compassion is not a one-shot deal. Rather, it's an ongoing dialogue in which you regularly engage your children on relevant issues related to compassion. You can discuss timely socially conscience issues that are occurring in your community, your country, and around the world. A quality newspaper, magazine, or website will offer many examples each day of compassion—and hatred and indifference—occurring throughout the world. You can further engage your children with more extensive resources, for example, books, television shows, films, and lectures that describe acts of compassion, hatred, and indifference in greater depth and give your children the opportunity to more fully delve into all aspects of compassion. The important part of exploring compassion is to evoke in your children the positive emotions associated with compassion (love, empathy, kindness, pride), the painful emotions connected to hatred (anger, fear, sadness), and the complete absence of emotions related to indifference.

Surround Yourself With Compassionate People

You are not, of course, the only influence in your children's lives. Extended family, friends, schoolmates, teachers, coaches, and others affect your children on a daily basis, as does American popular culture. Though you can't maintain control of all aspects of your children's social lives, you can exert a considerable influence over the critical mass of people who have an impact on them. Making deliberate decisions about who you surround your family with can help ensure that your children get messages of compassion from most of the people around them.

- The neighborhood you live in.
- The other families you socialize with.
- The schools your children attend.
- The activities your children participate in.

For example, having family friends (parents and their children) with whom you can share compassionate activities enhances the shared experiences and communicates to your children that compassion is not just a family value. Or having your children attend a school that incorporates compassion into its culture and curriculum further reinforces its importance to your children. Your children will implicitly think, "It's not just my parents who think this compassion stuff is important. Everyone seems to." You must actively explore each of these avenues to ensure that the values that your children are receiving from them, including compassion, are consistent with your own.

As your children move through middle childhood and into adolescence, your influence decreases and that of their larger social world (e.g., peers, teachers, popular culture) grows. Assuming an active role in shaping your children's early social environment is particularly important as they become increasingly immersed in American popular culture and become more vulnerable to peer pressure. By shaping your children's early lives, you increase the chances that peer influence later in childhood is generally positive and supportive of your values and encourages resistance to the messages from American popular culture.

Engage Your Children in Compassionate Activities

As your children gain an understanding of the value of compassion, you can further deepen their connection by having them engage in compassionate activities. These endeavors can begin within your family by encouraging acts of compassion toward siblings and toward you, for example, helping a sibling frustrated with her homework or being extra loving when you come home from a hard day at work. The value of compassion can be further fostered in your children by having them engage in activities outside the home that help others, such as participating in a food drive during the holidays or tutoring younger children. These compassionate activities can be further incorporated into the family-value culture by having the entire family participate. Discussions about the experiences, sharing stories about what each member of your family did, who they met, how they might have helped someone, and what emotions it evoked in them, all help to clarify and deepen the meaning of compassion in your family's lives.

One way that children can develop compassion as they enter adolescence is in their summer jobs. Unfortunately, there has been a noticeable shift over the past twenty years in the types of summer jobs that many parents encourage their children to undertake and that many children have done. It was common in years past for children, particularly those who were raised with some affluence, to work as manual laborers of some sort, for example, construction or landscaping, in local retail stores, such as those found in malls, or as a counselor at a summer camp. The manual labor and retail jobs fostered compassion because they taught children the meaning of hard work—physical exertion, long hours, low wages—and it showed them how the other half lived. Children had the opportunity to work with and get to know people for whom this work was not a summer job, but rather their life's work. They also learned what it meant to work hard, put in a day's work, and about the value of a dollar. As camp counselors, children learned not only about compassion and giving, but also leadership, mentoring, cooperation, and support, among other values.

These days, many parents who've been seduced by popular culture's definition of success and who are perhaps worried about the economic climate, want to jump start their children's careers with summer internships in corporate offices, law firms, or hospitals. Whether the work experience itself, the skills children learn, its appearance on college applications or résumés, or as a networking tool, many parents believe that these summer jobs will benefit their children in their future careers.

These "prepare for future career" experiences can be worthwhile. But as someone who worked as a carpenter, painter, roofer, and construction worker throughout high school and college, I'm a firm believer in the "old-school" summer jobs. These jobs teach children powerful lessons about essential values, such as compassion, hard work, responsibility, and financial prudence. These benefits, in my view, far outweigh the skills or "in's" that children gain from internships and will better serve them in later life. Also, there will be plenty of time for internships when your children get to college.

Emerging Values

Compassion is one of the most influential values you can incorporate into your family-value culture because, by its very nature, it fosters other important values that will not only serve your children in their later lives, but, more basically, it helps them become just plain good people. *Decency*, unfortunately, has gotten a bad rap in twenty-first-century America. When many think of good and decent people, the words wimp, loser, pushover, and sucker come to mind. American popular culture doesn't hold decency in particularly high esteem. More often than not, so-called "bad boys," such as the basketball player Latrell Sprewell (who attacked his coach, but still plays and makes millions of dollars) and the hip-hop artist, Snoop Dogg (who has gained fame and wealth despite alleged gang involvement, drug use, and jail time), are lionized by popular culture and idolized by impressionable young people. People believe that these bad boys walk all over the good people and get the money, celebrity, and "bling." The decent folks are left scraping for what they can get.

Raising your children to be decent will not make them soft or easy targets. To the contrary, decency these days takes courage and strength to resist the forces of American popular culture. Decent people are strong, independent, and willful, but these qualities are reflected in acts of compassion and goodness rather than attitude and aggressiveness. What separates the good from the bad is not their power, but rather the values underlying that power and how that power is exerted. The bad guys have bought into American popular culture and use it for selfish, greedy, and often destructive purposes. Decent people are raised in a positive family-value culture and use it for caring and giving ends.

Two of the most apparent values that emerge from compassion are *kindness and generosity*. Kind children are gentle, considerate, and sympathetic. They're responsive to others' needs, helpful, and motivated to do good. Kindness is such a good value because kind people are well-liked and appreciated by others, and are able to develop healthy long-term relationships that offer them so much in return. Compassionate children are also generous and willing to give of themselves to others. Though often thought of as giving something material to others, for example, money, gifts, or goods, generosity of spirit lies at its heart and is reflected in giving in many forms, both material and otherwise, such as love, caring, energy, time, and expertise. The wonderful thing is that acts of compassion, kindness, and generosity are returned many times over, so that both the giver and the recipient benefit.

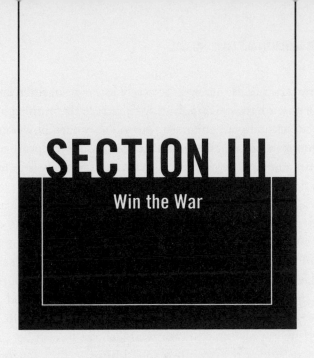

SECTION III

Win the War

To this point, you've learned where the battle lines have been drawn. You have a better understanding of what American popular culture is and how it hurts your children. You hopefully have a more clear idea of what values are and what specifically you value. You should also know whether your values are healthy and you are a stalwart ally of your children's battle against popular culture or you've been seduced by popular culture and have gone to the dark side. Importantly, you've learned how a family-value culture, in which your values are clear and suffused into your family's daily life, acts as a powerful defense system against popular culture.

You've seen where the war against American popular culture is being waged. I have identified six values that are essential for your children's healthy development and that are most under attack from popular culture. You've also learned how these values can be instilled in your children so the values can act as an armor to protect your children from popular culture. I've also shown how you can play an active role in helping your children to defend themselves from the ongoing and intense assaults.

Section III is devoted to showing you how to take the offensive in the war against American popular culture and make significant incursions into enemy territory. By acting proactively rather than reactively to popular culture, you have the opportunity to reduce the number and intensity of its attacks on your children. You will also learn how you can take the ammunition out of the armaments of popular culture—television, video games, the Internet, movies—and use them as tools to foster your children's development.

This section will also tell you what winning the war against American popular culture will mean to your children. The difference between losing and winning this war is no less than your children's futures and the kind of people they will become; their successes, happiness, the quality of their relationships, and the contributions they make to their families, communities, and the larger world in which they live. You will learn what happens to children who are primarily influenced by popular culture. You will also see how children develop when they're guided by a family-value culture and are taught the attitudes, beliefs, and skills necessary to resist the destructive messages of popular culture. This section concludes with a discussion of the wonderful, life-affirming gifts you give your children when you raise them in a family-value culture and you protect them from American popular culture.

CHAPTER 11

Taking the Offensive
(Going Behind Enemy Lines)

The 2003 film, *Thirteen*, tells the story of Tracy, played by Evan Rachel Wood, a bright, though naïve, 13-year-old girl being raised by a single, recovering-alcoholic mother. Tracy wants to feel grown up and accepted in her middle school, so she befriends Evie, played by Nikki Reed, another 13-year-old who is beautiful and popular, as well as manipulative and cruel. With this friendship, Tracy descends a slippery slope in which she transforms into a cold, uncommunicative, and self-destructive girl who threatens her relationship with her mother and her own life. One focus of the film is the relationship between Tracy and her mother, Mel, played by Holly Hunter. As the film's website describes, "Like many mothers, Mel is torn between the desire to be her daughter's best friend and the need to be an authority figure." Adds Ms. Hunter, "This culture of youth, this changing world where nothing is the same, and where there's tremendous confusion about how to be a parent, how to be a girl, how to connect when there's no real sense of what's right and what's wrong anymore." The *Thirteen* website also says that the movie illustrates a "Girl Culture. It's everywhere—in schools, malls, television, popular magazines—girls...living way too hard and fast for their adolescent years." Nikki Reed, who is also a co-writer of the screenplay, which is based on her own life, "began revealing a world fueled by confusion, anger, rebellion, and fear of not fitting in; a world rife with sex, high fashion, eating disorders, shoplifting, self-mutilation, and drugs."

Thirteen is a shocking and painful film that graphically illustrates the dangers to children of too much exposure to American popular culture without sufficient guidance and boundaries from parents. It shows the forces of popular culture that children are confronted with in twenty-first-century America and their inability to withstand the ongoing and intense assaults on their own. It's also an ultimately hopeful film that demonstrates the power that parents can have over their children to protect them from popular culture. It affirms the need for parents to be proactive rather than simply reactive to the pressures children face every day.

You alone as a parent can't change American popular culture, at least not in time to stop its assault on your children. The forces of popular culture are simply too numerous and too strong. I know that sounds awfully pessimistic, but I think I'm just being realistic. I'm not saying that American popular culture will win in the end, but it will be a long and difficult fight if it is to be defeated. What I am optimistic about is the power that you have to protect your children from popular culture and to inflict a little damage to this seemingly indestructible juggernaut. I'm optimistic that we can create an army of resisters that can halt the unrelenting march of American popular culture in its attempt to conquer our society. But it will take time.

In the meantime, there are other active steps you can take to help your children. These actions involve going behind enemy lines and using American popular culture against itself, and helping to grow the resistance movement. By doing so, you not only garner all of the resources at your disposal within your family and in your community, but you also surreptitiously enlist some of the forces of popular culture to fight for you rather than against you.

Pick Your Battles

Before you can go behind enemy lines to co-opt American popular culture, you must study the weapons it uses and decide which need to be disarmed and which you can turn against it for the benefit of your children. The best way to protect your children is to limit their exposure to popular culture. Though perhaps unrealistic for most American families, I have met parents who have no televisions in their homes, don't allow their children to own an Xbox (or PlayStation or Nintendo), and strictly control the types of movies that they permit their children to see. They also limit their children's toy selections, fast- and junk-food consumption, and clothing and shoe purchases. Even these highly protected children are vulnerable, though, because they can't avoid seeing popular culture every time they leave the house.

At a minimum, you should make conscious, rather than expedient, decisions about the battles you want to fight. You must give careful thought to the degree of harm that specific devices of American popular culture can inflict on your children and which battles are worth fighting, realizing that, given the size and force of popular culture, you will not win them all. It may be, for example, that you judge movies that have no commercial merchandising tie-ins to be okay for your children, but you don't permit them to watch any television (because of the seemingly endless stream of commercials) or you limit their video-game play to nonviolent, educational games. You may decide that you can live with sometimes explicit music lyrics, but draw the line at provocative clothing. You might even accept an earring for your son or navel earring for your daughter, but not allow tattoos under any circumstances, knowing that children tend to grow out of wearing extra earrings when they reach adulthood.

Deconstruct American Popular Culture

The minds behind American popular culture are sophisticated in the ways of deception and manipulation. If you just look at the surface of popular culture's messages, they usually appear quite benign; filled with entertaining characters, fun music, and eye-catching images. If you look no deeper, you may conclude that those messages are harmless or your children can simply ignore them. In either case, you expose your children to threats that exist below the surface. You need to deconstruct the media in which popular culture embeds its messages. You must look beneath the surface of the stimulation, fun, and entertainment that popular culture uses to disguise its real messages to attract your children, and determine what values it's really communicating to them.

You should do a litmus test for every piece of media your children are exposed to. A great exercise is to watch a television show, play a video game, or listen to music lyrics to which your children might be drawn. List what attracts your children to the particular medium (e.g., funny and bright images or cute and entertaining characters). Deconstruct the medium and list the value messages that it is really sending to your children. Compare these values to those that comprise your family-value culture; are they consistent with or contrary to the values that you hold most dear? If the messages from American popular culture are incompatible with your values, you must make a deliberate choice about whether you want to limit your children's exposure to that medium.

A final point about your children's exposure to American popular culture is that you don't have to openly endorse its messages for your children to be influenced by it. By allowing your children to play violent video games, listen to explicit music lyrics, or eat fast-food, you are conveying your tacit approval of the media and its underlying values. Because you typically express displeasure with your children when you don't like something they're doing, when you don't express it, they will assume that what they're doing is okay with you. The lesson here is that when you ignore something your children are doing, that is as good as encouraging it.

Be a Gatekeeper

One of the things that makes American popular culture so powerful is its weaponry: television, video games, movies, music, magazines. But these media aren't inherently dangerous. They're simply devices that are used by popular culture to communicate information that is harmful. The information that popular culture conveys through these media is the actual ammunition that hurts your children.

One way to disarm American popular culture is by becoming the gatekeeper of the types of information that your children are allowed to be exposed to. The role of gatekeeper involves making deliberate choices about how these media are used. You decide what your children are allowed to watch on television, what video games you let them play, and what websites they can view. As the gatekeeper, you must first look at how your children are using the media and whether their use is healthy. This involves becoming educated about popular culture and its role in your children's lives. What are your children watching, playing, listening to, and surfing? What messages are being communicated by the various forms of media to your children and what values are being conveyed? This process will take time, patience, and thoroughness because there is an extremely large—and increasing—number of television shows, music, video games, and websites out there. You need to look at what is unhealthy for your children and, importantly, what will be beneficial to them. You also have to take into account what healthy media are entertaining, for example, educational television shows, video games, and websites, and what your children's interests are— because if the healthy media aren't engaging, your children will quickly lose interest.

As an informed consumer of American popular culture, you're now ready to fulfill your two primary responsibilities as gatekeeper. First, establish limits on how much time your children are allowed to spend and what they're allowed to watch, play, listen to, and surf. For example, don't allow your children to watch more than one hour of television each day, play violent video games, or use the telephone or Instant Messaging during dinner or homework. If you begin this process early in your children's entry into American popular culture, they're likely accept your decisions and adopt the values that underlie those choices.

Second, you can't just take activities that your children enjoy away without replacing them with activities that they will find equally appealing, yet also consistent with your family-value culture. Your children will be left with a gaping hole in their entertainment lives. For you to get your children on a road away from American popular culture, you must introduce them to new forms of media that will hopefully interest them enough to make the transition less painful. For example, stimulating, nonviolent video games, such as Earthworm Jim, or entertaining movies that are aren't violent or sexually explicit. You may also need to assume some responsibility during this transition in which you spend more time actively sharing the new media with them and helping them to become engaged. You can also get them away from popular culture media altogether by having them spend their time reading, exercising, or playing a sport or musical instrument.

If you introduce limits midstream (i.e., when they have already been seduced by popular culture and there were few limits previously), your children may not like it and resist your efforts. For example, if your children are addicted to video games and you limit or remove them, they will be very unhappy and they will let you know it in no uncertain terms. If you're faced with this challenge, how you respond will determine whether your children ultimately buy into the change. You have to be firm and consistent in establishing limits, expectations, and consequences—follow-through is everything! When parents have followed my advice and thrown out their children's video games or limited their television viewing, they have told me that their children complain—loudly and persistently—for two to three months trying to wear them down. But when the parents stick to their principles, their children, in every case, finally gave up. Realizing that they can't win this battle, their children accept the situation, and, in time, change their own values and find new sources of entertainment that are consistent with their family-value culture.

Even with all this, though, allowing your children to use the media of American popular culture freely is still not the healthiest thing for them. The fact is that watching television, playing video games, and surfing the Internet, however much they can foster intellectual and creative development when used properly, are also sedentary, primarily solitary activities that can encourage obesity and social isolation. Because of the risks, you should not only act as the gatekeeper for how your children use these media, but also how frequently they are used, to ensure that your children maintain a balance of activities in their lives that fosters their overall healthy growth.

Finally, you have to recognize that you can't control what media of American popular culture your children are exposed to in the "real world," meaning at school, at their friends' houses, in malls, and the like. And you can't dictate how they will respond to these ongoing pressures from popular culture. But if you've raised your children in a family-value culture, you can trust that you've instilled in your children healthy values that will encourage them to make good choices when faced with the allure of popular culture and the pull of peer pressure.

Raise Healthy Skeptics

Your children are drawn to American popular culture's many media because of their inescapable exposure and popularity among their peers. Because of this attraction, you can use popular culture against itself to teach your children healthy values. What would happen if you co-opted American popular culture's weaponry for your own valued purposes? What if you turned those swords into plowshares, tools to help your children grow? Wouldn't that be a stealthy and beneficial way to protect your children from popular culture? In other words, you can use television, the Internet, magazines, and the like to advance your family-value culture instead of American popular culture.

Rather than just attempting to hold popular culture at the gates of your family, allow it to come into your house, but only to use for your purposes. With a clear understanding of your family-value culture and having deconstructed the media through which American popular culture imposes itself on your children, you're now in a position to use those media to promote your values rather than those of popular culture.

Too often, today's children are passive recipients of whatever messages they're exposed to. As such, children become victims of the messages that are loudest and most engaging. In other words, they'll believe almost anything that is entertaining. This gullibility will also cause them to be victimized throughout their lives because being naive in a world dominated by popular culture makes people susceptible to dishonesty, manipulation, and undue influence. You can help protect your children from this vulnerability by raising them to be healthy skeptics.

When I tell you to raise skeptics, I don't mean that I want you to teach your children to be cynical and mistrustful. Rather, I want your children to be critical observers and thinkers who don't just believe the messages they get from American popular culture at face value. I want your children to find a healthy middle ground between being naive and being suspicious of every message they receive from anyone. Healthy skepticism means that, rather than accepting messages from American popular culture, they ask tough questions about those messages. Why is the message so attractive? What is the real message? What am I getting out of the message? Would the message help or hurt me? Healthy skepticism is an essential part of being a value-driven, discerning, and thoughtful person, and will serve your children well as they become increasingly immersed in the seemingly inescapable quagmire of American popular culture.

You can foster this healthy skepticism by teaching your children to engage, rather than simply absorb, American popular culture. Instead of trying to protect your children constantly from popular culture—which, given its omnipresence, is an impossibility—you can teach them to combat it themselves. Just as you deconstructed some of the media of popular culture to help you understand its underlying messages, you can show your children how to be skeptical consumers for themselves. If, for example, there is a television show that your children like to watch—and that you're not thrilled about, but you decide that this battle isn't worth fighting—you should sit down and watch the show with them. Ask them what they like about it and what they find interesting. Then, see if they can dig below the surface and recognize the messages it is really communicating. If your children see the unhealthy messages, ask them about their purposes, for example, manipulation and selling products. If they don't see the messages, point them out as they arise, so they can see the messages more clearly. In either case, ask your children who is behind them and how they might hurt children like themselves and help the purveyors of the show. This discussion will help your children gain a better understanding of what they're really watching. They then can decide for themselves whether to accept the messages. At worst, your children may still watch the show because it's entertaining, but now, because they're healthy skeptics, they'll recognize and reject the unhealthy messages it's conveying. At best, your children will reject the medium and its values completely by choosing to no longer watch the show.

Expand Your Army

It can feel overwhelming sometimes when faced with having to battle an enemy that is ubiquitous, unrelenting, and seemingly invincible, with an apparently endless supply of soldiers and ammunition. It is especially frustrating if you're working so hard to instill a family-value culture, yet so many other influences in your children's lives have allied themselves with American popular culture and are working against you. When American popular culture recruits people and organizations that should be on your side—family, friends, schools—your efforts to protect your children seem hopeless. You can feel discouraged, helpless, and exhausted going it alone.

One of the best things you can do for yourself and your children is to actively recruit for your resistance movement against American popular culture. Make sure that the immediate influences in your children's lives are fighting with you rather than against you in protecting your children from popular culture. In this push to expand your value-driven army, you can shift the resistance movement to a new and larger scale in which you create a "community-value culture" that supports and augments your own family-value culture.

A community-value culture is an extension of your family-value culture because it shares your most fundamental values, enveloping your children in a sort of value-powered force field that can repel much of American popular culture when your children are outside your home. This shield acts to protect your children whenever they leave your house by keeping their immediate surroundings and inter-actions healthy even when the larger value messages raining down on them from billboards, stores, movies, and magazines are unhealthy.

A supportive community-value culture rarely materializes on its own. Rather, building a community-value culture means actively exploring the community in which your family lives and making deliberate choices about the world you want your family to live in outside of your home. Having already created a family-value culture, establishing a community-value culture to support it begins by identifying the people in your family's lives that influence your children. Then ask the following questions:

- Do your children's friends and their parents share and extend your family-value culture?
- Does the community in which you live support your family-value culture?
- Do the schools your children attend reinforce your family-value culture?
- Do the activities—cultural, athletic, religious, entertainment—in which they participate encourage your family-value culture?
- Simply put, do the people in your children's world foster the healthy, life-affirming values that reflect and reinforce your family-value culture?

If you answer "yes" to all (or at least most) of these questions, then you can feel confident that your children will have allies by their side when they leave the house. If you answer "no" to all (or most) of these questions, your children are entering a hostile world alone that they are ill-equipped to protect themselves from. You need to carefully consider the community in which you live and, as much as possible, make changes to that community so that its value culture is more consistent with your own family-value culture. My suggestion doesn't mean that, if your community doesn't support your family-value culture, you have to move. Such an uprooting is probably not realistic for most families (though I have seen it happen). At the same time, you can make changes within your community that can shift the preponderance of influence on your children in a healthy direction. Small changes can include a new sports league that emphasizes fun and participation over winning, a new piano teacher who is less demanding, or making the local mall off-limits to your children. Large-scale changes, though less likely, can include enrollment in a new school, attending a different house of worship, or not allowing your children to see friends (and their parents) who are bad influences on them.

Actively creating a community-value culture has significant benefits for both you and your children. You'll feel less alone and powerless, and more supported and empowered to face the daily attacks from American popular culture. You'll also be able to share encouragement, and problem-solving and practical assistance with other members of your value-based community. You won't have to worry as much about the messages your children will receive when they leave your home. You will be more confident that the messages that your children get from others will reinforce rather than undermine the messages you convey in your family-value culture. Your children will be surrounded by a community that supports their family-value culture, helping them to maintain perspective and reduce confusion and temptation. When they leave your home, your children will know that they are entering a world that is not quite as hostile and that is populated by like-minded people who will assist them in their daily battles with American popular culture.

Emerging Values

In teaching your children how to resist American popular culture, you implicitly communicate other emerging values that will reinforce their connection to your family-value culture. Learning to deconstruct the messages of popular culture and becoming a healthy skeptic encourages your children to develop the value and skill of *analytical thinking*. Analytical thinking involves being well-informed, judging the credibility of sources, evaluating motivations, asking the right questions, and making reasoned decisions. By making conscious choices about the people they allow into their community and the messages they receive from American popular culture, your children learn to not naively accept everything they hear. Instead, they're able to look beneath the surface of those messages, identify the unhealthy values that underlie the messages, and make deliberate choices about whether accepting those messages from popular culture are in their best interests.

In creating a community-value culture that extends your family-value culture, your children learn to appreciate the value of *community*. By making thoughtful decisions about the community in which your family lives, you communicate to your children that community is important and that they should value the relationships they develop with other family members, friends, neighbors, schools, and houses of worship. This valuing persuades your children to reach out for themselves to peers who share their values. It also encourages them to take responsibility for helping your family expand your community-value culture. The lessons they learn in fighting American popular culture also reinforce other values I discuss in this book, including respect, responsibility, family, compassion, and happiness, all of which have strong community components.

CHAPTER 12

Victory
(Winning the Big One)

American Popular Culture on the Offensive

To review American popular culture's "shock and awe" strategy for dominating twenty-first-century America:

- Violent media: Professional wrestling, Burnout 3: Takedown, 50 Cent, *The Terminator*, *CSI*.
- Sexually-oriented media: Britney-Madonna kiss at the 2003 MTV Video Music Awards show, Janet Jackson's breast-baring during the 2004 Super Bowl half-time show, "men's" magazines (e.g., *Maxim, FHM, Blender*).
- Celebrity-driven media: *Entertainment This Week, People, US*.
- Advertising: Budweiser's flatulence television commercial during the 2004 Super Bowl, political attack ads.
- Culture of beauty: *Glamour, Cosmopolitan, The Swan*.
- Fast-food: McDonalds, Burger King, Pizza Hut.
- Professional sports: Drug use and other criminal behavior.
- Corporate corruption and greed: Enron, Imclone, WorldCom, Tyco.

The list—and the assault—goes on…

American popular culture never rests. It's always looking for new ways to ramp up its forces and break down your family's defenses. Because many Americans, particularly children, are accustomed to the "sound-bite" world in which we now live and habituate so quickly to new messages, popular culture has to "turn up the volume" ever more to keep our attention. Much like a drug addict who needs increasingly greater doses to get high, Americans need stronger fixes from popular culture to stay interested. Because we have become so inured to what thirty years ago would have been considered truly objectionable, popular culture can't just hope to get our attention with bright lights and loud noise. Instead, it has to shock us!

Your Children Are Under Attack has shown you how to resist American popular culture and develop values that will act as the healthy foundation for your children's futures. These steps help your children to become compassionate and giving people, nurture healthy relationships, build successful and fulfilling careers, and lead meaningful and rewarding lives. The culmination of this process is the development of children who have the values, beliefs, attitudes, and skills to be vital members of your family, your community, our country, and the world. Victory is yours when you raise value-driven children who lead examined and satisfying lives.

Qualities of Value-Raised Children

Children who are raised within a family-value culture and who have been protected from American popular culture are different than those who have gone to the dark side of popular culture. They possess a variety of qualities that are becoming less and less common as popular culture expands its influence over our landscape. Yet you may not really understand the depth and breadth of these differences or, very specifically, what kind of adults your children can become when raised in a family-value culture.

From Immaturity to Maturity

An essential part of your children becoming healthy and mature adults involves letting go of immature ways of thinking (e.g., "I want it now and without any effort"), feeling (e.g., throwing temper-tantrums or sulking), and acting (e.g., taking without consideration of others).

Yet, American popular culture wants your children to stay immature. Immature children demand immediate gratification, are highly impressionable, dependent on others, have a strong need to be accepted, and are easily manipulated. These children are whiny, out of control, and inconsiderate because they never learn to be patient, control their emotions, or to be responsive to others.

Children who are raised in a family-value culture adopt ways of thinking (e.g., "How will I affect others?"), feeling (e.g., empathy, compassion, satisfaction), and behaving (e.g., putting others' needs ahead of their own) that are value-driven and that are in their own best interests while considering the interests of others. Mature children can delay gratification, think critically, are self-reliant, aren't gullible, make deliberate decisions, and are able to resist the allure of American popular culture. Mature children are trustworthy, dependable, and thoughtful because they've developed a perspective on life that is both realistic and best meets their needs without sacrificing the needs of others.

From Need to Want

Children who are guided by American popular culture are driven by what they believe are needs. These "needs" are created artificially by popular culture to ensure that children keep buying things that popular culture has convinced them that they must have. How many times have you heard children say to their parents about a toy, "But Mom, Dad, I need it. If I don't get it, I'll die!"? Popular culture encourages this confusion between want and need. For example, Circuit City, the electronics retail chain, has had an advertising campaign in which its slogan is, "Circuit City. Just what I needed." and in full-page ads it argues, "I need the latest technology...I need a great price...I need awe-inspiring expertise...basically, I need it all." Last time I checked, food, water, and shelter were needs, electronics was not. These children are needy, demanding, persistent, and irritating because they absolutely must have their "needs" met.

Children who are raised in a family-value culture aren't driven by such irrevocable needs. Rather, their lives are guided by what they want without the compulsive need driving them. These children don't confuse need and want, recognizing that, even though they may want something very much, they don't really need it. Value-raised children are patient, well-mannered, and disciplined because they're not driven by a compulsion to have their needs satisfied.

From Dichotomous Thinking to Continuous Thinking

Children who buy into American popular culture tend to think dichotomously; life is "either-or," black or white. Popular culture loves this simplistic thinking because it can control the few choices that children are presented with and can restrict the number of decisions that children have to make. Dichotomous-thinking children are narrow-minded, lack creativity, and are poor decision makers because they view their world in a restricted way and neglect to see the depth and breadth that life has to offer.

Value-raised children engage in continuous thinking in which they see a wide spectrum of options available to them in their lives. Continuous thinking allows these children to recognize, choose from, and experience the richness of life. It also forces them to deal with ambiguity and the complexities of decision making that are always present in adulthood. Continuous-thinking children are open-minded, creative, and deeply connected to their lives because they see many options and lead lives filled with diverse experiences.

From Selfish to Giving

The egocentrism that is common among children who are heavily influenced by American popular culture causes them to behave selfishly. These children are focused on themselves and have a fundamental disregard for others. They consistently act in ways that promote their own interests and either discount or undermine those of others. These children are spoiled, insensitive, needy, and generally irascible because they only care about themselves.

In contrast, value-raised children are unselfish and giving. These children set aside their own needs when necessary and make those of other people their priority. Their giving is expressed in every part of their lives, with family and friends, in school, and at their houses of worship. Giving children are the best defense against American popular culture and its ethos of "It's all about me." These children are caring, helpful, and supportive, because giving to others is one of their greatest joys.

Validation from Others to Affirmation of Self

Children who become victims of American popular culture typically have low self-esteem. So much of their lives, whether it is the conditional love and acceptance that they receive from their parents, their definitions of success and failure, or their perfectionistic expectations, instills in them feelings of inadequacy and low self-regard. This uncertainty causes them to depend on others for validation to feel good about themselves. This reliance on others for their self-esteem makes these children vulnerable to anyone or anything that will provide this validation. Popular culture is only too happy to help these children to feel good about themselves, if they will only wear the right clothes, listen to the right music, and eat the right foods. Gaining this validation meets their immediate self-esteem needs, but also creates a harmful dependence that limits their growth. These children are insecure, uncomfortable with themselves, and dependent because they don't feel good about themselves and rely on others to gain a sense of self-worth.

Children who are raised in a family-value culture believe themselves to be loved and competent people who are successful in their lives. Though these children receive support from others, they have the capacity to affirm their own self-esteem. These children gain affirmation directly from the life experiences and relationships in which they engage. This self-confirmation allows these children to have greater control over their self-esteem and keeps them from having to seek out unhealthy sources of self-esteem—like American popular culture—just to feel good about themselves. These children are confident, contented, and independent because they are happy with who they are and can gain self-worth from their own actions.

From Outcome to Process

American popular culture is all about outcomes—winning, straight A's, looking beautiful, getting rich, being popular. Children who gain their values from popular culture often look for shortcuts to what they want, and are impatient and unwilling to do what is necessary to earn their results. Or they commit massive amounts of time and effort toward achieving the outcomes, but find value only in the prize. This preoccupation with outcomes keeps these children from connecting with the meaning, satisfaction, and joy of the process in which they engage.

Because their self-esteem is based largely on the outcomes they achieve, these children are terrified of failing to gain the prize, making them vulnerable to taking a "whatever it takes" attitude toward obtaining those results. Children with this emphasis on outcomes are often selfish, untrustworthy, and unhappy because they don't fully believe that they can achieve the outcomes they want and will do anything they can to avoid failure.

Value-raised children are most interested in the journey that will lead them to their goals, recognizing that the prize at the end is only part of the experience. These children focus on what they need to do to obtain the desired outcome rather than only on the destination. They also have a healthy perspective about their successes and use the inevitable failures as opportunities to learn and progress toward their goals. This attitude allows them to enjoy the process deeply, regardless of the outcome. These children are passionate, committed, and joyful because their connection with their lives ensures that they enjoy the process as well as the achievement of their goals.

From Short-Term to Long-Term

One of the ways that American popular culture exerts its influence over children is its ability to keep them focused on the present. With its constantly changing images and sounds, popular culture prevents children from seeing any further than the next brief, entertaining moment. Children who fall for this attraction are expressly concerned with short-term concerns and needs. This limited perspective causes them to rely on their most recent past experiences and the most immediate ensuing activities to determine what they think, how they feel, and the way in which they behave. These children often act in ways that are not in their best interests in the long run. These children are impatient, easily distracted, and make poor choices because they're not able to look into the future and consider their actions with a long-term perspective.

Children who are raised in a family-value culture have a long-term perspective that allows them to weigh immediate benefits with long-term ramifications. This perspective enables these children to make better decisions because they're taking into account more relevant past, present, and future information. With this longer view of life, these children can recognize and accept the inevitable ups and downs in life.

This attitude also allows them to stay focused on the joy of the journey of life without being overly concerned with immediate events that arise. These children are patient, deliberate, and better able to handle the normal stresses of life because the breadth of the view of their lives puts everything that occurs in their lives in perspective.

To the Victor Go the Spoils

You may not fully appreciate the wonderful lifelong gifts that you give your children when you raise them in a family-value culture and you safeguard them from American popular culture. You may not even notice the gifts because they will be so embedded in your children. And what the gifts provide are often in terms of what you don't see: what your children don't think, what they don't feel, what they don't say, and how they don't act. Your children will certainly not be aware of these gifts as they're growing up because the gifts have been so woven into their lives and who they are.

Yet these gifts will exert a profound influence over your children, coloring every aspect of their lives; directing, guiding, and shaping their every thought, emotion, and action throughout their lives. If you look closely, you'll be able to see these gifts in the values they express in their lives, the perspectives they hold about the world, the quality of the life they establish for themselves, the way your children treat themselves and others, and the way they use their gifts to contribute to the world. You'll see these gifts in how your children are not: selfish, greedy, disrespectful, angry, or uncaring. And, hopefully, at some point in your children's lives, they will recognize these gifts and say, "Thank you for all you've done and for the wonderful gifts you've given me." At that point, your heart will skip a beat and you'll get a lump in your throat. You'll think back to when your children were young and you made the commitment to raise them in a family-value culture. And you'll smile and say, "You are most welcome."

Live a Rich Life

When most people hear about living a rich life, they think of being wealthy, having big houses, driving expensive cars, wearing fancy clothes and jewelry, and traveling first class. That, I would argue, is a moneyed life, not a rich one. When I talk about a rich life, I'm suggesting a life not measured in monetary terms, but rather one that is like a fine piece of cloth: layered, textured, intricately woven, interestingly patterned, and pleasing to the eye and touch. A rich life is built on a family-value culture and is expressed in the breadth and depth of the life that your children live as they enter adulthood.

A rich life is characterized by deep, satisfying, and lasting relationships with family, friends, schoolmates, coworkers, neighbors, and members of the community in which you live. These connections are usually based on shared values, beliefs, interests, and activities. Healthy relationships offer love, caring, encouragement, emotional support, practical assistance, and stress release. These relationships give your children opportunities to reach out, connect, and give to others who, in turn, can give so much back to them. Also, as I talked about in chapter 8, relationships are an essential contributor to happiness.

A rich life is typified by activities that your children have a passion for and a deep connection with. School, work, hobbies, sports, and cultural and religious activities provide your children with experiences and challenges that give their lives meaning and offer them satisfaction, joy, fun, inspiration, and pride. These activities give your children a reason to get up in the morning, capture their attention and imaginations, and stimulate ideas, creativity, and action.

A rich life is deep, diverse, and balanced. Children who lead rich lives are deeply involved in one or two activities, yet are involved in many. This diversity provides children with many sources of meaning and fulfillment, and gives them many directions from which to choose in the journey that is their life. This variety of activities creates children who have balanced self-identities and lives so that, if one area isn't going well, they are sustained by gratification in other areas.

A rich life is both comfortable and stimulating. Children who lead rich lives feel a sense of comfort because the life they live gives them feelings of contentment, security, and "I'm in a good place." This comfort enables these children to be calm and contented when they aren't doing anything, and encourages them to pursue stimulation when they want it. Their comfort also prevents them from feeling compelled to seek stimulation out of boredom, need for acceptance, or validation. From this place of comfort, these children can direct energy toward their interests—intellectual, physical, social, artistic, spiritual. This energy is not lost, but rather recirculated, in which the experience of those interests acts to reenergize them and, at the same time, ground them in the feeling of comfort. These children are connected, enrapt, and stimulated as they immerse themselves in these interests, yet are at ease when such opportunities aren't present.

A rich life allows children to dream. Children who lead rich lives have the opportunity to find areas of their lives that they're passionate about and vigorously pursue their dreams. These children have a sense of security and support from their family-value culture that provides them with a safe haven from which they can to explore their world. They also feel support from others and a sense of freedom to seek their dreams and fully realize whatever ability they've been endowed with.

A rich life is hereditary. When I say hereditary, I don't mean that it's passed from parents to children genetically. Instead, I mean that when parents create a family-value culture, they teach their children healthy values and perspectives who, in turn, are better equipped to create rich lives of their own. Just as abused children may repeat the abuse with their own children, children raised in a family-value culture are likely to repeat those life-affirming values with their children. The real test of the strength of a culture, whether family, community, or societal, is its ability to replicate and sustain itself across generations.

Love of Self and Others

Children who are raised in a family-value culture love themselves. I don't mean in the narcissistic and self-absorbed way that you find so often among children—and many adults—these days. Those children don't actually love themselves, but rather are driven by the need to gain love and validation from others. Children with this unhealthy love are also incapable of loving others, which means that they don't receive the healthy love that they crave.

The self-love I'm talking about gives children confidence in who they are, what they believe, and how they want to live their lives. This healthy self-love puts children in a position of security and strength from which they can explore, take risks, and strive toward their goals. This love comes from parents who make love an important part of their family-value culture and express healthy love to their children (as I talked about in chapter 4). By experiencing healthy love from their parents, children learn to love themselves and express their love for others in a positive way. This self-love allows them to be vulnerable and to have the comfort to express love and other emotions to others without fear of rejection or condemnation.

This self-love and the ability to express emotions in a healthy way helps these children to develop loving relationships with others. The openness that other people sense from children with this type of self-love encourages them to reciprocate love and other emotions they feel toward the children. These emotional expressions foster deep connections between these children and others that bring them meaning, satisfaction, and happiness in their lives.

Power to Effect Change

As I discussed previously, we live in a culture of victimization, the purported benefits of which are that children will never feel bad about themselves and their self-esteem will be protected because nothing is ever their fault. Being a victim is easier in a distorted sort of way because children can let others do everything for them and they can just follow along. The costs, however, for this so-called protection are profound. Children who are raised as victims have little self-regard, no sense of responsibility, are fearful, powerless to change things they don't like, and dependent on others to lead their lives. These children also lack initiative and creativity, and are poor problem-solvers. So when they get bored or frustrated, they look to others for stimulation and solutions. Most painfully, children who are victims are entirely at the mercy of others and are helpless to effect change in their lives.

Children who are raised in a family-value culture have a strong sense of ownership of their lives. Their parents establish clear expectations and consequences, hold them accountable for their actions, and require them to take the initiative in their lives. Growing up in this environment fosters self-esteem, responsibility, and decision-making capabilities. These children learn that they have the power to effect change in themselves and others. The most important benefit of this ability is that, when something is not going well in their lives, these children have the ability to make changes. This power is essential because our world is constantly in flux and there are so many areas over which we have little control. Children's belief in their ability to control their lives reduces doubt and fear when unwelcome changes occur, gives them confidence that they can effect beneficial changes, and spurs them to action to make the necessary changes. This power enables children to act on other values that are part of their family-value culture.

This power also helps children be better citizens of the world. Knowing that they can effect change in themselves, children gain the belief that they can also positively influence others. This belief is so important because it allows children to act on the value of family by becoming involved members of their family, contributing to their family's value culture, and acting in ways that support their values. This power also enables the value of compassion to come to life. Empathy, caring, and consideration are nice values, but they have limited worth if children don't believe that they can act on them and perform compassionate deeds toward others.

Healthy Perspective on an Unhealthy World

Perhaps the greatest gift you give your children by raising them in a family-value culture is a healthy perspective on a decidedly unhealthy world. This perspective acts as a protective shield against everything that American popular culture tries to throw at your children and as a filter for everything that they see, hear, think, feel, experience, and learn in their lives. It gives them the ability to view the seductive messages of popular culture critically rather than being naively sucked in by the bright lights, loud noises, and charismatic characters. This healthy view enables your children to see popular culture for what it is: a dishonest, manipulative, and unhealthy force that cares nothing for them. This perspective allows your children to make deliberate choices about what they think, feel, and do in their lives that are in their best interests.

With this healthy perspective, you're giving your children an opportunity to create their own "personal-value culture" that will ensure that they do what is best for themselves as they move toward adulthood. The values that they embrace from your family-value culture also shape the specific direction that their lives take, their educational and career pursuits, as well as their relationships, hobbies, cultural activities, and religious involvement.

This perspective determines what kind of people your children become. Children who lose the battle against American popular culture could grow up to be selfish, shallow, unkind, disrespectful people who care for little beyond themselves and what popular culture has told them is important. These children perpetuate all that is ugly about popular culture and, rather than just being its victims, become newly minted members of their ever-growing army that spreads its path of destruction in an even larger swath. In contrast, children who are raised in a family-value culture mature into thoughtful, responsible, caring, and contributing members of our society whose values propel them to make the world a better place than it is now. These children repudiate all that American popular culture represents and become the latest inductees into the growing underground army determined to overthrow the popular culture that has hijacked our country and instill anew the values that make our country great.

In claiming victory, you can take great pride and satisfaction in knowing that you are raising children who will be truly exceptional people in a culture in which mediocrity and homogeneity are the standard. You can also be heartened that you are raising children who can continue to fight the good fight against American popular culture and will be at the forefront of a revolution. I am confident that, in time, we will turn back the forces of popular culture and return America to a place that once again cares about its children and a place of which we can again be proud.

Emerging Values

Your children will develop three emerging values when you join forces with them in the war against American popular culture. They will learn the value of *fighting for what they believe*. This value, though not often considered, is one on which our country was founded and it has been the catalyst for many of the positive changes that have occurred in America's history, for example, the suffragist and civil rights movements. And we have seen this value create a tidal wave of change throughout the world (e.g., the end of the former Soviet Union, the fall of the Berlin Wall). There may be no more irresistible force on Earth than people believing deeply in something and being willing to fight for that belief.

This value will also benefit your children because it fosters the emerging value of *mission* in their lives. There are few things more powerful or inspiring than people on a mission, seeing them intensely devoted to something meaningful in their lives. When children have a purpose to their lives, they are driven to pursue it relentlessly. A mission may be the ultimate outcome of raising value-driven children and the best defense against American popular culture. Children with a mission will let nothing stand in their way, least of all something as obviously harmful as popular culture. Success (as your children come to define it), meaning, satisfaction, and joy are inevitable in pursuit of their mission.

Finally, when you raise your children to be guided by their values, you instill one last value that will enable them to endure—and even thrive—in the ongoing and seemingly unending war against American popular culture, *faith that good will prevail.* Without this faith, it would be easy to lose hope and give in to the relentless forces of popular culture. But leading a life directed by deeply felt values means having the belief that the greatest power on Earth is the power of good and knowing that, in the end, the values on which our country were founded and those that make life worth living will triumph.

AFTERWORD

Creating a New American Value Culture

Your children's futures are in your hands. What a marvelous—and scary!—responsibility you have. Do you ally yourself with American popular culture and push your children toward values that will hurt them? Or do you join forces with your children, teach them healthy values, and protect them from the harmful messages of popular culture? The choice is simple, obvious, but decidedly not easy. But the decision is all yours nonetheless.

Thankfully, you're not alone. There are indications that pockets of resistance against American popular culture are forming in communities around the U.S. More and more parents are recognizing the destructive force of popular culture on their children. They aren't just sitting back and idly allowing their children to be overrun. Instead, they're taking a stand against the values expressed by popular culture, determined to put up a fight in defense of their children's futures. These parents are choosing to alter their family's current course—that may be controlled by popular culture—and to create a family-value culture that will allow them to raise children they can be proud of.

Recent media reports describe the efforts by parents to band together and build a community-value culture aimed at derailing

American popular culture's influence on their children. For example, a group of parents in Ridgewood, New Jersey, organized a community-wide night off for families in which all homework and extracurricular activities were cancelled. Even the school system agreed not to assign homework and to cancel sports practices. The response was overwhelming. Parents in Greenville, South Carolina, chose to pass up formal soccer-league participation for their children—along with the long commutes and missed dinners—and, instead, organized pick-up games at their neighborhood park. As one parent described it, they wanted to "step off the high-pressure merry-go-round" of childhood achievement and slow down the pace of their family's lives. Organizations have emerged, such as Family Life First, National Family Night, Take Back Your Day, and Turn Off TV, whose aim it is to encourage parents to ratchet back their children's schedules and return some sanity to the lives of twenty-first-century American families.

Schools are stepping up to the plate as well. In response to increased concerns about the epidemic of obesity among school children, in January, 2004, the Philadelphia School District banned the sale of sodas in lunch rooms and vending machines throughout its school system. The schools were ordered to replace the sodas with water, fruit juice, milk, and other healthier alternatives. With a growing concern for not only obesity, but also for Type-2 diabetes and tooth decay, last year New York City stopped the sale of soda, candy, and other unhealthy snacks in its school system. In both cases, the school districts placed their students' health ahead of their own (sometimes desperate) fiscal needs. Bravo!

Sports programs are also contributing to this new American value culture. The La Jolla Country Day School in San Diego responded to concerns about very young children feeling the pressure to specialize in one sport by requiring its athletes to play at least two sports. They also require school and club team coaches to have a plan for how they resolve practice and game conflicts to protect the athletes from being over-stressed. Says Bruce Ward, San Diego public schools' director of physical education and athletics, "The shame of it is you see how hardened these 14-year-olds are by the time they get to high school. They're talented, terrific players, but I don't see the joy. They look tired. They've played so much year-round, they are like little professionals." The state of Connecticut has prohibited high-school athletes from playing on both high-school and traveling teams during the same season.

There are also signs of change within American popular culture as a whole. Since the September 11, 2001, terrorist attacks, the "tarting up" of female entertainers (e.g., Britney Spears, Christina Aguilera, Jennifer Lopez, and Pink) to sell more music has failed to increase sales. As Dr. Terry Pettijohn, a social psychologist at Mercyhurst College in Erie, Pennsylvania, suggests, "When social and economic times are more threatening and pessimistic, we actually prefer others with more mature facial, body, and personality characteristics." He adds that "In times of trouble, strong, stable, and supportive people are favored. When times are good, we tend to favor the fun person." This shift has benefited performers, such as Avril Lavigne, Norah Jones, and Alicia Keys, who write songs that emphasize values, emotions, character, and introspection, and perform in ways that are more subtle and genuine rather than blatant and trashy.

A New American Value Culture

Raising your children in a family-value culture and helping to foster a community-value culture is not just about resisting American popular culture, but also creating a new "American value culture" with which to replace it. A new American value culture is grounded in and driven by life-affirming values on which this country was founded, but, sadly, has lost sight of in the last several decades. Examples include integrity, accountability, hard work, kindness, fairness, primary concern for children, and a fundamental emphasis on always acting in the public interest. An American value culture identifies, highlights, and pursues values, goals, interests, and priorities that reflect the highest common denominator of American society, not the lowest. It involves persuading families, schools, houses of worship, big business, and local, state, and federal governments to return their priorities to those that care deeply for children. An American value culture is devoted to creating an environment that places your children's needs and best interests ahead of all else.

Because of the wealth that is invested in sustaining and expanding American popular culture and the power that comes with it, effecting change from the top down is probably impossible. Enlisting government as an ally in this war becomes less likely every day as special interest groups from all segments of popular culture exert lobbying and financial influence to maintain the status quo or alter its direction to serve their own agendas. American popular culture simply has too great an arsenal to overwhelm and defeat it with a frontal attack.

Much like the suffragist movement of the early 1900s and the civil rights movement of the 1960s, starting a revolution against popular culture and replacing it with a new American value culture has to begin at the grassroots level—in families, schools, houses of worship, neighborhoods, and communities. You must recognize that America is heading down a bad road that can only lead our children—and our society—to a disastrous end. You must find a new and better road with a positive destination and a value-driven road map—a new American value culture—and direct your children to exit the bad road and begin life's journey on the good route. You must commit to traveling this road with your children to ensure that they aren't seduced by the popular-culture billboards and exit ramps that will entice them to return to the bad road.

If you join the resistance, along with other converts, an army willing and capable of fighting against popular culture and for an American value culture will grow. As this groundswell builds, resistance to and repudiation of American popular culture will also increase. Over time, the tide will turn against popular culture and, just as it has for past movements, the values of a new American value culture will emerge victorious.

Bibliography

Adams Business Media. *Liquor Handbook.* New York: Adams Business Media, 1998.

Adderholdt-Elliott, M. "Perfectionism and the gifted adolescent." In M. Bireley and J. Genshaft (Eds.), *Understanding the Gifted Adolescent: Educational, Developmental, and Multicultural issues.* Education and psychology of the gifted series (pp. 65–75). New York: Teachers College Press, 1991.

The Alan Guttmacher Institute. 1998. "Facts in brief: Teen sex and pregnancy." *1995 National Survey of Family Growth* and *1995 National Survey of Adolescent Males.*

American Academy of Pediatrics report. 1998. "Alcohol advertising: fiction vs. fact."

American Dream 2000 poll by Interprise for Junior Achievement. http://www.ja.org/files/polls/american_dream_2000.pdf.

Americana: The Journal of American Popular Culture. Fall 2002. "Conversations with scholars of American popular culture: Ray B. Browne." http://www.americanpopularculture.com/journal/articles/fall_2002/browne.htm.

Anderson, Craig A. October 22, 2001. "The impact of violent video games." Iowa State University: The impact of entertainment media and violence on children and families. www.extension.iastate.edu/families/media/program.anderson.html.

Anderson, C. A. and B. J. Bushman. 2001. "Effects of violent video games on aggressive behavior, aggressive cognition, aggressive affect, physiological arousal, and prosocial behavior: A meta-analytic review of the scientific literature." *Psychological Science,* 12, 353.

Anderson, C. A., N. L. Carnagey and J. Eubanks. 2003. "Exposure to violent media: The effects of songs with violent lyrics on aggressive thoughts and feelings." *Journal of Personality and Social Psychology,* 84, 960–971.

Anderson, C. A. and K. E. Dill. 2000. "Video Games and Aggressive Thoughts, Feelings, and Behavior in the Laboratory and in Life." *Journal of Personality and Social Psychology,* 78, 772–790.

Andrejevic, M. 2003. *Reality TV: The Work of Being Watched.* Lanham, MD: Rowan & Littlefield.

Astin, A. W., W. S. Korn, and E. R. Rigg. 1993. *The American Freshman National Norms for 1993.* University of California at Los Angeles Graduate School of Education Higher Education Research Institute.

Aurthur, K. October 10, 2004. "Reality stars keep on going and going..." *New York Times,* 2, 20, 34.

Bahrke, M. S. and C. E. Yesalis. 2002. "Anabolic-androgenic steroids." In M. S. Bahrke and C. E. Yesalis (Eds.), *Performance-enhancing substances in sport and exercise.* (pp. 33–46), Champaign, IL: Human Kinetics.

Better, N. M. November 21, 2003. "How long a drive? *Finding Nemo* or *Harry Potter?*" *New York Times,* D3.

Brooks, D. 2004. *On Paradise Drive: How We Live Now (and Always Have) in the Future Tense.* New York City: Simon & Schuster.

Brown, J. D. 2002. "Mass media influences on sexuality." *Journal of Sex Research,* 39, 42.

Brown, S. and L. Eisenberg. 1995. *The Best Intentions.* Institute of Medicine, National Academy Press, 192.

Buchman, D. and J. Funk. "Children's time commitment and game preference." *Children Today.* 1996, 24.

Bushman, B. J., and L. R. Huesmann. 2001. "Effects of televised violence on aggression." In D. G. Singer and J. L. Singer (Eds.), *Handbook of Children and the Media* (ch. 11, pp. 223–254). Thousand Oaks, CA: Sage.

Carver, C. and E. Baird. 1998. "The American dream revisited: Is it *what* you want or *why* you want it that matters?" *Psychological Science,* 9, 289–292.

Center for a New American Dream. May 2002. "Kids and commercialism." http://www.newdream.org/campaign/kids/press-release2002.html.

Center for Media Education. 1999. "Youth access to alcohol and tobacco web marketing: The filtering and rating debate." Center for Media Education, Washington, DC.

Cohen, P. and J. Cohen. 1996. *Life Values and Adolescent Mental Health.* Mahwah, NJ: Lawrence Erlbaum.

Common Sense Media. 2003. Media poll of American parents. http://www.commonsensemedia.org/information/polls.php.

Congressional Public Health Summit. July 26, 2000. "Joint statement on the impact of entertainment violence on children." www.aap.org/advocacy/releases/jstmtevc.htm.

"Copycat" Crimes. 2000. Issue Brief Series. Studio City, CA: Mediascope Press.

Council of Economic Advisers to the President. May 2000. "Teens and their parents in the 21st century: An examination of trends in teen behavior and the role of parental involvement." http://www.whitehouse.gov/WH/EOP/CEA/html/Teens_Paper_Final.pdf.

Crane, D. 1992. *The production of culture: Media and the urban arts*. Newbury Park, CA: Sage.

CyberAtlas. 2001 "Search engines, browsers still confusing many web users." http://cyberatlas.internet.com/big_picture/traffic_patterns/ article/0,,5931_588851,00.html.

Dennison, B. A., T. J. Russo, P. A. Burdick, and P. L. Jenkins. 2004. "An intervention to reduce television viewing by preschool children," *Archives of Pediatric & Adolescent Medicine*, 158, 170–176.

Diaz, J. March 30, 2003. Editorial: "Reclaiming childhood." *San Francisco Chronicle*, D4.

Diener, E., and M. E. P. Seligman. 2002. "Very happy people." *Psychological Science*, 13, 81.

"Directing the pitch: Do smart marketers to children target kids or their parents?" *Youth Markets Alert*, July 1, 1998.

Distefan, J. M., E. A. Gilpin, J. D. Sargent, and J. P. Pierce. 1999. "Do movie stars encourage adolescents to start smoking? Evidence from California." *Preventive Medicine*, 28, 1–11.

Donahue, D. October 1, 1998. "Struggling to raise good kids in TOXIC TIMES." *USA Today*, 1D.

DuRant, R., E. S. Rome, M. Rich, E. Allred, S. J. Emans, and E. R. Woods. 1997. "Tobacco and alcohol use behaviors portrayed in music videos: A content analysis." *American Journal of Public Health*, 87, 1131–1135.

Engh, F. January 11, 2002. "Stop the madness." *San Francisco Chronicle*, A23.

Ericsson, K. A., and N. Charness. 1994. "Expert performance: Its structure and acquisition." *American Psychologist*, 49, 725–747.

Ewing, M. E., and V. Seefeldt. 1996. "Patterns of sport participation and attrition in American agency-sponsored sports." In F. L. Smoll and R. E. Smith (Eds.), *Children and Youth in Sport: A Biopsychosocial Perspective* (pp. 31–45). Madison, WI: Brown & Benchmark.

Extreme Makeover 2004. Show description. http://abc.go.com/primetime/extrememakeover/show.html.

Farkas, S., J. Johnson, A. Duffett, L. Wilson, and J. Vine. 2003. "A lot easier said than done: Parents talk about raising children in today's America." Public Agenda.

Federal Trade Commission 2000. "Marketing violent entertainment to children: A review of self-regulation and industry practices in the motion picture, music recording, and electronic game industries." Washington, DC: Federal Trade Commission.

Field, A. E., L. Cheung, A. M. Wolf, D. B. Herzog, S. L. Gortmaker, and G. A. Colditz. 1999. "Exposure to the mass media and weight concerns among girls." *Pediatrics,* 103, 660.

Flett, G. L., P. L. Hewitt, K. R. Blankstein, and S. W. Mosher. 1991. "Perfectionism, self-actualization, and personal adjustment." *Journal of Social Behavior and Personality,* 6, 147–160.

Frank, R. H. 2000. *Luxury fever: Money and happiness in an era of excess.* Princeton, NJ: Princeton University Press.

Fritz, G. K. January 2004. "Children and adults need family traditions." *Brown University Child & Adolescent Behavior Letter,* 20, 8.

Frost, R. O., P. A. Marten, C. Lahart, and R. Rosenblate. 1990. "The dimensions of perfectionism." *Cognitive Therapy and Research,* 14, 449–468.

Gelmis, J. May 11, 1999. "Shoot to thrill or shoot to kill?: The Littleton massacre has reopened the debate about violent video games." *Newsday.*

Gentile, D. A. July 1999. "Teen-oriented radio and CD sexual content analysis." National Institute on Media and the Family. http://www.mediafamily.org/research/report_radiocontentanalysis.pdf.

Gilbert, S. March 18, 2003. "Scientists explore the molding of children's morals." *New York Times,* D6.

Goldstein, J. 2003. "The value of play." http://www.btha.co.uk/publications/ntc/valueofplay.html.

Green, H. May 7, 1999. "Children's ads under threat of EU ban." *Campaign.*

Greenberg, B. S., M. Siemicki, S. Dorfman, C. Heeter, C. Lin, C. Stanley, and A. Soderman. 1993. "Sex content in R-rated films viewed by adolescents." In B. S. Greenberg, J. D. Brown, and N. Buerkel-Rothfuss (Eds.), *Media, Sex, and the Adolescent* (pp. 45–58). Cresskill, NJ: Hampton Press.

Grigoriadis, V. November 19, 2003. "Princess Paris." *Rolling Stone.* http://www.rollingstone.com/features/featuregen.asp?pid=2156.

Gross, J. November 26, 2003. "Exposing the cheat sheet, with the students' aid." *New York Times,* A1, 26.

Grube, J. W. and L. Wallack. 1994. "Television beer advertising and drinking knowledge, beliefs, and intentions among schoolchildren." *American Journal of Public Health,* 84, 254–259.

Harmon, A. August 26, 2004. "Internet gives teenage bullies weapons to wound from afar." *New York Times,* A1, 21.

Hedegaard, E. July 6, 2000. "Ozzy." *Rolling Stone*, 112.

Heffernan, V. November 3, 2004. "Another lesson in humiliation, taught by a British nanny." *New York Times*, B4.

Hewitt, P. L., and G. L. Flett. 1991. "Perfectionism in the self and social contexts: Conceptualization, assessment, and association with psychopathology." *Journal of Personality and Social Psychology*, 60, 456–470.

Hinson, H. November 4, 1994. "Hoop dreams." *Washington Post*, http://www.washingtonpost.com/wp-srv/style/longterm/movies/videos/hoop-dreamsnrhinson_a01b70.htm.

Hofferth, S. L. 2001. "How American children spend their time." *Journal of Marriage and the Family*, 63, 295–308.

Holson, L. M. October 4, 2004. "A finishing school for all, Disney style." *New York Times*, C1,11.

Howard, J. 1997. "You can't get there from here: The need for a new logic in education reform." *Journal of the American Academy of Arts and Sciences*, 124, 23–25.

Irish, O. April 6, 2003. "Four tennis dads to rival Damir Dokic." *The Observer*. http://observer.guardian.co.uk/osm/story/0,6903,929107,00.html.

Irvine, M. June 18, 2002. "Kids able to figure out at an early age that nagging usually works." *San Francisco Chronicle*, A2.

Julien, A. December 16, 2002. "Parents turn up the heat." *Hartford Courant*, A1, A6, A7.

Kanner, D. A., and T. Kasser. July 2000. "Stuffing our kids: Should psychologists help advertisers manipulate children?" Society for Industrial and Organizational Psychology Inc. http://siop.org/tip/backissues/TipJuly00/34Kanner.htm.

Kasanoff L., R. Sanchini, and R. Shriver (Executive Producers), S. Austin (Producers), P. Easley (Associate Producer), and J. Cameron (Producer/Director). 1994. *True Lies* [motion picture]. United States: Lightstorm Entertainment and 20th Century Fox.

Kasser, T. 2000. "Two versions of the American dream: Which goals and values make for a high quality of life?" In E. Diener and D. Rahtz (Eds.) *Advances in quality of life theory and research*. Dordrecht, Netherlands: Kluwer.

Kasser, T. Winter 2001. "Kids and values." *Kids Newsletter*. http://www.kidscanmakeadifference.org/Newsletter/nw2001b.htm.

Kasser, T. and R. M. Ryan. 1993. "A dark side of the American dream: Correlates of financial success as a central life aspiration." *Journal of Personality and Social Psychology*, 65, 410–422.

Kasser, T. and R. Ryan. 1996. "Further examining the American Dream: Differential correlates of intrinsic and extrinsic goals." *Personality and Social Psychology Bulletin*, 22, 280–287.

Kirn, W. and C. Cole. April 30, 2001. "Whatever happened to play?" *Time*, 56–58.

Klein, J. D., J. D. Brown, K. W. Childers, J. Oliveri, C. Porter, and C. Dykers. 1993. "Adolescents' risky behavior and mass media use." *Pediatrics*, 92, 24–31.

Kluger, J. and A. Park. April 30, 2001. "The quest for a super kid." *Time*, 50–55.

Kornblum, J. November 11, 2003. "Effects of TV on kids becoming less remote." *USA Today*, 10D.

Kunkel, D., K. Cope, W. Farinola, E. Biely, E. Rollin, and E. Donnerstein. 1999. "Sex on TV: A biennial report to the Kaiser Family Foundation." Menlo Park, CA: The Henry J. Kaiser Family Foundation.

Lazarus, R. S., and B. N. Lazarus. 1994. *Passion and Reason*. New York: Oxford University Press.

Leonard, D. The Adelphia story. *Fortune.com*. http://www.fortune.com/fortune/ceo/articles/0,15114,371110,00.html.

Leone, M. L. April 2002. "The Enron difference." *CFO*, 21.

Lewin, T. October 29, 2003. "A growing number of video viewers watch from crib." *New York Times*, A1.

Loomis, C. J. February 9, 2004. "Dick Grasso's pay: The sequel." *Fortune*, 22.

Loewenstein, G. and S. Frederick. 1997. "Predicting Reactions to Environmental Change." In M. Bazerman, D. Messick, A. Tenbrunsel, and K. Wade-Benzoni (Eds.), *Environment, Ethics, and Behavior*. San Francisco: New Lexington Press.

Long, J. November 26, 2003. "An athlete's dangerous experiment." *New York Times*, C15–16.

Madden, P. A., J. W. Grube. 1994. "The frequency and nature of alcohol and tobacco advertising in televised sports, 1990 through 1992." *American Journal of Public Health*, 84, 297–299.

"Mauled to Death: Glamour Investigates the Horrific Dog Attack in San Francisco That Killed Diane Whipple in an Exclusive Interview With Victim's Partner." May 10, 2001. *Glamour*.

McCabe, D. Winter 2001–02. "Cheating: Why students do it and how we can help them stop." *American Educator*, 38–43.

McDonald, N. October 15, 2002. "Video games." *The Alestle*.

McGinn, D. and G. Gagnon. September 16, 2002. "Jack is paying for this." *Newsweek*, 42.

McKee, B. September 25, 2003. "Parents schedule in a little dawdle time." *New York Times*, F1.

McLean, B., N. Varchaver, J. Helyar, J. Revell, and J. Sung. December 24, 2001. "Why Enron went bust." *Fortune* (Europe), 52.

Mead, M. 1963. *Sex and Temperament in Three Primitive Societies.* New York: Perennial, an Imprint of HarperCollins Publishers Inc.

Mediascopes. March 2000. "Teens, Sex, and the Media." http://www.mediascope.org/pubs/ibriefs/tsm.htm.

Murphy, A. May 1998. "Taking His Medicine." *Sports Illustrated,* 56.

Myers, D. G. and E. Diener. 1995. "Who is happy?" *Psychological Science.* 6, 10.

NCAA. 2004. Estimated probability of competing in athletics beyond the high school interscholastic level. http://www.ncaa.org/research/prob_of_competing/.

Nanny 911 (2004). Profiles. http://www.fox.com/nanny911/.

National Institute on Media and the Family. August 2001. *Fact sheet: Effects Of video game playing on children.* http://www.mediafamily.org/facts/facts_effect.shtml.

Nelson, A. M. S. 1999. "Popular culture: What everyone needs to know." *Symposium on American values.* http://www.angelo.edu/events/university_symposium/1998/Nelson.htm.

Office on Smoking and Health, Centers for Disease Control and Prevention. 1994. "Preventing tobacco use among young people: A report of the Surgeon General." U.S. Department of Health and Human Services.

Ozer, E. M., C. D. Brindis, S. G. Millstein, D. K. Knopf, and C. E. Irwin Jr. 1997. *America's Adolescents: Are they Healthy?* San Francisco, CA: University of California, San Francisco, National Adolescent Health Information Center.

Packer, J. I. 1993. "Leisure and Life-Style: Leisure, Pleasure, and Treasure," in *God and Culture: Essays in Honor of Carl F. H. Henry,* edited by D. A. Carson and J. D. Woodbridge. Grand Rapids, MI: William B. Erdmans.

Parents Television Council. 2003. *Culture watch.* http://www.parentstv.org/PTC/publications/culturewatch/2003/0718.asp.

Pennington, B. November 12, 2003. "As team sports conflict, some parents rebel." *New York Times*, A1.

Peterson, J., K. Moore, and F. Furstenberg. 1991. "Television viewing and early initiation of sexual intercourse: Is there a link?" *Journal of Homosexuality,* 21, 93–118.

Peterson, K. S. November 19, 2002. "Extracurricular burnout." *USA Today*, 7D.

Presley, C. and P. Meilman. July 1992. "Alcohol and drugs on American college campuses." Student Health Program Wellness Center, Southern Illinois University.

Putnam, R. D. (2002) *Bowling alone: The collapse and revival of American community*. New York: Simon & Schuster.

Quittner, J. May 10, 1999. "Are video games really so bad?" *Time*.

Reich, J., E. Diener, D. G. Meyers, and A. C. Michalos. July/August 1994. "The road to happiness." *Psychology Today*, 32.

Rendon, J. October 10, 2004. "Rattling the windows without breaking the bank." *New York Times*, 5, 8.

Ressner, J. April 1, 2002. "Justice bites back." *Time*, 63.

Reuters 2004. "Does sex still sell?" http://www.cnn.com/2004/SHOWBIZ/Music/01/21/music.sex.reut/.

Reuters. 2004. "Philadelphia schools ban soda sales." http://www.cnn.com/2004/EDUCATION/01/16/health.soda.reut/index.html.

Rideout, V. J., U. G. Foehr, D. F. Roberts, and M. Brodie. 1999. "Kids & media @ the new millennium." *The Henry J. Kaiser Family Foundation Report*.

Rideout, V.J., E. A. Vandewater, and E. A. Wartella. 2003. "Zero to six: Electronic media in the lives of infants, toddlers, and preschoolers." *The Henry J. Kaiser Family Foundation Report*.

Robinson, T. N., H. L. Chen, and J. D. Killen. 1998. "Television and music video exposure and risk of adolescent alcohol use." *Pediatrics*, 102, 5.

Ruskin, G. 1997. "Why they whine: How corporations prey on our children." *Mothering*. http://www.mothering.com/10-0-0/html/10-3-0/10-3-whine97.shtml.

Sargent, J. D., M. L. Beach, M. A. Dalton, L. A. Mott, J. J. Tickle, M. B. Ahrens, and T. F. Heatherton. 2001. "Effect of seeing tobacco use in films on trying smoking among adolescents: cross-sectional study." *BMJ*, 323, 1394–1397.

Schooler, J., D. Ariely, and G. Loewenstein. 2003. "The pursuit of happiness can be self-defeating." In. J. Carrillo and I. Brocas (Eds.) *Psychology and Economics*. Oxford, GB: Oxford University Press.

Senate Committee on the Judiciary (1999, September 14). "Children, violence, and the media: A report for parents and policymakers." Available at: http://judiciary.senate.gov/mediavio.htm.

Shapiro, H. D. March 1998. "Making allowances." *Hemispheres*, 37–38.

Sheldon, K. M., J. E. Elliot, Y. Kim, and T. Kasser. 2001. "What is satisfying about satisfying events? Testing 10 candidate psychological needs." *Journal of Personality and Social Psychology,* 80, 325–339.

Shepard, C. October 17, 1997. *News of the Weird.* http://www.langston.com/Fun_People/1997/1997BHJ.html.

Silver, A. 2003. "Overexposed celebrities: Paris Hilton." http://www.askmen.com/fashion/austin/43b_fashion_style.html.

Sirgy, M. J. 1999. "Materialism and quality of life." *Social Indicators Research,* 43, 227–260.

Slobogin, K. April 5, 2002. "Survey: Many students say cheating's OK." http://www.cnn.com/2002/fyi/teachers.ednews/04/05/highschool.cheating/.

Smith, S. L., and E. Donnerstein. 1998. "Harmful effects of exposure to media violence: Learning of aggression, emotional desensitization, and fear." In R. G. Geen and E. Donnerstein (Eds.), *Human aggression: Theories, research, and implications for social policy* (pp. 167–202). New York: Academic Press.

Stepanek, M. J. T. 2004. "Welcome to Mattie's website." http://www.mattieonline.com/.

Subrahmanyam, K., R. Kraut, P. Greenfield, and E. Gross. 2001. "New forms of electronic media." In D. G. Singer and J. L. Singer (Eds.), *Handbook of children and the media* (pp. 395–414). Thousand Oaks, CA: Sage.

Swain, S. January 7, 2004. "Importance of fashion to one Brooklyn teenager and her peers." *National Public Radio.*

Tanner, L. December 3, 2001. "Teens head pressure not to smoke." *San Francisco Chronicle,* A2.

"Teenagers and tobacco use." 1998. Issue briefs. Studio City, Calif.: Mediascope Press.

Thirteen. 2003. http://www2.foxsearchlight.com/thirteen/thirteen.html.

Tillich, P. 1959. *Theology of Culture,* Robert C. Kimball, editor. New York: Oxford University Press.

Torgan, C. June 2002. "Childhood obesity on the rise." *Word on Health.* http://www.nih.gov/news/WordonHealth/jun2002/childhoodobesity.htm.

Unger, J. B., D. Schuster, J. Zogg, C. W. Dent, and A. W. Stacy. 2003. "Alcohol advertising exposure and adolescent alcohol use: A comparison of exposure measures." *Addiction Research and Theory,* 11, 17–193.

University of California–Berkeley English Department. "Post–World War II American literature and culture database: Pop culture." http://english.berkeley.edu/Postwar/pop.html.

University of California, Los Angeles Center for Communication Policy. 1996. "Entertainment industry's perspectives on sex in the media." *U.S.News and World Report.* http://ccp.ucla.edu/u_s.htm.

Varma, S. J. 2003. Plot summary of *Thirteen.* http://www.imdb.com/title/tt0328538/plotsummary.

Waiters, E. D., A. J. Treno, and J. W. Grube. Winter 2001. "Alcohol advertising and youth: A focus group analysis of what young people find appealing in alcohol advertising." *Contemporary Drug Problems,* 28, 695–718.

Wallack, L., J. W. Grube, P. A. Madden, and W. Breed. 1990. "Portrayals of alcohol on prime-time television." *Journal of Studies in Alcohol,* 51, 428–437.

Walsh-Childers, K., A. Gotthoffer, and C. R. Lepre. 2002. "From 'Just the Facts' to 'Downright Salacious': Teen's and women's magazines' coverage of sex and sexual health." In J. D. Brown, J. R. Steele, and K. Walsh-Childers (Eds.), *Sexual Teens, Sexual Media* (pp. 153–172). Mahwah, NJ: Lawrence Erlbaum.

Walsh D. 1998. 1998 "Video and Computer Game Report Card." National Institute on Media and the Family. http://www.mediafamily.org/research/report_vgrc_1998-1.shtml.

Webster's New Universal Unabridged Dictionary. New York: Random House.

White, F. A. 2000. "Relationship of family socialization processes to adolescent moral thought." *Journal of Social Psychology,* 140, 75.

Whitley Jr., B. E. and P. Keith-Spiegel. 2002. *Academic Dishonesty: An Educator's Guide.* Mahwah, NJ: Lawrence Erlbaum.

Wigand, J. (October 13, 2000). Statement of Jeffrey S. Wigand, PhD, MAT. Public hearings for the Framework Convention on Tobacco, World Health Organization, Geneva, Switzerland. http://www.jeffreywigand.com/insider/who.html.

Wyllie, A., J. F. Zhang, and S. Casswell. 1998a. "Responses to televised alcohol advertisements associated with drinking behavior of 10- to 17-year-olds." *Addiction,* 93, 361–371.

Yesalis, et al. 1997. "Trends in anabolic-androgenic steroid use among adolescents." Archives of Pediatric and Adolescent Medicine, 1512, 1197–1206.

Yochim, D. "Our credit crunch." *The Motley Fool.* http://www.fool.com/ccc/secrets/secrets01.htm.

Index

About the Author

Jim Taylor, PhD, has worked with young people, parents, and educators for twenty years. He has been a consultant and frequent speaker to numerous elementary and secondary schools, youth-sports programs, and performing-arts organizations around the country.

Dr. Taylor received his bachelor's degree from Middlebury College and earned his master's degree and PhD in psychology from the University of Colorado.

A former alpine ski racer who competed internationally, Dr. Taylor is a 2nd-degree black belt in karate, a marathon runner, and an Ironman triathlete.

Dr. Taylor is the author of five books, including *Positive Pushing: How to Raise a Successful and Happy Child* (Hyperion, 2002). He has published more than four hundred articles in scholarly and popular publications, and has given over five hundred workshops and presentations throughout North America and Europe.

Dr. Taylor has appeared on NBC's *Today Show*, ABC's *World News This Weekend*, UPN's *Life & Style,* and major television network affiliates, and has participated in many radio shows. Dr. Taylor has been interviewed for articles that have appeared in *Family Circle*, the *Christian Science Monitor*, *Parents*, the *Miami Herald*, the *Ft. Lauderdale Sun-Sentinel*, and the *Baltimore Sun*, and many other newspapers and magazines.

For more information, please visit www.drjimtaylor.com.